GLOBALIZING PRACTICES AND UNIVERSITY RESPONSES

GLOBALIZING PRACTICES AND UNIVERSITY RESPONSES

European and Anglo-American Differences

Jan Currie, Richard DeAngelis, Harry de Boer,
Jeroen Huisman, and Claude Lacotte

Studies in Higher Education
Philip G. Altbach, Series Editor

Westport, Connecticut
London

Library of Congress Cataloging-in-Publication Data

Globalizing practices and university responses : European and Anglo-American
    differences / Jan Currie ... [et al.].
        p.cm. — (studies in higher education)
    Includes bibliographical references and index.
    ISBN 0–89789–868–0 (alk. paper)
    1. Education, Higher—Cross-cultural studies.   2. Comparative education.
    3. Globalization—Cross-cultural studies. I. Currie, Jan.
  LB2322.2.G58   2003
    378—dc21   2002066337

British Library Cataloguing in Publication Data is available.

Library of Congress Catalog Card Number: 2002066337
ISBN: 0–89789–868–0

First published in 2003

Praeger Publishers, 88 Post Road West, Westport, CT 06881
An imprint of Greenwood Publishing Group, Inc.
www.praeger.com

Printed in the United States of America

The paper used in this book complies with the
Permanent Paper Standard issued by the National
Information Standards Organization (Z39.48–1984).

10 9 8 7 6 5 4 3 2 1

Published in cooperation with the Center for International Higher Education and the
Program in Higher Education, Boston College, Chestnut Hill, Massachusetts.

We dedicate this book to our spouses and partners:
Paul, Françoise, Sjoukje, Louisa, and Jacqueline

Contents

Tables

Series Foreword

Studies in Higher Education publishes current research and analysis on higher and postsecondary education. Higher education in the twenty-first century is a multifaceted phenomenon, combining a variety of institutions and systems, an increasing diversity of students, and a range of purposes and functions. The challenges of expansion, technology, accountability, and research, among others, require careful analysis. This series combines research-based monographs, analysis, and reference books related to all aspects of higher education. It is concerned with policy and practice in a global perspective. Studies in Higher Education is dedicated to illuminating the reality of higher and postsecondary education in contemporary society.

Higher education is a central enterprise of the twenty-first century and a key part of the knowledge-based economy. Universities are the most important source of basic research, and are therefore key to the development of technology. They are also the repositories of the wisdom of society—their libraries and other facilities are in many ways the institutional memory of civilization. University faculty provide not only education and training, but are involved in the creation and interpretation of knowledge. Universities are central to the civil society. Higher education is a key to the social mobility and progress of large numbers of people.

Universities and other postsecondary institutions are increasingly complex. They are large and multifaceted. Academe is also diverse, with a wider range of institutions, a less homogenous student population, and a mixture of public and private support. This series is dedicated to illuminating these complexities. It is also committed to the improvement of one of the most important parts of society—postsecondary education.

Philip G. Altbach

Acknowledgments

We are all working in universities that are undergoing change. For some of us, the impact of globalizing practices in our universities has been quite dramatic. For others, there have been changes, but they have had less of an impact on us. In this book we interviewed academics and administrators in four countries and gathered information from our participant observations to analyze the kind of changes, if any, that have altered universities. We were curious to discover the impact that globalizing practices may have had on the higher education system in France, Norway, the Netherlands and the United States. We also wanted to know how and if these changes altered the internal structures of universities and the impact various reforms have had on the working lives of academics.

The Australian Research Council funded the study. In addition, we received support for our visits to the institutions from the Center for Higher Education Policy Studies (CHEPS) at the University of Twente; the Center for International Higher Education at Boston College and its Director, Professor Philip Altbach, and a graduate student, David Engberg; the Institute for Educational Research at the University of Oslo and a colleague, Professor Arild Tjeldvoll, who assisted with interviews and gathered information for us; the Department of Sciences and Applied Languages at the University of Avignon; and the School of Education at Murdoch University that assisted with secretarial support. A number of colleagues read and made suggestions on our manuscript. We thank David Dill, Guy Neave, Bjorn Stensaker, Arild Tjeldvoll, Ingvild Marheim Larsen, and Christine Musselin for their constructive comments.

We would also like to acknowledge the excellent assistance we had with data analysis, using NUD.IST and editing from Paul Snider, with specialist, NUD.IST expertise from Harriett Pears, with transcription from Steve Robson, with interviewing from Lynn Meek, with translating the French transcripts from Natalie Westcott, and with myriad activities from Karyn Barenberg. We especially want to thank Loraine Abernethie for her initial work on this book and Claire Pickering for editing, indexing and producing the final print-ready version of the book—a formidable task.

Finally, we want to thank the 131 academics and administrators from Boston College, the Universities of Avignon, Oslo, and Twente, who gave generously of their time to be interviewed. We acknowledge their insights during the interviews and their suggestions after the case studies were completed. It is our hope that the findings we generated about globalizing practices in universities will initiate deeper discussions about the issues we raised in this book.

February 2002
Jan Currie, Perth
Richard DeAngelis, Adelaide
Harry de Boer, Enschede
Jeroen Huisman, Enschede
Claude Lacotte, Avignon

Chapter 1

Introduction

Globalization is a contested term, having different meanings for different people, having strong supporters and strong opponents. For instance, recent antiglobalization protests[1] were aimed at corporate globalization or neoliberal globalization. These protesters argue that inequalities within the world are growing due to the free trade movement. Conversely, those embracing globalization believe that free trade will increase world prosperity. In addition, there are those who perceive globalization as a neutral instrument, allowing easier and faster communication between populations. They may also see the Internet as a global tool; a mechanism potentially increasing democratization of information, interconnectedness of the world's cultures, and integration of the global economy. Concurrently, however, globalization tends to segment and divide societies and the world into three types of players: those who globalize, those who are globalized, and those who are excluded by globalization (Yang & Vidovich, 2001). There are winners and losers in the globalization process. Globalization is not a simple, neutral term, and needs to be explored in its ideological and material forms. This is discussed in greater depth by examining its impact on universities. Yet it is important to understand why the term *globalization* has not been included in the book title. This was a conscious choice, to focus instead on actual globalizing practices witnessed in a study of universities.

The globalizing practices examined in this book began appearing, unevenly around the globe, 30 years ago in the field of higher education. Initially, these practices arose in the United States, then spread to Commonwealth countries such as Australia, Canada, New Zealand and the United Kingdom, and further to European countries. Around the globe, these practices intensified in the last decade of the twentieth century. It is not certain whether these globalizing practices were caused directly by globalization itself or by neoliberal economic policies; nevertheless, these were developing at the same time. For instance, many governments initiated public sector reforms, introducing greater institutional autonomy for universities in a more deregulated, economic environment, and new controls, such as "steering from a distance mechanisms," resulting in disguised governmental control. What is surprising is how rapid and universal these changes were, seeming to occur in almost every country, though not always with the same visibility, intensity, or timing. Observation has shown the interrelation between many globalizing practices and institutional reforms. Yet it is problematic to assume a direct, causal relationship between these. For instance, some practices, such as privatization, may be more directly related to globalization than others, such as democratization or massification of higher education.

It is beyond the scope of this book to unravel in detail the causality of these practices. Instead, this book is mainly interested in the consequences of certain globalizing practices for the institutions and the individuals within, for instance the changing nature of the academic profession (Porter & Vidovich, 2000). Hence, this book focuses largely on these consequences at the university level and for the academic staff.

As systems move increasingly from elite to mass higher education, many governments reduce their per capita university funding. As universities are given greater institutional autonomy, many governments demand greater accountability. As the student-to-staff ratio increases in many universities, the maintenance of quality becomes an issue. Concurrently, many universities or stakeholders, such as governments and students, begin to demand that staff demonstrate quality assurance, despite the impact of increased workloads. These practices change academic work and often lead to lower morale and less job satisfaction. For instance, academics are required to be increasingly skilled in areas such as online teaching, general computing, marketing, and legal processes for the selling of intellectual property and development of overseas markets. In addition, more part-timers are hired to increase flexibility in the staffing profile, changing the traditional culture of a scholarly community consisting of permanent members.

This book will specifically focus upon privatization, governance, accountability, tenure and permanency, and new technologies. These issues do not cover all the new ground in higher education; however, they do appear to be the relevant areas policy makers are confronting in many countries. A number of questions are posed concerning these issues. How are university administrators and academic staff responding to the challenges, opportunities, and problems related to the issues of globalization? Are staff resisting, adapting, manipulating, or acquiescing to governmental demands and changes? To what extent are universities developing novel or hybrid forms of governance structures, retaining some older, traditional values and blending these with new management processes? How is the Internet changing the function of universities? These are a few of the questions investigated in this book. Initially, however, it is important to understand the intellectual journey prompting this investigation of globalizing practices.

INTELLECTUAL JOURNEY

How did a diverse group of authors unite to write this book? The authors are of three nationalities (American, Dutch, and French), located in three countries (Australia, France, and the Netherlands), investigating universities in four countries (France, Netherlands, Norway, and the United States). In the early 1990s, one author, Jan Currie, troubled by changes occurring at her university in Australia, gained an Australian Research Council grant to study the changing nature of academic work in Australia and the United States, resulting in six case studies of public universities between 1994 to 1996. During this study, Currie met researchers from many countries who were concerned about the same changing practices. One important meeting involved Janice Newson, from York University in Canada, provoking this statement: "We recognized instantly that we were talking with the same passion and urgency about the consequences of globalization for our universities" (Currie & Newson, 1998, p. ix). They agreed to organize a commission on globalization and universities for the World Congress of Comparative Education in 1996, held in Sydney, Australia. During this congress, they decided to edit a book, *Universities and Globalization: Critical Perspectives*, which consisted of papers from the conference and others by researchers investigating similar phenomena in their respective countries. Following this publication, Currie applied for a further Australian Research Council grant to explore contrasting European and Anglo-American university responses to globalization. This grant included three associate investigators: Richard DeAngelis, Janice Newson, and Arild Tjeldvoll, who had presented papers at the World Congress of Comparative Education. This grant also included Claude Lacotte, who participated in a case study of the University of Avignon (Université d'Avignon), and Lynn Meek, who was closely associated with the University of Twente (Universiteit Twente) and had previously compared Australian and Dutch higher education.

The general aim of this project was to gain an intimate understanding of the widely assumed trend towards uniformity and homogeneity, and the concurrent, conflicting evidence of microlevel variations that led towards greater localization and resistance within higher education policies and practices. The specific aims were to investigate the extent to which universities in different countries reflect common global trends in the areas of governance (towards corporate managerialism); accountability (towards performance indicators and quality reviews); funding (towards privatization, marketization, and increased competition); and the use of new technologies (towards increased use of Internet, satellite television, and online teaching). The research involved case studies of four universities, chosen to represent a range of responses to global trends.

Jan Currie conducted most of the interviews in the universities, aided by the invaluable assistance of Philip Altbach, Center for International Higher Education, Boston College; Claude Lacotte, Faculty of Sciences and Applied Languages, University of Avignon; Arild Tjeldvoll, Institute for Educational Research, University of Oslo; and Jeroen Huisman, Center for Higher Education Policy Studies, University of Twente. These contacts assisted in choosing the respondents, accessing key informants at the highest level of administration, providing an office, and accessing computers, libraries, and other facilities.

When we began applying for research grants, many writers were emphasizing the dual nature of globalization: first, as promoting homogenization, and second, as creating localized responses striving to resist pressure towards uniformity. Cunningham, Tapsall, Ryan, Stedman, Bagdon, and Flew (1998) noted that, "Converging technologies and the potential for global reach have led some to assume the existence of one 'global market.' Conversely, this investigation would support the notion of the fragmentation of world markets and the development of numerous niche markets on an international and regional, rather than global scale" (p. xv). In addition, Henry, Lingard, Rizvi, and Taylor (1997) argued that, "There is no essential determinacy to the ways in which globalization processes work, since for various globalization pressures there are also sites of resistance and counter movements" (p. 68). The contradictory tensions emerging within globalization are intriguing, including universalization and particularization, homogenization and differentiation (Porter & Vidovich, 2000).

GLOBALIZATION

According to Scott (1998), globalization is the fundamental challenge facing contemporary universities. He believes the threat of globalization is more serious than the challenges faced by universities during the rise of humanism and the scientific revolution; more serious than industrialization, urbanization, and secularization; and more serious than the totalitarianism of the last century. What is the nature of this challenge, and how has it affected universities? The responses of universities to globalizing practices are unique, yet are often forced by globalizing politicians and bureaucrats. For instance, some universities respond quickly and internalize the practices, while others act cautiously, adapting or resisting the practices.

Before examining the effect of globalizing practices on universities, it is necessary to understand globalization as a process. From the outset it must be recognized that not all countries follow the Anglo-American model, an alternative being the French model. The French often show outward opposition to globalization, expressed towards the hegemony of the United States and ubiquity of the English language, and shown by opposition to McDonald's and the dominance of American movies. Turnbull (1999) describes France's reduction of working hours, from 39 to 35 per week, as an outward defiance and reaction against Anglo-Saxon efficiency and the global economy, which maintains long working hours. A French lawyer explains that, "It had to stop. France has always been known for its high quality of life, and it's good that we are sending a signal—even if it's a silly one. We want to lead a civilized life" (cited in Turnbull, 1999, p. 32).

Contrary to the American Chamber of Commerce in Paris and other critics, who believed the 35-hour week was a retrograde step, the first year of *les 35 heures* coincided with a 3 percent growth in the economy, increased consumer confidence, and a nine-year low of unemployment at 9.2 percent (Anderson, 2001). In addition, a survey of French workers found that personal and family life had improved (86 percent), personal growth and development had regenerated (74 percent), and work morale had increased (50 percent).

In a recent publication, French Foreign Minister Hubert Védrine expresses what he perceives as the problem of exclusive world dominance by the United States: "This situation is unprecedented: what previous empire subjugated the entire world, including its adversaries?" He suggests that France should work towards a "multipolar world" that would undo the "uniformity and the unilateralism" resulting from American supremacy (cited in Perlez, 2000, A9).

It is not the French alone who find the American drive to globalize economies disturbing. In an open letter to the incoming President George W. Bush, Mikhail Gorbachev explains that, "Globalization is a given—but American globalization would be a mistake. In fact it would be something devoid of meaning and even dangerous" (2001, p. 17). Particularly, he expresses a failure of American policy to address the heightening of inequalities and abject poverty within the world.

In addition, former Australian Prime Minister Malcolm Fraser stresses the need to restrict the excesses of globalization, stipulating that "Government has failed to draw a line in the sand where Australia's national interest transcends the cause of globalization" (cited in Wilson, 2001, p. 24). However, Australia appears to be embracing the notion of free trade, welcoming the Bush administration and hence, anticipating a strengthening of free trade ties.

Images of Globalization

There are many different images of globalization within current literature. This section examines some of these images, while exploring how globalization differs from internationalization, utilizing examples from mainly Anglo-American universities.

How is globalization described within current literature? Many writers discuss globalization in economic terms: the global economy, fast capitalism, market forces, economic liberalization and free trade regimes. Some discuss the phenomenon of a global culture: Westernization, Americanization, modernization, and homogenization of values. Others discuss globalization in political terms: democratization or the spreading of democratic practices, but rarely world government. There are particular global media agencies, such as CNN, that help globalize information and the English language; and particular organizations associated with globalization, such as the World Bank, the International Monetary Fund (IMF), the Organization for Economic Cooperation and Development (OECD), and the World Trade Organization (WTO). The United Nations and its agencies, such as the United Nations Educational and Scientific Cooperation Organization (UNESCO) and the United Nations Development Program (UNDP), may also be included. However, they tend to operate on internationa assumptions and are *not* necessarily focused on free trade and globalizing business practices. It is important to distinguish organizations that have an international focus from those aimed at creating a growing capitalist economy.

In addition, there are global communication tools, such as the Internet, that may lead, not to increased homogenization of news, but to wider access to a range of information and the coalescing of people to protest against the neoliberal form of globalization, evident in Seattle at the WTO talks and in Washington, DC, at the World Bank. Paradoxically, the Internet enables minority groups with little or no capital to access a worldwide audience, while simultaneously enabling those holding the capitalistic means of broadcasting or publishing (the press, television channels, publishing companies) to concentrate information into the hands of a few global actors (CNN, AOL, Microsoft, etc.) who become the gatekeepers. Therefore, globalization can lead to greater diversity and greater homogeneity, social activism, and social control. In addition, globalization arouses many dichotomies: with a global culture comes the loss of local culture; with a global economy comes less democracy, the likely loss of the welfare state and eventually the nation-state itself. However, not all literature advocates these dichotomies, instead pointing to evidence that globalization stimulates some local cultures to resist the intrusion of dominant cultures, and that a market economy stimulates a freer political culture and promotes the establishment of democratic societies.

Sklair (2001) suggests that it is "a widely-held misconception that globalization and localization are mutually exclusive and contradictory processes." Nevertheless, he admits that "global forces certainly change local cultures but this does not necessarily mean that they destroy them, though sometimes they do" (p. 256).

Sassen (2000) reiterates this, asserting that there is significant overlap and dynamic interaction between the global and national. There is global within the national and national within the global. For instance, she explains that "global processes are often strategically located in national spaces where they are implemented usually with the help of legal measures taken by state institutions" (p. 218). Nonetheless, she acknowledges a partial unraveling of the national space, perceiving the global as a novel order, distinct from the national. It is evident that nations take action and establish legislation leading to economic liberalization, and equally evident that nations are not totally separate from global forces. As Sassen asserts, "the idea of the nation-state as a container," as a fixed entity in space and time, is erroneous (p. 215). Thereby, the global and national are intertwined: "A country's central bank can be a key institution for implementing—in its national economy—some of the new rules of the global game, notably the standards of IMF conditionality. This means that national institutions can become home to some of the operational rules of the global economic system" (Sassen, p. 228).

Thus, partly supranational organizations, such as the World Bank and the IMF,[2] play an increasing role in nation-states and their engagement in implementing global processes. This is evident in many Third World countries, caught in the web of supranational organizations that steer them in certain directions. In turn, these governments have to provide legislation enabling IMF conditionality or structural adjustment principles to become law. It is through the nation state that globalizing practices seep into economies.

Many of these countries do not have the latitude to refuse IMF funding. The World Bank assesses and determines how these countries can be remunerated using neoliberal economic principles. The vision is global economic integration through free trade, which is, Daly (1994) suggests, a self-evident good. He notes, in a farewell lecture to the World Bank, "the word 'globalist' has politically correct connotations, while the word 'nationalist' has come to be pejorative." He asserts, "to globalize the economy by erasure of national economic boundaries through free trade, free capital mobility, and free or at least uncontrolled migration is to wound fatally the major unit of community capable of carrying out any policies for the common good" (p. 116).

Similar concerns emanate from Appadurai (2000), particularly regarding the possible impact of globalization on the poorest nations. He describes globalization as a world of things in motion, a world of flows. There are flows of ideas, ideologies, people and goods, images and messages, technologies and techniques. He stresses that these flows are not equivalent or spatially consistent, but are in relations of disjuncture; for example, the flow of media across national boundaries espouses images of well being, which cannot be satisfied by national standards of living and consumer capabilities. Therefore, globalization "produces problems that manifest themselves in intensely local forms but have contexts that are anything but local" (p. 6).

Conversely, Appadurai (2000) perceives a possible emancipation from globalization through the influence of imagination on social life, whereby collective patterns of dissent and new designs for collective life emerge, even though modern citizens are disciplined and controlled by states, markets, and other powerful interests through the imagination. He describes a counter to "globalization from above" as "grassroots globalization" or "globalization from below," taking the form of non- government organizations (NGOs) or the new, transnational advocacy networks (TANs). The emergence of these "globalization from below" organizations and networks contest the current form of globalization, by developing arguments for an international civil society, on behalf of the poorer 80 percent of the world population, totaling 6 billion in 2000.

Many commentators are writing about the economic crises affecting Russia and Asian, Eastern European, and South American countries, which many Western economists hoped were heading towards economic growth and prosperity. How-ever, current indicators suggest there is doubt concerning the continuation of eco-nomic growth within these countries, and even fear of an uncontrollable collapse of the global economy. In the *Guardian Weekly*, Elliot (1998) writes about "capi-talism on a fast road to ruin," and Gray (1998) comments that "unfettered capi-tal spells global doom." Similarly, in *Le Monde Diplomatique*, Halimi (1998) con-tributes an article translated as "The shipwreck of liberal dogma," and Balligand (1998) contributes an article translated as "Globalization, the state and the mar-ket." Halimi remarks:

Furnished with this poor intellectual logic [the neoliberal economic paradigm] and a box of tools which contains only four big hammers (deregulation, privatization, lowering taxes, and the free market), international economic organizations have been busy trans-forming the world into the image of the Anglo-Saxon model. The cult of the 'new' per-mitted them to ignore all the precedents; the market and the opening of markets would guarantee everyone prosperity and democracy. (p. 18)

Halimi (1998) quotes a disillusioned neoliberal: "To propagate capitalism does not constitute simply an exercise of economic engineering. It is also an assault against the culture and the politics of other nations which will almost always guarantee a collision" (p. 18).

Balligand (1998) notes a difference between the latest economic crisis in 1998, particularly in Asia, and the previous crises in 1987 and 1994, in areas includ-ing Eastern Europe, Brazil, and Mexico. The present crisis indicates increasing difficulty to stabilize world financial markets. Balligand identifies one benefit of the latest financial crisis:

It reminds us that factors such as regulation and stabilizing the markets allows the mar-kets to develop in a more peaceful environment. The banking sector is in need of stable guidelines in time and space (regional, national and European), just as the public sector is in need of financial innovations from the private sector which could ameliorate the quality of its interventions. (p. 26)

He further states, "The law of the market does not exist and neither does the invisible hand of the market" (p. 26), thus outlining the necessity for regulation based on a code of good conduct for the financial sector.

The OECD has developed a more cautious attitude towards a free market. Al-though many OECD publications are openly biased towards utilizing market forces, there is a recognition that curbs should be placed on unfettered capital-ism. The OECD agrees with Rodrik (1997) who suggests that the greater the openness of an economy, the greater the need for intensified social expenditure. Hence, one effect of globalization could be to increase the demand for social pro-tection. The OECD (1998a) summarizes the argument, stipulating that "increased international trade and investment is, thus, an additional reason to improve the efficiency of public social protection systems, rather than a ration-ale to reduce overall levels of protection" (pp. 58–59).

Globalization is described as being a positive and negative force, depending extensively upon one's vantage point. This depends upon geographical and occupational location: residing in a high growth economy in the North or a stagnating, vulnerable economy in the South; working as a high-tech knowledge producer or being an unemployed person. This also depends upon one's sense of justice and basic values: joining the protesters against corporate globalization or becoming a free trader amassing profits.

Globalization and Internationalization

At this juncture, some distinctions should be drawn between globalization and internationalization, due to the frequent slippage and interchangeability of these terms used by many writers. Scholte (2000) views global relations as conceptually distinct from international relations: "Whereas international relations are *inter*territorial relations, global relations are *supra*territorial relations. International relations are *cross*-border exchanges over distance, while global relations are *trans*-border exchanges *without* distance. Thus global economics is different from international economics; global politics is different from international politics, and so on. Internationality is embedded in territorial space; globality transcends that geography" (p. 49).

Sklair (2001) distinguishes between internationalization and globalization by succinctly stating that "if it is to mean anything more than internationalization, globalization must at least mean that capitalists (or any other globalizing forces) seek to transcend the national in search of the global" (p. 16). He restricts the term *global* to the processes of globalization, including the "establishment of a borderless global economy, the complete denationalization of all corporate procedures and activities, and the eradication of economic nationalism" (p. 3).

Within this book, we use the term globalization to represent neoliberal economic ideology and its material strategies that aim to increase profits and power for transnational corporations, and similar strategies enabling government agencies to gain economic advantages and be competitive. This often leads to the homogenization of cultures and promotion of so-called "world best practice," where one idea is considered the best strategy to progress within the world economy. However, global tools such as the Internet enable the exchange of ideas regarding neoliberal globalization and the organization of protests against free trade. These tools minimize the world, compressing time and space regularly, although not always, resulting in negative consequences, such as creating greater income inequalities and not reducing the plight of the world's poor, or making organizations leaner and meaner and individuals work faster and more intensely. This may result in considerable productivity, yet the poor and the workers do not appear to gain many benefits.

Generally, internationalization involves agreements between or among nations or regions, such as the European Community, furthering cultural or diplomatic exchanges. It represents a positive exchange of ideas and people contributing to a more tolerant world. Ideally, internationalization should lead to a world where neither one culture nor economic system dominates, but rather, where a plurality of cultures and ethnic diversity are recognized and valued. The organizations that promote internationalization, such as the United Nations and its agencies (UNESCO, for instance), are more likely to allow equal representation among nation-states and humanitarian goals. However, domination by key players, such as the United Nations Security Council, remains. Nevertheless, there is increasing recognition of sovereignty and the need to listen to the concerns of all nations on a more equal basis.

Developments in Europe illustrate elements of globalization and internationalization. For instance, in the last decade, political, cultural, and academic rationales have been driving internationalization. Recently, however, economic rationales have assumed primary importance, explained by Haug (1999) as a shift from cooperation to competition. The 1999 Bologna Declaration reflects these rationales, stressing student and staff mobility, and the competitiveness, quality, and attractiveness of European higher education (van der Wende, 2001). Countries involved in the European Economic Community including long-standing members, newcomers, and aspiring members, have developed policy initiatives related to these objectives. A striking structural change concerns the implementation of an undergraduate-graduate program (Bachelor-Master) and the development of national and European quality assurance mechanisms. Van der Wende (2001) highlights the diversity of internationalization approaches: "Anglo-Saxon countries have chosen an explicit (and sometimes even aggressive) *competitive* approach to internationalization of higher education, by contrast, most continental European countries seem to pursue a more *cooperative* approach" (p. 255). This latter approach resembles the academic and cultural values of continental academics and administrators.

The OECD (1996) encouraged universities to think of internationalization as preparation for a global economy. This represents a shift from thinking of internationalization as a means to promote tolerance and cosmopolitanism to thinking of internationalization as globalization.

Internationalism should be seen as preparation for twenty-first century capitalism. If the goal of making government policies more supportive of these objectives is to be realized, then the educational policies of the higher education institutions must become more integrated with the economic policies of government and of the private sector. Higher educational institutions must become more oriented to the demands of trade and markets in terms of their educational content, approach, and outlook (OECD, 1996, p. 11).

Significantly, the OECD is one institution favoring neoliberal globalization and encouraging cross-border trade in educational services. Thus, it is important to identify the underlying purpose and motivation for particular interpretations of terms like internationalization and globalization. The goal of the OECD is economic growth and free trade, leading to increasing trade in university education. Therefore, using the terms interchangeably is beneficial for the OECD.

For our purposes, *globalization* represents *neoliberal*, market-oriented forces enabling a borderless world, and *internationalization* represents arrangements between nation-states primarily cultivating greater *tolerance* and exchange of ideas.

A similar interchange of globalization and internationalization occurs in literature concerning universities. Scott (1998) argues that universities have not been international organizations in the past and continue not to be in terms of cultivating tolerance or exchange of ideas. He suggests that internationalist rhetoric cannot be accepted at face value. In Western Europe, universities emerged as distinctive institutions in a world where nation-states did not exist; therefore, they could not be truly international institutions. Scott argues that the modern university is a national and a novel institution:

Now, at the very end of the twentieth century, the university faces a new environment—an environment in which the older neo-imperialist notions of internationalism are by no means dead but have been overlaid by new processes of globalization. And these processes ... cannot simply be seen as a reiteration of the old internationalism, still dysfunctionally dominated by the West but are now intensified by the new information technologies. Globalization cannot be regarded simply as a higher form of internationalization. Instead of their relationship being seen as linear or cumulative, it may actually be dialectical. In a sense the new globalization may be the rival of the old internationalization. If this is true, the role of the university becomes more problematical. (p. 124)

There are numerous programs in universities throughout the world trying to cultivate international exchanges that foster greater tolerance, which are to be applauded as expressions of genuine internationalization. However, recently initiated programs gaining revenue from international students should not be considered a form of internationalization but a part of the university's neoliberal globalization agenda. Some universities are involved in both types of programs: student/staff exchanges, and providing scholarships to Third World students in the spirit of cooperation and internationalization while simultaneously recruiting overseas students to gain revenue.

GLOBALIZATION AND UNIVERSITIES

When considering the impact of globalization on universities, it is imperative to acknowledge the latest transformation of the nation-state into a competitive player within the new global marketplace. Primarily, this new competitive state creates markets where none existed and encourages public institutions to behave in market-rational ways (Lingard & Rizvi, 1998; Sassen, 2000). Therefore, education becomes less a part of social policy and more a part of economic policy. During the past two decades, governments have attempted to coerce universities to become more enterprising and competitive. This has affected the institutions' funding and management concerning the types of research undertaken, student profiles, teaching loads, and collegial relations.

Governments require universities to serve national interests within the global marketplace, emphasizing the practical and technical value of higher education. Consequently, students begin to view universities in an instrumental way, as serving their individual economic goals. Key economic elements include building partnerships between universities and industries, and recognizing that educational products commute easily across borders, creating a borderless higher education system. This gives an advantage to universities and enables them, like transnational companies, to form alliances and deliver education on a global scale, using Internet technology.

The impact of globalization on universities is exemplified in Australia, where a decade of reforms deregulated and commercially oriented the higher education system. This pattern may not occur in all countries; however, Anglo-American countries, such as Britain, Canada, New Zealand and the United States, follow this model to a certain degree. From the mid-1980s through the 1990s, Australian governments and legislative agencies introduced numerous initiatives aimed at privatizing the costs of education. In 1985, the Labor government ended the Overseas Student Program, which provided scholarships for Third World students, and instead encouraged universities to charge overseas students full fees. Essentially, this was a system deregulation, allowing universities to individually market themselves, recruit overseas students, especially from neighboring Asian countries, and charge self-appointed fees. This resulted in one of the largest increases in the proportions of international students studying in any country. For instance, from 1994 to 1998 the number of international students in Australian universities doubled (41,244 to 84,304) and continues to increase each year. There are close to 100,000 international students in Australian universities in 2001. In addition, in 1989 certain postgraduate courses became liable to fees; by 1994 these restrictions were almost entirely removed, effectively making postgraduate coursework a fee-paying domain. In 1998, the Coalition (Liberal and National political parties) allowed universities to enroll and charge fees to a small proportion of private Australian undergraduates. Crucially, this was accompanied by a lowering of government support for individual students, payments were reduced, and income tests tightened. From 1984 to 1996 the proportion of students unable to obtain government support almost doubled, from 35.1 to 61.9 percent (Marginson, 1997a).

Due to these measures, in the decade following the Dawkins (former Labor minister for education) reforms, the proportion of higher education income (HECS and other fees) contributed by students rose from 3 to above 24 percent, while the proportion contributed by government fell from 91 to 62 percent (Marginson, 1997a). However, from 1988 to 1998 student enrollments increased by over 45 percent, while the real operating funds per full-time student fell by approximately 15 percent (Marginson, 1997a:, p. 220). Since 1998, government funding has fallen further, currently representing only 50 percent of funding for many universities. Also, the managerial level experienced changes in style, structure, and nomenclature directed towards streamlined administration, increased control over spending, and flexible staffing practices. In addition, there was an explicit attempt to move universities from collegial to executive decision making.

Due to these developments, Marginson and Considine (2000) suggest that universities in Australia have changed "more in the 1990s than in the previous 40 years" (p. 39). They also argue that "neoliberal policies have been enforced with greater rigor in Australia than in the United States. Fiscal constraints have been tighter and competition reform has been harder" (p. 54). Many academics agree, and believe that intellectual traditions are being forcibly displaced by market directives. Coady (1996), professor of philosophy at Melbourne, explains that these new practices threaten "intellectual virtues such as honesty, intellectual courtesy, indifference to the mere fashion in ideas, and a dedication to the regulative ideal of truth" (p. 51).

These concerns are particularly echoed in Anglo-American countries. For instance, in discussing the impact of corporatization on Canadian public universities, Polster (2000) proposes that academics may favor advancing profitable links with industry, at the expense of real interests, due to the incentives and penalties involved. Moreover, she warns:

As for corporate links, they are not an add-on to the university, such that after their establishment one has the old university plus these links. Corporate links are an add-into the university, which produce the qualitative changes that pervade its multiple and interacting aspects and dimensions including its culture, operating practices, funding systems, reward structures, etc. (p. 183)

Tudiver (1999), another Canadian academic, suggests that:

Operating universities like businesses changes their essence. Gearing to the market means redefining relevance. Social values that have shaped higher education are replaced by measures of financial viability. Research and teaching are assessed in narrow market terms. Profit becomes the guiding principle for deciding which services and products to offer.... Corporations draw faculty into a search for sales rather than truth, favouring projects with strong market potential over theoretical or basic research. Inherent value of the work is less important than its potential to generate revenue. (p. 168)

Similarly, in the United States, Press and Washburn (2000) contend that commercially sponsored research puts disinterested inquiry at risk. They describe university administration as co-capitalist, systematically downgrading arts faculties where many academics remain disengaged from market values. The humanities have been "neglected, downgraded, and forced to retrench" due to the "market-model university" which prioritizes those subjects that "make money, study money, or attract money" (p. 52). Likewise, Miyoshi (1998) describes how the function of the university has become industrial management with an "unmistakable reduction of its public and critical role" (p. 263). He further reflects upon this endangered tradition: "From Fichte and von Humboldt, through Newman and Arnold or even Thorstein Veblen, the university was thought of as a part of national culture, national history, national identity, and national governance. The construction and maintenance of the coherent nation-state was at the core of its agenda" (p. 262).

Pragmatically, a well-documented consequence of university corporatization is the increase in workloads. In 1993 Australian academics worked an average of almost 48 hours per week, an increase of approximately 3 hours since the 1970s (McInnis, 1996). Coaldrake and Stedman (1999) report that from 1993 to 1998, the system became increasingly strained as student enrollment rose by 17 percent, while academic staff numbers remained static or decreased. In 1999 McInnis (2000) surveyed academics and found that, in the last five years, overall working hours had increased by 1.5 hours. He also reported a steep decline in the level of overall satisfaction from 76 to 51 percent, and a rise in the level of work-induced stress from 52 to 56 percent. He noted that the majority of academics mentioned loss of morale and the deterioration of working conditions. These findings were corroborated by the National Tertiary Education Union (2000), that found the majority of academics worked, on average, 52.8 hours per week. In addition, the majority of staff reported increased workloads since 1996, most working in departments that had staff reductions.

Perhaps the most marked characteristic of the "corporatized" university is its downgrading of collegiality. As a result, success is tenuous, individualized, and highly tailored to the needs of the entrepreneurial institution. Another potential casualty of the corporatized university is academic freedom. It appears that abuses of academic freedom are on the increase in Anglo-American universities and are taking different forms than they did half a century ago, when loyalty oaths and political ideology were questioned. The commercialization of research and partnerships with industry are limiting the public sharing of research findings (Graham, 2000; Oliveri, 2000). When academics have tried to publicize results unfavorable to industry partners, university managers have not supported the academics, acting to silence them (Currie, 2001a). When academics have challenged these selective disclosure policies, publishing their findings, they have been dismissed or suspended. Industry partners try to get confidentiality agreements in their contracts with universities, delaying publication of research findings until patents are obtained or they secure other rights over the intellectual property.

Newson (1992) discusses similar shifts in Canadian universities, showing that marginalization of faculty is "rooted in the complex changes that must be understood as more than simply the adoption by university administrators of a corporate style of management" (pp. 239–240). She argues that these changes and the links between universities and the corporate sector are interwoven. Yet not all academics oppose these connections; rather, they benefit from the increased flow of industry funds into their areas for research and development. This differentiation among faculty is another consequence of globalization; as flexibility of work patterns increases, some faculty are paid handsome salaries while others barely survive on their incomes. Slaughter (1993) writes about retrenchments within U.S. universities, the simple rule being that those who are closer to the market are deemed sacrosanct and those who are not battle to survive, thereby fragmenting the scholarly community and weakening the social contract.

Many have written about the increasing part-time and temporary academic workforce. Rhoades (1998) describes how managers are restructuring the academic profession due to privatization:

The terms and position of faculty's professional labor are being renegotiated as managers seek to reform, reinvent, re-engineer, redesign, or reorganize colleges and universities.... Higher education executives have sought greater flexibility in shaping and controlling the configuration, distribution, activity, and output of the academic work force. Such efforts have implications for faculty's reward structures, their job security, the ratio of part- to full-timers, the use of technology in delivering curriculum, outside employment, and intellectual property rights. (p. 3)

The attack on and elimination of tenure is another example of how managers and legislators use their power to reform academic work. In the 1990s, tenure was eliminated in numerous American and all U.K. universities. Currently, post-tenure reviews are common in many American universities, giving management greater flexibility over employees. Rhoades (1998) argues that managerial discretion is broad and expanding, heightening the hierarchy and divisions within the American academic profession. He also indicates that faculty are no longer involved in allocating university budgets, particularly noting that faculty do not purchase or establish new instructional technologies. Rhoades, focusing on unionized faculty, explores whether unions have negotiated rights, controls, and limits surrounding the use of instructional technology.

Newson (1998), discussing an eight-week strike at York University in Toronto, identifies management's imposition of new technologies on academic and general staff as a pivotal issue. The striking staff voiced concerns about the overbearing and overly corporate style of management, the increasing commercialization of campus culture, and the influence of corporations on research and teaching programs. As part of the negotiated settlement ending the strike, faculty gained greater control over the use of new technologies in the university and acquired aspects of intellectual property rights regarding developing online courses. However, most academics are unaware of the intellectual property issues of online courses and the implications of new technologies on their work.

Around the globe, many universities are jumping on the online education bandwagon, the epitome of globalizing universities. In an article titled, "The Globalization of Education," Langlois, Litoff, and Iiacqua (2001) describe a joint project, using the Internet, between an American college and two Belarusian institutions. The project coordinators describe the use of Internet technologies and interactive teaching as a powerfully democratizing influence on Belarusian learners. This suggests a culturally myopic view that American models of learning are superior to Belarusian teaching styles, and also provides an example of cultural interpenetration of educational institutions through online education (Marginson & Mollis, 1999/2000).

Since the Internet began, universities have led information and communication technologies (ICTs) experimentation in research and teaching. Harley (2001), director of the Higher Education in the Digital Age Project at Berkeley, describes some challenges facing universities in this "uncertain future," and various models that have developed: "We are all aware of the emergence in the past few years of a diverse array of online education models—for-profit ventures (Fathom.com, NYUonline), equity stakes in external companies (University of Chicago, Columbia University, Unext.com), university consortia (Universitas 21, WGU, University Alliance for On-line Learning), licensing agreements (Pearson, McGraw-Hill), and most recently, the MIT OpenCourseWare initiative" (p. 12).

Harley (2001) does not view online education as a panacea, predicting an ongoing market for residential higher education and expecting an innovative blend of ICTs into courses, on-site or off-site. However, as with other global practices, there are proponents and opponents of online education. Interestingly, shortly after the publication of Harley's article, NYUonline and other online for-profit ventures, such as Virtual Temple and UMUC online, were closed by their universities. Carlson and Carnevale (2001) in an article titled, "Debating the Demise of NYUonline," question whether the trend of venture companies going under would continue due to the economic recession or whether NYUonline was just poorly managed. The university had already invested $25 million and decided not to sink more into a losing venture. The article notes that online enrollments grew in other universities, such as Penn State and the University of Maryland, where enrollments continue at a healthy rate, and the University of Phoenix, where enrollments doubled. It will be some years before it is known whether the investments in online education will pay off for universities.

The impact of globalization on institutional policies in the Netherlands serves as a contrast to those of Anglo-Saxon countries. It is important to note, however, that their policies are not necessarily representative of continental European trends. The Dutch government, similar to those of Anglo-Saxon countries, is aware of the economic importance of higher education. Two recent policy documents, *Borderless Learning* (2001) and *Towards an Open Higher Education System* (2000), refer to a 1997 European Council decision in Lisbon, stressing knowledge, innovation, and social cohesion as the means to make Europe the most dynamic and competitive region in the world. Following this convention, the Dutch government ambitiously sought a means for Dutch universities to become part of the elite among universities in Europe and to contribute to the strengthening of the knowledge economy. Noneconomic elements were also stressed in the policies, the central concepts being quality, accessibility, and efficiency. The policy issues and instruments proposed and applied reflect the dual approach of the Dutch government. Issues high on the political agenda are implementing the Bachelor-Master structure, developing accreditation, establishing adequate information and communication technology infrastructure, increasing flexibility in teaching and learning, and developing excellence in research and teaching. Most of these issues can be considered a mixture of economic and noneconomic rationales, in which one rationale may be more profound than the other.

When investigating the proposed policies and those actually implemented, the Dutch government remained loyal to traditional instruments already in place for approximately two decades. These policy instruments consist of "steering from a distance" and planning and control, meaning that the government seriously assumes the role of being constitutionally responsible for higher education. Therefore, the government regulates and controls elements of the higher education system, but concurrently leaves considerable autonomy to the institutions. Market mechanisms are visible in the policies, but not as extensively as in Anglo-Saxon countries. Increases in student fees and changes to grant eligibility mean that students have to pay a larger share of higher education costs, and that higher education institutions are expected to earn a larger share of their income from nongovernment agencies. In addition, due to funding changes within higher education, the amount of money granted to an institution is increasingly determined by specific outcome-based performance measures, such as the number of graduates and Ph.D. completions, instead of student enrollment numbers. The introduction of these mechanisms indicates a neoliberal perspective of higher education. However, many of the changes comprise only small steps towards the neoliberal model, and to some extent proposals are thwarted in the corporate-pluralist model of consultation and decision making. In sum, the Dutch example illustrates that there are countries where the economic globalization perspective is not predominant, and where economic rationales are coupled with cultural and academic rationales. Thus the impact, including negative consequences, will not be as profound as in many Anglo-Saxon countries.

This chapter has mainly concentrated on the negative consequences of globalizing practices, with continental European developments indicating a smaller impact overall. This chapter has focused on the introduction of corporate business practices into universities and their potential threat to traditional university values, noting with concern the decline of collegiality and the rise of a corporate managerial culture. Administrators are borrowing "best practice" techniques from corporations, including various forms of accountability mechanisms and employee flexibility policies, leading to a decline in morale and grave concern for the future of the traditional university.

However, there can be positive outcomes and benefits of globalization—new technologies transforming communication processes in higher education; the reduction of world distance due to the rapid exchange of information; the development of global networks through the Internet, enabling greater collaboration in research and teaching; and the increasing mobility of students and scholars. The world can benefit from international knowledge exchange, possibly developing more open-mindedness and tolerance towards a pluralistic world. In addition, collaboration between private and public research laboratories may enable faster problem solving, hence finding cures for illnesses. Thus, the use of technology is instrumental to the speed of discovery.

The tools of globalization can be used both constructively and destructively, with unwarranted globalizing practices resisted, adapted, or accepted without question. The underlying thesis of this book is that globalization is *not* an inexorable force. Yet certain aspects—the more material and structural aspects—actually and undeniably exist. For instance, national economies are becoming integrated into a global economy, the Internet enables faster communication, compressing time and space, English is becoming a world language, and certain television networks are dominating the airwaves.

Academics can be at the forefront of questioning the ideological underpinnings of globalization, and analyzing the complex intertwining of economic, political, and cultural dimensions of globalization and their impact on universities. We collected empirical data to discover how globalizing practices are penetrating universities. We were curious to investigate whether uniformity and fragmentation are occurring simultaneously, and whether academics are becoming more individualized or similar in terms of their work organization and structure. Most importantly, we wanted to know if academics are adapting to or resisting particular globalizing practices.

CASE STUDIES

Case studies are a method of establishing, at the grassroots level, how university academics are responding to specific global trends. Through university documents, national statistics, reports, and historical and contemporary accounts,[3] universities can be contextualized within their national settings. This allows the question: How do the contexts in which these universities are situated alter their responses? Having key respondents in each university to check the case study reports, our confidence increased that we are presenting a fairly accurate picture of these universities. The respondents gave their opinions and thoughts about what was occurring at their universities. Therefore, this is a qualitative, systematic study of how certain globalizing practices affect these four universities. It is not a definitive study of how all the managers and academics in these institutions see the impact of these globalizing practices, nor is it a comprehensive survey with scaled responses to questions. Due to time constraints, students or general staff could not be interviewed. However, what will be presented is a clear picture of how diverse academic and administrative staff cope with rapid change in their university.

We interviewed between 31 and 37 individuals at each site. Chapter 2 details the sample, provides methodological information, and discusses the university context. By interviewing a range of senior administrators and academic staff, it was possible to determine if a person's position, discipline, age, or gender affected his/her responses. Basically, the aim was to discover if academics and managers respond similarly to their changing environments.

One hunch we had at the beginning of the study was that European universities were responding differently than Anglo-American universities to these globalizing practices. There was curiosity as to whether this was the case and, if so, why. Why were some universities more willing to adopt these globalizing practices? Why did some universities perceive globalization as inevitable and other universities resist the process? Were some universities keen to stand by their traditions and not take the globalizing path? Was the future of the universities that were resisting globalization doomed if they did not adopt certain globalizing practices?

OVERVIEW OF THE BOOK

Chapter 2 contextualizes the study, giving a brief overview of the national system of each country studied and a description of each university, discussing the methodology used, and describing the sample. (For a more detailed depiction of the sample see Appendix I.) Each of Chapters 3 to 7 takes one globalizing practice and explores it theoretically and empirically.

Chapter 3 analyzes responses to questions on privatization, competition, and entrepreneurialism. Globalizing practices have impacted all four universities, even France and Norway, where funding cuts have been minor. There is increasing competition for research funds in each university, with most respondents being encouraged to become more entrepreneurial. There is greater privatization and acceptance of its inevitability, even desirability, than anticipated. However, there is a clear difference between the continental public universities and the competitive private universities, with the University of Twente standing between as the entrepreneurial public university, accepting privatization reforms. In all four universities, market reforms were perceived to have advantages and disadvantages. Only in Boston and less so in Twente are the reforms internalized. Resistance remains strong, change is uneven, and hybrid mixes of public and private appear to be the wave of the future.

Chapter 4 takes the political dimension of globalization as a point of departure, addressing the issue of institutional governance in relation to globalizing practices and neoliberal ideologies, often accompanied by managerialism (McBurnie, 2001). The key question is whether managerialism leads to increased homogeneity in institutional governance. Managerialism consists of a strengthened executive leadership, instrumental rationality, and centralized decision making in universities. Using a sophisticated analytical framework, country reports with historical views, and the four case studies, the chapter concludes that the impact of managerialism cannot be denied. However, differences among universities remain due to the maintenance of traditions.

Chapter 5 addresses the concomitant change in accountability systems partly resulting from changes in the governance of universities, usually giving universities greater autonomy. This chapter analyzes which developments related to globalization have an impact on national and institutional policies and on the daily practices of academics and administrators. What is the intended impact of increasing attention to quality assurance? To which constituents are universities becoming more or less accountable? Two crucial elements in the analysis are the possible gap between policies and practices and the dynamics that accountability produces in relationships among higher education actors. This chapter summarizes national developments and describes the practices within the four university systems. Respondents were asked how they dealt with accountability mechanisms and whether they would like to see changes to the current situation.

A further consequence of privatization relates to the need for greater employment flexibility in universities. Anglo-American universities have adopted globalizing practices leading to more part-time workers and less security for university staff. Simultaneously, European universities have maintained the tradition of the civil service and lifetime employment. Chapter 6 reviews the literature addressing tenure and permanent employment in American and European universities, describing responses to the question of whether tenure is an important principle to maintain in their university. This chapter explores why the respondents feel that keeping tenure is important and the possible results of abandoning tenure.

Perhaps the greatest change universities are facing concerns integrating new technologies into teaching and research programs. Chapter 7 explores the impact of new technologies on these universities. Should instructional technologies be viewed as instruments of the globalization process or as its antidote? Whether viewed from the student's or teacher's point of view, e-learning and e-teaching tend to generate new types of pedagogic models where interactivity replaces interaction. The four universities have strong policies concerning technological equipment. However, it was equally evident that buildings are more easily wired than minds, with most academics remaining suspicious of the didactic implications of the technological revolution. The danger is that universities will be bypassed by the moneymaking strategies of multimedia publishing conglomerates where e-teaching is simply a profitable form of e-commerce.

Chapter 8 summarizes the findings, demonstrating the interrelatedness of globalizing practices and their impact upon universities. It is not assumed that neoliberal globalization is inevitable; however, it is understood that certain globalizing practices will persist, and universities will have to adapt their practices to a changing global environment. A final question posed concerns the future role of universities in their respective societies. Most academics want universities to maintain their core, traditional values of basic research, academic freedom, critical thinking, and social critique. Yet concurrently, academics want universities to embrace changes to become more relevant within a global world, by undertaking entrepreneurial and applied research, serving the region and community, and developing skills for a global society.

NOTES

1. Between 2000 and 2001, major demonstrations were held against the World Trade Organization in Seattle, the World Bank in Washington, DC, the World Economic Forum in Melbourne, the expansion of NAFTA to the Americas in Quebec, and the G8 in Genoa. These were mostly peaceful demonstrations, only becoming violent due to police provocation.

2. The extent to which the World Bank and the IMF are supranational organizations can be questioned, as they are often highly influenced by key rich states, such as the United States and certain Western European countries.

3. One by Burtchaell (1998) on Boston College, and one by Clark (1998) on the University of Twente.

Chapter 2

Context and Design of the Study

This research project analyzes qualitative data gathered through in-depth interviews with academics and managers from four diverse universities in France, the Netherlands, Norway, and the United States. The involvement of individuals located within each institution enables a greater understanding of the formal structures and operations in practice, and how the specific context mediates the impact of globalizing trends. Data on Australia is added to contrast with these four countries, demonstrating that Anglo-American countries, rather than European countries, are leaders in globalizing trends. It is important to emphasize that this research is not a strictly comparative study because we did not control the sample of institutions or the interview respondents to enable a statistical or explanatory comparison of our findings (see Ragin, 1987; Goedegebuure & van Vught, 1994). Nevertheless, some trend comparisons are revealed through the empirical data.

COMPARISONS OF NATIONAL SYSTEMS

Similar Economic and Social Levels

This brief comparison includes five countries belonging to the Organisation for Economic Cooperation and Development (OECD). These countries are mainly high-income, high standard of living, industrialized nations and, according to 1998 OECD figures, have a mid to high Gross Domestic Product (GDP) per capita. Table 2.1 compares these per capita incomes using two measures: their current exchange rates and their purchasing power parity. For instance, Norway recorded the highest GDP per capita based on the current

Table 2.1
GDP per capita 1998 (in US dollars)

Country	At Current Exchange Rates	At Purchasing Power Parity
Norway	33,174	27,391
USA	32,184	32,184
Netherlands	24,921	24,141
France	23,954	21,132
Australia	19,900	24,192

Source: Organization of Economic Cooperation and Development (OECD) 1998c.

exchange rate, while the United States recorded the highest based on purchasing power parity. In contrast, Australia recorded the lowest GDP per capita based on the current exchange rate but a higher one based on purchasing power parity than France. Overall, this table shows the high standard of living enjoyed within these five countries.

In 2000, the growth rate percentages of these countries were fairly similar: the United States high with 5, Norway low with 2.7, France with 3.1, the Netherlands with 4, and Australia with 4.7. In addition, inflation rates were similarly modest, below 4 percent. Yet population sizes varied enormously: the United States with 278.1 million, France with 59.5 million, Australia with 19.3 million, the Netherlands with 15.9 million, and Norway with 4.5 million. However, all had a lower population growth rate than replacement rate, in percent: Australia at .99, the United States at .90, the Netherlands at .55, Norway at .49, and France at .37.

An additional measure often used to judge national well-being is population life expectancy, which in Table 2.2 shows little difference between men and women within respective countries. In 1999, the difference between highest and lowest for men and women was two to three years. Interestingly, for men, Australia had the longest life expectancy at 75.6 years, and the United States had the lowest at 73.6 years. For women, France had the longest life expectancy at 82.3 years, and the United States had the lowest at 79.4 years.

In addition, all have high rates of literacy, some degree of welfare provision, and democratic government forms, based on competitive two-party or multi-party electoral systems. Of the countries investigated, three are constitutional monarchies (Australia,[1] Norway and the Netherlands) and two are republics (France and the United States). Within the three European countries there are many varying political parties, including communist, liberal democratic, conservative, green/environmental, and nationalist or xenophobic, extreme-right parties. In contrast, the United States and Australia basically have two-party systems, although within Australia third parties have more political leverage,

Table 2.2
Life Expectancy at Birth, 1997

	Women	Men
Australia	81.3	75.6
France	82.3	74.6
Norway	81.0	75.4
Netherlands	80.6	75.2
USA	79.4	73.6

Source: Organization of Economic Cooperation and Development (OECD) 2000.

due to preferential voting and proportional representation in the Senate. Moreover, the political parties within the United States and Australia are more to the economic right than European countries.

Mass Higher Education

According to Trow (1996), mass higher education refers to a system that educates over 15 percent of an age cohort. Today the figure is closer to 25 percent of an age cohort. The United States has provided mass higher education for at least three decades, and European countries have started to provide it during the past two decades. However, some countries have surpassed the United States in the percentage of students graduating from high school and commencing tertiary studies. In 1998, the net entry percentages for tertiary education showed Norway at 62, the United States at 58, Australia and the Netherlands at 53, and France at 52 (OECD, 1998b). However, Table 2.3 depicts an alternate participation measure, examining the participation rate for ages 25 to 64. This shows similar rates among countries, with a 3 percent difference between the highest and lowest, the United States at 26.6 and Norway at 23.7.

Recently, higher participation rates in tertiary education have led to policies aimed at increasing efficiency and completion; for instance, contracting in France, consolidation and institutional profiling in Australia, and funding formulas in Norway (Wagner, 1996). During the 1970s, the United States introduced user-pays and competitive policies. In 1989, Australia introduced the Higher Education Contribution Scheme (HECS), allowing students to defer fees until earning a reasonable income. However, over the past decade fees have steadily increased, and the reasonable income required before repaying has steadily decreased. Currently, these fees are among the highest *public* fees in the world, ranging from A$2,500 to A$5,000 per year. In addition, only low income earners are given government grants for living costs. In the 1980s, the Netherlands

Table 2.3
Participation Rates for Tertiary-Level Education Overall for Ages 25–64, 1999

Country	Participation Rate
USA	26.6
Australia	25.8
Netherlands	24.2
France	24.0
Norway	23.7

Source: Organization for Economic Cooperation and Development (OECD) 2000.

began charging higher yearly tuition fees, increasing annually by NLG 100, reaching NLG 2,250 in 1994. During 1996, fees were further increased by NLG 500, reaching NLG 2,750 by 1998 or approximately US$1,380 at 1998 currency rates. In addition, students receive government grants and loans for living and tuition costs. Dutch fees are relatively low compared to those in Australia or the United States. In Norway, higher education remains virtually tuition free. Likewise, in France, modest fees are charged and living allowances supplied.

During the past decade, there has been a doubling of higher education enrollments virtually worldwide. However, only the public funding in Norway and Singapore has kept pace, allowing Norway to support students with grants or loans, to be repaid after graduation. In contrast, the University of California receives a low 23 percent of its revenue from the state of California. It is not surprising to learn that in the United States what were formally called state-supported universities are now called state-assisted (Aitkin, 2000).

Different Economic and Social Policies

Despite broad similarities between these countries in standard of living, quality of life, and tertiary education participation, there are indications of differences in their economic and social policies. From a U.S. perspective, the Central Intelligence Agency (CIA) discusses the adaptation of a country's economy to pressing globalization (CIA, 2001). It describes "the US as the largest and most technologically powerful economy in the world. In this market oriented economy, private individuals and business firms make most of the decisions, and government buys needed goods and services predominantly in the private marketplace." It suggests France is "in the midst of transition from an economy that featured extensive government ownership and intervention to one that relies more on market mechanisms" CIA, 2001, Web site). The report critiques France's generous unemployment and retirement benefits and the reduction of the standard working week to 35 hours.

Likewise, the report critiques Norway, labeling it the prosperous bastion of welfare capitalism, combining free market activity and government intervention. In contrast, the Netherlands is described positively, as a prosperous and open economy with stable industrial relations, moderate inflation and a sizable account surplus. The report praises the Netherlands for the implementation, in 2001, of comprehensive tax reform, designed to reduce high income tax levels and redirect the fiscal burden onto consumers. Finally, the report describes Australia as having similar economic policies to the United States, as "a prosperous Western-style capitalist economy, with a per capita GDP at the level of the four dominant West European economies" (CIA, 2001, Web site). The CIA praises the economic reforms as allowing Australia a reasonably high growth rate, despite the Asian crisis and general world economic downturn.

It is evident from the CIA's descriptions that European economic policy has not moved as far right as that of the United States or Australia (Kim & Fording, 1998). For instance, in France both right and left parties want the market regulated: "French voters, of both right and left, have an instinctive mistrust of globalization" (*The Economist*, 2001c, p. 42). In 1993, Edouard Balladur, a conservative prime minister, argued: "What is the market? It is the law of the jungle, the law of nature, and what is civilization? It is the struggle against nature" (cited in *The Economist*, 2001c, p. 42). Recently, President Chirac similarly stated, "Our democracies clearly cannot be mere spectators of globalization. They must tame it, accompany it, humanize it, civilize it" (cited in *The Economist*, 2001c, p. 42). Prime Minister Jospin, a former Trotskyite in his youth, commented that France should celebrate a citizens' movement against globalization.

The Dutch and Norwegian politicians do not as often express sentiments like this and are loath to abolish welfare policies. In an article discussing French resistance to globalization and Americanization, Lawday states, "You won't catch the French throwing schools, jails, trains and the Paris Metro into private business hands" (2001, p. 3). These are still being run by the Dutch and Norwegian governments. Meanwhile, Australia and the United States have privatized jails, trains, and have encouraged the development of private schools. In addition, within the United States private universities are flourishing, and a few have begun to emerge in Australia.

Within these countries, the movement to privatize the public sector varies depending upon the current economic situation and the political parties in power. For instance, in 2001, France and Norway were social democratic in political orientation, and Table 2.4 shows their higher levels of public sector funding as a percentage of GDP in 1990 and 1996. There has been some decline over that period for the Netherlands and Norway, bringing them closer to the OECD average. Australia and the United States are clearly below the OECD average. Since 1996, government spending in the Netherlands has further declined with changes in its political orientation and economic conditions (CIA, 2001, Web site).

All three European countries still remain committed to the welfare state, although certain aspects are disappearing due to governments moving towards

Table 2.4
Government Spending as a Percent of Gross Domestic Product

Country	1990	1996
France	49.8	54.5
Netherlands	54.0	49.9
Norway	53.8	49.9
OECD Average	46.1	47.1
Australia	34.7	36.6
United States	33.3	33.3

Source: International Monetary Fund (IMF) cited in The World Economy Survey 1998.

the Third Way, between the dogma of free-market capitalism and big-government regulation. During the Cold War, Sweden exemplified the Third Way, between American capitalism and Soviet communism. However, the new Third Way lies between Sweden and the United Sates. The Third Way, according to proponent Anthony Giddens, developed due to declining traditional class politics and the dilemmas facing liberal, social democratic governments concerning the global market. "Giddens distinguishes between the old left's version of the mixed economy, which outside the United States included state ownership of industry, and the Third Way's acceptance of state intervention to help individuals within an economy that is privately owned and managed" (Dionne, 1998, p. 6). As Dionne asserts, "The simple fact is that the regulatory state championed by American liberals and European social democrats has great difficulty working its will in a global market" (p. 6).

French prime minister and socialist Lionel Jospin adopted a managerial, socialist administration retaining strong state regulation. As James (1998) writes, "While being prepared to accept some ideas from the right, such as the privatization of state industries, Mr. Jospin has derided capitalism as 'a force that moves, but which does not know where it is heading.' It is, he believes, the state's role to supply the necessary direction and protect fundamental values of egalitarianism and justice" (p. 1). Recently, Jospin stated that without state guidance there would be "an explosion of inequality, the erosion of the social bond, the menacing of our environment, the enfeebling of our cultural wealth, [and] the loss of long-term perspectives" (cited in James, 1998, pp. 1, 7).

Norway is one of the few countries within Western Europe vetoing European Union membership. Tjeldvoll and Holtet (1998) suggest this does not indicate a wish to withdraw from Europe, but it is illustrative of Norwegian self-confidence and a wish to preserve its unique culture. Tjeldvoll (1998) states, "just before the year 2000 and under the strong influence of a globalized market economy ideology, Norway is still a distinct welfare state" (p. 1). Although there is political consensus concerning the maintenance of welfare state principles, the informal coalition of Conservative, Progressive, and Labour parties is gradually pushing towards neoliberal market reform. For instance, currently the government is considering selling part of its national petroleum company to the private sector. Furthermore, the minister of education has publicly signaled that he prefers the American model, leading to privatization of universities, increasing competition, and making tenure more difficult to obtain.

Norway is one of few countries within the world where public revenue exceeds public spending, thereby giving government greater leeway in social policies. In contrast, the Netherlands is not in surplus and does not have external debt, while Australia, France, and the United States have sizable external debt. In addition, the unemployment rates vary slightly, all remaining under 10 percent. In 2000, the unemployment rates of Norway, the Netherlands and the United States ranged from 2–4 percent, Australia's was 6.4 percent, and France's was 9.7 percent.

The level of technology use is high in most countries, with a lower usage in France (CIA, 2001, Web site). The percentage of population using the Internet is highest in the United States (53) and Norway (52), followed by the Netherlands (43) and Australia (40), and is lowest in France (15). Additionally, the number of Internet providers is largest in the United States (7,800), given its much larger population, followed by Australia (264), France (62), the Netherlands (52), and Norway (13), given their smaller populations.

Table 2.5 highlights a further difference between the European and Anglo-American countries, concerning the distribution of funding from public and private sources for tertiary education. This table shows the influence of privatization on higher education. For instance, the percentage of funds from public sources is greater in European countries (Norway, 97; the Netherlands, 87; and France, 85) than Anglo-American countries (Australia, 58, and the United States, 51), which have to rely increasingly upon private sources.

Table 2.5
Distribution of Public and Private Sources of Funds to Tertiary Education, 1997

Country	Public Sources	Private Sources
Norway	93.0	7.0
Netherlands	87.0	13.0
France	85.0	15.0
Australia	58.0	42.0
USA	51.0	49.0

Source: Organization for Economic Cooperation and Development (OECD) (2000).

Differences in Higher Education Policy and Governance Structures

When addressing higher education governance, McDaniel (1996) stresses the irrelevancy of the old paradigm of differences, the Continental, Anglo-Saxon, or United States models, instead finding that Australia, Norway, and the United States are alike, being "predominantly decentralized," and that France is different, being "predominantly centralized." Goedegebuure and van Vught (1994) make similar observations when comparing models of government steering. For instance, in France higher education institutions are more directly controlled by the state and rely less on incentive funding. Although incentive and formula funding are becoming increasingly attractive to all the countries in this study, each has unique policies concerning competition and privatization of funding.

A study of university autonomy in 20 countries found that within Anglo-American countries, the governments have less authority to intervene and exert direct influence (Anderson & Johnson, 1998). The universities therein are semi-public, often operating as public–private corporations that are outside of government bureaucracy, yet not completely private, for-profit institutions. However, these universities remain in the web of government accountability, being required to lobby legislators for public funding. Conversely, in European countries, government authority to intervene is more apparent. Australia, France, and the United States were included in this study, contributing results between the low to mid range. For instance, to the statement, "Government exerts significant influence on university operation," the United States polled 27 percent; Australia, 35 percent; and France, 43 percent. To the statement, "Government has legal authority to intervene," the United States polled 30 percent; Australia, 32 percent; and France, 78 percent. Almost all countries in this study reported changes towards greater deregulation and exposure to market competition. Concurrently, some countries using the "steering from a distance mechanism" reported increases of government influence in strategic areas. For instance, in the Carnegie study, Australia ranked second on the statement, "There is too much government interference in important academic policies" (Glassick, 1997).

Turner (1996) utilized case studies to examine institutional responses to changing patterns of funding in European higher education, identifying significant trends pertinent to questions pursued in this book, such as how external forces are changing the nature of academic work. He found that external funding has a profound impact on the internal organization, leading to increased managerialism and workplace pressures as responsibilities are passed to departments and individual academics. In addition, institutions respond differently: some comply, others subvert or resist policy directives, depending upon their historical and political context.

In a recent review of tertiary education, the OECD (1998b) encouraged globalizing practices in member countries. These included quality assurance practices, management practices derived from business (namely financial management and strategic institutional profiling), entrepreneurial practices (especially linked with industry and professional communities increasing student access to work situations), and technology in teaching practices. In addition, the review investigated American universities' dynamism, noting their quick decision making, year-round operation, and flexible personnel. Despite the praise for some corporate world practices, there was also hesitancy in totally surrendering universities to market forces: "However, maximizing profit is not the purpose in education, and it is necessary to ask whether the adoption of practices from the business world is consistent with the multiple services expected of educational institutions" (OECD, 1998b, p. 77).

HIGHER EDUCATION SYSTEMS IN THE CASE STUDY COUNTRIES

This section gives a general overview of the higher education system structure in each case study country, beginning with the continental systems (France, the Netherlands, and Norway), and finishing with the United States, the most complex system in terms of public and private sectors and range of institutions. Due to the increasing pressure from organizations like the OECD, the pervasive power of the media, and popular trends, it is necessary to examine the extent to which national systems have adopted and been influenced by globalization.

France

In France, higher education is diverse, with different levels and types of institutions, most part of a bureaucratic, centralized, national, public system. There are 90 universities, over 174 specialized professional schools (*grandes écoles*), numerous university-level technical and professional institutes (*Instituts Universitaires de Technologie* [IUT], and *Instituts Universitaires Professionnalisés* [IUP]) often attached to universities, a non-university technical sector (*Sections de Techniciens Supérieur*), and a few private university-level institutions. Approximately 90 percent of students, or 1.4 out of 1.9 million, are in public universities. All those passing the *Baccalauréat* exam are given automatic entry into higher education, paying registration fees ranging from US$125 to $750. The private institutions are mainly business and specialized professional schools catering to some French and international students. According to the French Science and Technology Policy (2001), over the past four years, the government increased the science budget by 6.8 percent, placing France fourth among OECD countries for research and development spending, and second for public sector spending in 2001.

In 1981, the first left-wing coalition in the history of the Fifth Republic came into government and was committed to democratization, participation, and higher education reform. After the May 1968 turmoil and aftermath, the government began extending the research base, opening universities to surrounding regions and industry. In addition, it began undergraduate and doctoral study reform and restructured the governance and management systems at the institution level. Interestingly, socialists and nonsocialists agreed that the internal efficiency of the French higher education system needed considerable improvement (Neave, 1991, pp. 68–69).

The 1984 Higher Education Guideline Law (*Loi sur l'enseignement supérieur* or *Loi Savary*) gave universities autonomy and independence regarding research activities. However, this autonomy was circumscribed by the limited funds available to universities, since the minister appointed and continues to appoint teacher-researchers and administrative/technical personnel as permanent civil servants. Nevertheless, increasing options for institutional policies and strategic directions have become possible with the implementation of "the contractual policy and the new system of funding which began in 1993" (Neave, 1991, p. 113).

According to Kaiser and Neave (1994), the legislation concerning higher education has often changed during the past 25 years. In 1968, *The Law of Orientation for Higher Education (Loi Faure)* highlighted three elements: autonomy, pluridisciplinarity, and participation of students and staff, giving universities a new status by changing faculty organization and creating a representative council responsible for managing institutions (see Chapter 4). In addition, three councils were designated for university governance: the Administration Council, the Scientific Council, and the Council of Study and University Life. Each consisted of teacher-researchers, students, administrative/technical/worker/service (ATWS), and external representatives. The most important of these is the Administration Council which, for example at the University of Avignon, consists of 18 teacher-researchers, 9 students, 4 ATWS staff, and 9 external representatives, totaling 40 members. The vice president presides over the councils, while all three councils combine to elect the university president. The president is elected for a five-year term and cannot serve subsequent terms after this period. The president assumes financial and administrative authority and is the university representative to the external world and the ministry, where contracts, staff positions, and development schemes are negotiated, prioritized, and passed. In addition, each faculty and institute has a council consisting mainly of teacher-researchers and representatives from various university sectors that elect the dean and director. External representatives hail from local government, business, unions, scientific and cultural organizations, public service organizations, schools and lycées.

In May 1991 France adopted an improvement and development program, *Programme Universités 2000*, for the higher education sector, espousing the following objectives:

To bring more students into higher education and accommodate them.

To adapt higher education economic needs developing vocationally oriented educational programs in all higher education structures and levels.

To work towards regional improvement involving the higher education institutions in the dynamics of regional development.

To prepare for full participation in the European Union and the competition that this membership has caused in intellectual and educational fields (CEPES, 1993; Kaiser & Neave, 1994).

These objectives were developed and implemented due to an immanent shortage of highly skilled technicians/engineers (CEPES, 1993). However, the limited vocational capacity made achieving these objectives particularly challenging. The mismatch between capacities has made vocational institution enrollment difficult and universities overcrowded with an increasingly heterogeneous student population unable to qualify for prestigious higher education institutions. Consequently, French universities are facing more or less contradictory functions: to take all students that do not or cannot enter selective types of higher education, and to maintain a high standard of research and to educate and train high-level researchers (Kaiser & Neave, 1994).

In 1985, the Ministry of Education began external evaluations of universities, establishing the National Evaluation Committee, and by 1994, all universities had been evaluated at least once (Abecassis, 1994). These evaluations were aimed at improving teaching and administrative procedures. In addition, the Ministry asked universities to develop teaching evaluation mechanisms to be introduced in 1998 to 1999. However, any system attempting to monitor teacher-researchers is likely to face resistance in France (see Chapter 5 on accountability).

The Netherlands

The Netherlands has distinctive social and welfare policies and has recently successfully adapted these policies to the neoliberal, cost-cutting climate. Reforms to the tax system and university system have occurred internally without major conflict and without sacrificing growth, exports, or welfare rights (CIA, 2001, Web site).

In the Netherlands, higher education comprises higher professional education and university education, with 59 higher professional education institutions and 14 universities, including an Open University providing distance education. Since 1993, all higher education has been regulated by a single piece of legislation, the Higher Education and Research Act. This provided the statutory framework within which each institution operates, although each can decide its teaching and examinations regulations. Like Norway, Dutch universities are modeled on Humboldtian traditions of powerful chairholders, namely full professors who occupy a dominant position within each research unit and preserve links between teaching and research. In addition, like France and Norway, most academic staff are drawn from within the borders, only 5 percent originating from outside the country (Geurts, Maassen, & van Vught, 1996).

Dutch university education, as in France and Norway, is accessible to all who pass a high school exam. Students are supported by a four-year government grant, and are able to cover living costs by acquiring a loan. Initially, students receive the grant as a loan, becoming a nonrepayable grant if certain performance criteria are met, such as graduating. For example, if a student graduates within six years, the four-year loan is cancelled and the student only repays the extra two years. Basing grants on performance criteria is indicative of the global trend, which aims to make students and universities operate more efficiently.

In 1997, some 259,000 students attended higher professional education institutions, providing theoretical and practical training, with almost 169,000 students pursuing a theoretical education, which may contain some practical and work components. Between 1980 and 1991, student enrollments increased, slowed down, and then stabilized. The percentage of enrollment within the 18 to 23 age cohort increased from 29.3 in 1980 to 50.2 in 1996. Concurrently, similar increases in enrollment occurred in other European countries. For instance, Finland had the highest percentage increase in enrollment of the age cohort, from 32.2 in 1980 to 71.1 in 1996. Also, France had a percentage enrollment increase similar to the Netherlands, from 25.3 in 1980 to 52.2 in 1996 (Boezerooy, 1999).

During the three decades after World War II, Dutch universities were fairly homogeneous and espoused open access and equality policies. In the 1980s and 1990s, the policy goals became quality and differentiation. Open access is still an underlying government goal, but change towards increasing institutional autonomy led to greater accountability and an impetus to differentiate and develop niche markets (Geurts, Maassen, & van Vught, 1996). The Dutch government policy document, Higher Education: Autonomy and Quality (1985), replaced the traditional "controlling" strategy with increased institutional autonomy. The implementation of increased autonomy consisted of lump-sum funding, decentralization of staff policies, and undertaking new financial initiatives (Vossensteyn & Dobson, 1999).

Another important change came with the introduction of the University Government Modernization Act, on 1 September 1997, which strengthened the position of university managers. Each university is run by the executive board, which is established by a supervisory board, which is in turn appointed by the minister. The changes reduced the power of the university council, where staff and students participated in running the university. For instance, the university budget is no longer approved by the university council, but by the supervisory board (see Chapter 4).

Globalizing practice has reduced funds for universities, which has led to the need for greater efficiency in university management. Between 1980 and 1996, Boezerooy (1999) investigated the Gross Domestic Product (GDP) and the percentage of higher education expenditure in nine European countries, finding that most countries' expenditure increased with corresponding growth in enrollments. The Netherlands was the only country where public expenditure decreased markedly, namely a 40 percent decline in public funding of universities, from 1.9 percent of GDP in 1980 to 1.16 percent in 1996. In addition, between 1985 and 1997, there was a decrease in the number of academic and nonacademic staff (3 percent and 1 percent respectively). A report addressing higher education market type mechanisms noted that 80 percent of initial higher education is funded by public resources. "A small but increasing amount is financed through tuition fees. In addition an increasing amount is privately financed as part of a teaching contract" (Kaiser, et al., 1999, p. 87).

Norway

Unlike many Anglo-American countries, Norway has not taken the privatization route. Recently, however, the government has begun to steer the higher education system towards market mechanisms, resulting in a slight reduction in public funding of universities (Tonder & Aamodt, 1993). However, higher education remains a public concern and is publicly financed. In Norway, higher education is regarded as a social right, thereby it is accessible and free of charge to all who qualify. Additionally, interest-free loans are available to students to cover living costs while studying.

During the last decade, Norway has undergone a number of reforms, including:

Norway Network.
The Legal Act of May 12, 1995, No. 22, *On Universities and Higher Education.*
Standardized principles of governance.
Reorganization at the level of basic units.

During 1994, structural ties were formed between college and university sectors and institutions, when 98 state colleges were reorganized into 26 institutions. *Norway Network* was established by the Ministry to increase efficiency and introduce systematic cooperation between institutions, incorporating four universities, six university colleges with professional specializations, and 26 regional colleges. The Ministry encouraged institutions to develop research in limited fields while continuing specialized research in others. In addition, national crediting and admission were to be simplified and standardized to ease student flow between institutions and programs. In 1995, new laws introduced decisive, independent leadership, incorporating small executive boards with external representatives,[2] streamlining decision-making and administrative matters. Universities implemented several changes to promote efficiency: standardized principles, such as management by objective and activity planning; accountability procedures, such as evaluation and performance control; and bigger units, reorganizing the level of basic units (Kyvik & Odegard, 1990).

According to Bleiklie (1996), the most influential higher education import during the past decade has been "new public management" (NPM), enabling universities to be governed like corporate enterprises. However, a University of Oslo case study concluded that NPM, even though mandatory, was unsuccessful, having a minor influence upon internal patterns of influence and behavior. Nevertheless, NPM altered the power relationship between the state and institutions, through state demands for cost effectiveness, accountability, assessment, and surveillance, resulting in decreased institutional autonomy: "The NPM philosophy champions the idea that both *decentralization* of responsibility and a stronger *central control* can be achieved at one and the same time" (Bleiklie, 1996 p. 20). In addition, *Norway Network* and NPM are regarded as important indicators of *decentralized centralized* structure within the higher education system. In a Norwegian tertiary education review, the OECD reinforces this, noting, "the Ministry has substantial power especially over budgets. It is expected that there will be increased pressure for results and greater visibility, in line with the overall governmental policy of results-oriented planning and budgeting" (OECD, 1997, p. 8).

Prior to the institutional reforms during the 1990s, academics in Norway, as in many countries, enjoyed considerable autonomy. However, increasing student enrollments and economic constraints, enacted accountability, and associated government controls have eroded the autonomy once enjoyed. Nevertheless, by world standards, Norwegian academics have significant freedom and control over their daily work patterns. Yet what may have changed, and continues to change, is the amount of money academics can obtain for essential and curiosity-driven research, from sources such as the Ministry, research councils, contracts, and industry. A study of higher education uncovered a decrease in funding for some disciplines, during the 1980s and 1990s, while other disciplines, such as technology, mathematics, and natural resources, are remunerated by external resources—for instance, the oil industry (Kyvik & Odegard, 1990).

Norwegian universities have been challenged by an increasing student population and reforms, leading to conditional funding based on postgraduate completion rates and greater government intervention designating priority research areas (Aamodt, Kyvik, & Skoie, 1991). These indicate an erosion of working conditions, also evident in the changing student-to-staff ratio from 7.8 students per staff member in 1979 to 8.4 in 1993, increasing further during the 1990s (Bleiklie,1996). According to Kyvik (2000), from 1987 to 1997 the total number of students rose by approximately 70 percent, from approximately 44,000 to almost 83,000, while the expenditure per student decreased by 6 percent. In particular, the increased student numbers have negatively affected the student-teacher ratio in the humanities and social sciences. For example, at the University of Oslo the student-teacher ratio was much higher at 14.6 in 1998.

In the mid-1960s, a group of professors initiated a process leading towards democratic decision making. This occurred before the 1968–69 student revolts at the University of Oslo but was not instituted until 1972 when a decision-making system based on elected boards replaced the professorial autocracy. Other universities followed suit. In 1990 an official act was passed covering all four universities and six university colleges that maintained democratic decision making. It also granted institutions greater autonomy, such as responsibility for teaching and research content and appointing professors; formerly all these aspects were controlled by the government.

In October 1985, the OECD review team visited Norwegian universities and concluded that they were moving in line with international trends. The reviewers noted that, "The recent legislation has resulted in streamlined governance arrangements, greater external participation in smaller governing bodies and increased executive power.... A major challenge, but by no means an insuperable one, is to ensure a blending in practice of modern governance, managerial and executive leadership approaches with the direct democratic mode of collegial decision making" (OECD, 1997, p. 10).

According to Kyvik (2000), academic leaders currently have less administrative responsibility and a stronger political role within the governing system, but are under increasing pressure to become managerially oriented. Kyvik concludes that, "Despite the fact that the [Norwegian] higher education sector has been exposed to a large number of reforms, changes and challenges during the last decade, ... minor adjustments in role patterns and role performance [of academics], rather than large changes, are the predominant tendency in the universities" (p. 68).

The United States of America

According to DeBats and Ward (1999), the crucial aspects of American higher education are its size (3,885 institutions), its complexity, its diversity, and its strong private sector. The American education system includes technical and community colleges, liberal arts colleges, public and private institutions, and comprehensive and elite research universities. During 1997, *The Chronicle of Higher Education Almanac* reported that there were 1,657 public institutions, 1,625 nonprofit private institutions, and 603 for-profit private institutions. In 1998, 36.6 percent of the 18 to 24 age cohort were enrolled, and approximately 78 percent, or 11.5 of 14.8 million, were enrolled in public institutions, even though there are more private than public institutions. In 2000, the cost (tuition, fees, room, board) of a four-year, private college education ranged from $80,000 to $100,000, and a public college education ranged from $30,000 to $45,000 (Kong, 2000). There are Pell grants, scholarships, loans, and tax credits to offset the costs, but the average student still has to pay a substantial amount for a college education.

During the 1970s, the U.S. government introduced market forces to public higher education, giving aid to students rather than to institutions, thus making students "consumers" of tertiary education (Slaughter & Leslie, 1997). In addition, the Bayh-Dole Act of 1980 encouraged academic capitalism, permitting universities and small businesses to retain titles to inventions developed with federal research and development money. Slaughter (1998) noted that other laws introduced during the 1980s promoted competitiveness and encouraged deregulation, privatization, and commercialization of public university activities. The changes shifting colleges and universities towards academic capitalism were more incremental in the United States than in England and Australia. However, unlike these countries, the U.S. federal government has limited influence on higher education policies, due to changes filtering through states rather than enacted in a White Paper, as occurred in England in the early 1980s and Australia in the late 1980s. In the United States, each state acts individually, deciding whether to enact legislation altering the higher education system. A number of states developed quality assessment systems, standardized teaching evaluations, and performance-based budgeting, which, during the 1980s and 1990s, began regulating academic work more closely and introducing greater competition into the college system.

Though some larger states, such as California and New York, have systems of higher education similar to a national system, such as France or Germany, each university or college within these states has considerable autonomy, many founded as private institutions with their own governing bodies. Nevertheless, all institutions, whether public or private, resemble the English "corporation" model, the key characteristic being autonomous institutions, often having a buffer layer, such as a board of trustees or regents, that is not controlled by academic staff. This board determines most major financial decisions for the university, with the senior administrators (presidents and vice presidents) making major decisions on a daily basis. Some recently selected administrators have nonacademic backgrounds, such as business, military, or government. Often a faculty senate can counterbalance the power of the president; yet in many universities the senate powers have been reduced to a consultative role. Nevertheless, there is still considerable autonomy, at the faculty and departmental level, in determining who is hired and granted tenure, and in course teaching and content. However, power over financial decision making, curriculum, and granting of tenure is shifting to the management level and boards of trustees. The trustees are becoming increasingly prominent in curricular decisions and employment practices. Many institutions have multiple stakeholders, including trustees, academic and general staff, parents and students, alumni and government agencies—all wanting to influence decision making.

DESCRIPTION OF UNIVERSITIES

We chose particular universities to study globalizing practices and their impacts on tertiary institutions. Focusing on four institutions enabled us to examine the similarities and differences in their responses to global impulses. Boston College is a medium-sized (12,500 students), private, Jesuit university located in the United States, which became highly managed due to a brush with bankruptcy in the early 1970s. The University of Avignon is a small (7,100 local and regional students), provincial, liberal arts university located in France and is mainly an undergraduate institution. The University of Oslo is a large (34,400 students) university located in the capital of Norway and is mainly research focused. The University of Twente is a small (5,500 students), entrepreneurial university located in the Netherlands and combines technology and social sciences. Oslo and Twente determine their futures, having greater autonomy than Avignon, yet not as much as Boston College with its need and capacity to garner private funds. However, Twente is becoming less dependent on government funding, becoming an "entrepreneurial" university, building up money from research and consulting contracts. Avignon and Oslo staff are beginning to embrace and serve local community economic interests, yet their traditional nature remains more intact than Boston College or Twente.

Before presenting and addressing the findings, it is necessary to outline the context of each university, beginning with the European public universities—Avignon, Twente, and Oslo—and ending with the American private university, Boston College. As previously noted, the old paradigm of differences based on the Continental, Anglo-Saxon, or U.S. models is not as valid today, with universities adopting characteristics from each model. Interestingly, two universities trace their origins to the University of Paris (Avignon and Boston College), and two universities follow the German research model devised by Humboldt (Oslo and Twente). In addition, the Humboldtian tradition influenced many American research universities via Johns Hopkins, undoubtedly influencing the development of Boston College as it moved from a mainly undergraduate liberal arts college to a research university.

University of Avignon

The original institution was founded in the fourteenth century during the Papacy's stay in Avignon; however, it only lasted until the French Revolution and was then abolished. Hence, the University of Avignon is young, having only been reconstituted after World War II. From 1962 until recently, it was a protected, dependent offshoot of other institutions, relying upon local municipal and regional authorities for financial support. Academically, it was a branch of the larger, older, prestigious University of Aix-en-Provence/Marseilles. It now competes with Aix and Marseilles as well as the University of Montpellier, all three attracting students from across southwestern France. Being hemmed in by competitive giants and having only limited, though often crucial, municipal resources from Avignon city, the University of Avignon has remained one of the newest and smallest of France's 90 universities, which may be considered advantageous. Within 13 years, it had increased student numbers from approximately 2,500 to 6,480 by 1998. In addition, the student-to-staff ratio improved, as the Ministry became aware of the lack of posts being created, these compared to larger universities, the rate dropped from 26 students per staff in 1991 to 24.7 students per staff in 1997.

Visiting the University of Avignon 10 years ago required considerable walking, as the various faculties were widely scattered in old buildings provided by the town government, some inside the old medieval city walls and some in the suburbs. However, currently the University of Avignon is situated on a large site, where a thirteenth-century hospital formerly stood, within the city walls and surrounded by graveled open space and sycamore trees. There is now an almost totally new campus for the University of Avignon faculties of law, humanities, and social sciences. The science faculty is in an adjacent historical building near the renovated hospital. The technological and IT campus is outside the inner city. This campus was heavily funded by the regional council as a *technopole*, attracting research and high technology firms to the site. The old hospital was sandblasted to restore the classic stone façade, while the contents are new, consisting of modern technology, furnishings, and teaching equipment. Adjacent to the renovated hospital is a wholly new glass, steel, and concrete building for the modern library, amphitheaters, student facilities, and restaurant. In addition, for the first time teaching staff have offices, telephones, and Internet/e-mail access, albeit shared. The University of Avignon has one of the nicest and best-positioned campuses in France, achieving a level of infrastructure and user friendliness usually only found in well-appointed and well-funded universities abroad.

Apart from its relatively small size and new campus acquisition, other crucial aspects of the Avignon context are:

its relative lack of autonomous control over the bulk of its own staff salary budget, due to the Ministry determining the number of jobs created, yet its ability to choose whom to hire from a national list;

its institutionalized separation, like other French universities, from the best funding, teaching conditions, and cutting-edge research found in the Center for National Scientific Research (CNSR), technological training (IUT), or elite government training (*grandes écoles*);

the modest level (a few hundred dollars only) of administrative fees for students, most of whom are local to the region, and the generous subsidies for student restaurants, yet relative lack of student accommodation;

the electoral democracy of its internal governance systems, with few managerial prerogatives;

the civil, stable, and relatively well-paid academic staff, teaching quite limited, formal contact hours with few administrative or student-services responsibilities;

the new contractual relationship with the national state, guiding growth over the coming years, partly breaking with former bureaucratic inflexibility and uniformity.

The academics are predominantly French nationals with permanent civil service status, whose recruitment and promotion are decided by nationally determined panels, guidelines, and authority. Since 1968, there has been a movement towards the American model, yet the structure of universities remains primarily a bureaucratic, public service model. Over the past two years, new strategies have been developed, creating a significant proportion of jobs, *Attachés Temporaires d'Enseignement et de Recherche* (ATER) that offer a two-year, permanent term, and are mainly filled by postgraduate students finishing their theses. This has developed a new category of untenured academics teaching in universities, having the same workload as *Maîtres de Conférences* (192 hours of teaching). Along with its public service model, the French higher education system is rooted in the democratic traditions of the French Revolution, therefore abiding by a fairly collegial model. However, without as much autonomy as Dutch or Norwegian universities, it has power over a much smaller budget and makes fewer employment and curricular decisions.

University of Twente

The University of Twente is one of the youngest of the 13 Dutch universities, founded and established in 1961, in an economically depressed area near the eastern region of the German border. Survival required a synergy with the region, aiming to rejuvenate the economy. Interestingly, a main focus of Twente concerns labor market needs, ensuring that graduates have little difficulty finding employment. It is a unique institution, encouraging students to combine technological and social sciences, to develop majors and minors and interdisciplinary study.

In its mission statement, Twente describes itself as "an entrepreneurial university for academic education and research, offering training courses in both technical and social disciplines" (1998, p. 9). Likewise, Clark (1998) used the term entrepreneurial to describe Twente, choosing it as one of five European universities that has successfully transformed its organization into a vigorous, entrepreneurial culture. This idea of being entrepreneurial dates back to the early 1980s in the Netherlands because of Twente's success in developing links to regional industries. Twente also aspires to be the leader in Information and Communication Technology (ICT), engaging in substantial research concerning telematics and computer-assisted learning. This indicates its pragmatic nature and the speed with which it has developed a market niche.

Throughout the years, the executive board has attempted to restructure its faculties. In the 1998 *Annual Report*, it proposed to cluster the ten faculties and rationalize its service departments (15 central service departments being reduced to 8) to increase efficiency and reduce costs. In 2001, ambitious plans were developed to reduce the number of faculties from 10 to 5. Given the delicacy of the issue, it remains to be seen whether these plans will be implemented. The university continuously monitors and engages in quality assessment, involving various accountability mechanisms, from outside national agencies and within universitywide or faculty procedures. Also, Twente has a long history of decentralized budgeting, which from the early 1990s has allocated its education budget based on outputs rather than inputs. Also, a system of internal charging is used, making faculties aware of the costs associated with office space, lecture halls, libraries, and computing facilities (Jongbloed & van der Knoop, 1999).

In research, Twente has adopted some similar competition practices to those developed within Anglo-American universities. In the late 1990s, an initiative involved the selection of spearheads or centers of excellence, which were given extra funding by the university. Twente also distributed internal research funding according to the way it came to the university, partly based on the number of Ph.D. graduates, enrollments, and national competitive grants, which meant that the most productive areas received an equivalent amount of research funding. This made the internal funding as competitive as that distributed through the national budget allocation.

In 1997, the Ministry of Education, Culture and Science initiated major changes to university governance and management, passing the so-called Modernization of the Universities Governance Act. These changes were imposed upon universities; however, they appeared to suit the Dutch university entrepreneurial culture (de Boer, Denters, & Goedegebuure, 2000). From 1997 to 1998, the University of Twente established new governing bodies; for instance, a supervisory board, a central management team composed of the executive board and the deans. This management team is not a legal entity, but is nevertheless a powerful body within the new governance setting. Since 2001, the executive board, consisting of five members including the *rector magnificus*, has increased its power.[3] In December 1997, the university council was dissolved, and in its place a central staff council and central student council were established. These representative advisory councils lost many powers compared to the former university council, such as the budgetary powers. A reevaluation regarding the separation of these councils prompted the initiation, within two years, of a joint council—the "university council new style." However, this did not regain the power held by the university council in the heyday of the "democratic university," the 1970s and 1980s.

During the 1980s enrollment increased, followed by a slight decline of student numbers to 6,383 in 1993 and 5,515 in 1998. Despite public funding decreasing in 1998, Twente maintained a fairly low student-to-staff ratio at 17.5 students per staff member. By 2000, most staff (80 percent) were full-time, permanent civil servants, proud of the quality of education they offer and the innovations they have initiated in teaching methods. The university is regarded as a pioneer in tele-learning: "For several years now UT education has consistently ranked amongst the highest scorers in the Netherlands. These results were confirmed in January 1999, in a survey of the quality of university education, conducted by the Dutch weekly, *HP/De Tijd*. The UT scored 3.3 on a scale of 4, a result that was equaled only by the University of Maastricht" (University of Twente, 1998, p. 16).

University of Oslo

The University of Oslo is the oldest of four public universities in Norway, situated in the capital city. In 1811, the Danish monarch King Frederick VI granted Norway the right to found a university, hence establishing the Royal Frederick

University in Oslo, consisting of 71 students and six teachers. In 1931, the university name was changed to the University of Oslo or Universitas Osloensis. Initially, the university had four faculties: theology, law, medicine, and philosophy. In 1861, the philosophy faculty split into the Faculty of Arts and the Faculty of Mathematics and Natural Science. In 1959, the College of Dentistry was established, in 1963 the Faculty of Social Sciences formed, and in 1996 the Faculty of Education developed.

University education is free for Norwegians, but expensive for foreigners unless on a scholarship, and the cost of living is high. Teaching staff are civil servants with life tenure, and are appointed by the university. In 1998, enrollments totaled 34,450, with a student-to-staff ratio of 20 students per staff member, smaller at 14.6 students per staff member if research staff are included.

The university draws its ethos and mission from the Humboldt tradition, stressing dedication to pure research and freedom to criticize all established truths and societal institutions (University of Oslo 1995). In addition, professors are given much autonomy, many preferring to work on questions of curiosity within the university rather than being overinvolved with community questions or applied research.

A common characteristic of the university governing system is its colleague-based decision making, evident at each level: central, faculty, and department. Each level has a parallel administrative leadership. According to Tjeldvoll (1998), the University of Oslo is very democratic, holding elections for important academic positions at least every three years. The boards and councils are particularly constituted to ensure that all groups are represented. Since 1996, external representation, from state bureaucracy and corporate life, has been required on university boards: "According to the political authorities, external representation on university boards is a means to make the universities more accountable to the problems of real life" (Tjeldvoll, 1998, p. 119). The university board decides most strategic research issues, while the National Research Council, with increasing funds to distribute, can now influence the direction of strategic research in Norwegian universities.

Boston College

In 1540, Ignatius of Loyola and his nine companions founded the Society of Jesus, which began educational ministry in 1547, founding schools and colleges in many parts of the world. Interestingly, the founders were all Masters of the University of Paris, hence their pedagogy and curriculum followed the pattern established during that time. In 1863, the Society of Jesus founded Boston College, situated at the South End of Boston. It began as a small, streetcar institution under the Jesuits' firm control, providing sons of immigrants, particularly those from poorer neighborhoods, with a Catholic education. The classical Jesuit curriculum was based on a humanistic education with a heavy emphasis on philosophy and developing the moral and intellectual faculties of students.

Over time, Boston College changed in many respects, described by Burtchaell (1998) in *The Dying of the Light*. He argues that many colleges and universities have disengaged themselves from Christian churches, becoming secularized and losing their sectarian focus. Burtchaell notes that in 1951 "Jesuits were firmly in place at the head of the School of Arts and Sciences, the graduate school and the college itself. Twelve of the academic deans were Jesuits, and two were lay people (in nursing and graduate business administration)" (1998, p. 576). Philosophy was considered an imperative part of Jesuit education, and students were required to take 10 courses (28 credits) during their final 2 years. In 1971, this was reduced to two courses (six credits), which could be taken at any time. From 1942 to 1964, 95 percent of students were Catholic, before World War II 41 percent of the faculty were Jesuits, and 93 percent of lay faculty were Catholics. However, from 1964 to 1965 a downward shift began appearing, with Jesuits comprising only 21 percent of the faculty (Burtchaell, 1998, pp. 578–579).

In 1913, the college moved to Chestnut Hill, located partly in Boston and partly in Newton, changing from a commuter college to a residential college. Thus, residence halls were constructed, and recruitment began extending beyond the city and state. In 1970, the undergraduate level became coeducational, with graduate schools already admitting women. By 1975, there were 5,065 female and 4,779 male undergraduates. In 1998, 74 percent of students lived on campus; of these, 8 percent were Asian, 4 percent black, 5 percent Hispanic, 80 percent white, 3 percent international. Only 28 percent were from Massachusetts, and 53 percent of the undergraduates were female. As tuition fees increased, Boston College began attracting an increasingly heterogeneous and affluent student body, becoming increasingly selective in its freshman admissions. During the late 1990s, tuition and boarding costs were almost US$30,000 a year (in 1998–99 tuition and fees were US$21,304). New university scholarships, federal grants, and student loans enabled less affluent people to attend Boston College, with 46 percent of undergraduates receiving an average annual aid package of US$16,614.

U.S. News & World Report (1999) ranked Boston College at 36 out of 228 national universities offering a full range of undergraduate majors, master, and doctoral degrees, placing strong emphasis upon research. This ranking is based on many features, one of which is the selectivity of students. In 1997 to 1998, Boston College was ranked "most selective" due to applications for freshman admission totaling 16,455 with acceptance of only 6,455. A further indicator of academic quality is the student-to-staff ratio of 13 students per staff member. In 1996, full-time enrollment totaled 12,561, consisting of 9,528 undergraduates and 3,033 graduates; full-time faculty totaled 615, full professors comprising 21 percent, compared to the national average of 14 percent; and in 1993 to 1994 faculty pay was in the national top 10 percent, though female faculty were only paid 85 percent of the male salary.

A further change occurring during the past three decades concerns the increasing control by central management over the budget and major organizational decisions. A precarious budget in the early 1970s prompted the board to introduce more professional administrators, which has led to an expansion of vice presidents and a more professional approach to administration.

In 1990, *Standard & Poor's* upgraded the university rating to A+, indicating excellence in financial management practices. In 1986, *Barron's Guide to Colleges* elevated the university ranking from very competitive to highly competitive, the second highest category, indicating excellence in selectivity of incoming freshmen. On September 5, 1972, Fr. J. Donald Monan became university president, inheriting a debt of US$30 million and an endowment of US$6 million. In 1996, his term ended, leaving a building debt of US$350 million and an endowment of US$500 million. The endowment reached approximately US$1 billion by 2000. The Monan presidency was regarded as very successful by almost every quantifiable measure.

Burtchaell (1998) highlights that the enrollment of full-time students at Boston College is larger than the other 28 Jesuit campuses, with undergraduates being 79 percent Catholic. Larger numbers of students are earning doctorates, compared to other Jesuit universities. Jesuits are still a presence on the campus, though in dwindling numbers. In 1998, there were 44 trustees including nine Jesuits, and there were 48 Jesuits on campus including 18 administrators and 30 full-time faculty. There were 130 Jesuit residents on the campus, the largest community in the United States. Only the Departments of Philosophy and Theology have significant Jesuit numbers, about one-fourth of each department.

Since 1972, the physical campus has grown phenomenally, from 59 buildings on 112 acres to 90 buildings on 185 acres. In 1996, Project Agora was completed, making the college the first to enable undergraduate residents to access communication tools in their hall rooms, including Internet access, voice and electronic mail, cable TV, and phone services.

DESCRIPTION OF THE METHODOLOGY

This is a qualitative study, based on 131 interviews with a small number of senior administrators and an approximately equal number of academic staff from professional schools (education, applied languages, and/or law), sciences, and social sciences (arts). The interviews were conducted face-to-face during 1998 to 1999, almost entirely by a single person, Jan Currie, ensuring consistency in questioning and depth of probing. The sample included 37 individuals from Boston, 32 from Avignon, 31 from Oslo, and 31 from Twente. The academics interviewed ranged from professors to assistant professors, consisting of more men than women, particularly at Avignon and Twente, with a more equal representation at Boston College and Oslo (see Appendix I for a detailed description of the sample breakdown for each university).

The length of the interviews ranged from 30 minutes to one hour. People graciously gave of their time, which was much appreciated. There was no hesitation in answering the questions, as participants were assured their responses would remain anonymous. All signed a consent form indicating their willingness to participate in the interview and were given the opportunity to withdraw from the study at any time. The respondents are identified by their university, position or location (manager in senior administration, academic and subject area), gender, and age (junior = below 45 and senior = 45 and above). Each participant received a copy of the Trends Report for his/her university and consented to the use of the quotes within those reports.

The software program NUD.IST was used to analyze the interview data, and Excel was used to enter the demographic details, which were then integrated into the NUD.IST program. Several research team members devised response codes, which, in conjunction with NUD.IST software, enabled responses and respondent demographic information to be efficiently correlated. The factors used were gender, rank, discipline, and location or position cross-tabulated with individual answers. Surprisingly, few cross-tabulations were significant, indicating consensual responses to questions.

Utilizing numbers raises questions about the ability to generalize from this sample. It is not possible to generalize from this study because there are very small numbers in some categories and the sample is not a representative one in the first place. Generally, numbers are used in this study to illustrate trends within the sample. The tables record *responses,* not *respondents,* hence the totals may not always equal the number of respondents interviewed.

In addition, this book presents quotes from participants, giving more depth and feeling to the findings. The participants were asked a similar set of 20 questions in the areas of governance, accountability, competition and generating funds, and new technologies, ending with a few questions regarding the role of tenure and the future of the university. The questions varied slightly to accommodate the country and university context (see Appendix II for the interview protocol). For instance, the interviews in Avignon were conducted in French and translated into English before coding, whereas the interviews at the other three universities were conducted in English.

The following five chapters are structured similarly, presenting the findings for university responses to globalizing practices. Each chapter investigates a particular practice, initially reviewing the literature and theoretical positions, then analyzing the policies adopted within the four countries and respective universities, and finally presenting the empirical findings and discussing differences in the responses between universities to these globalizing practices. We begin in Chapter 3 discussing privatization, competition, and entrepreneurialism.

NOTES

1. Australia, an independent state of the Commonwealth since 1901, is not often considered a monarchy, though its chief of state is the British monarch. Australia has conducted a referendum to become a republic, yet the latest attempt, in 1999, was defeated.

2. These are refinements from a preceding law in 1990.

3. According to the national higher education law, the executive boards of Dutch universities are composed of three members, including the rector. The University of Twente asked the minister to extend this number to five and permission was granted on a five-year trial basis.

Chapter 3

Privatization, Competition, and Entrepreneurialism

INTRODUCTION: PUBLIC AND PRIVATE: SHIFTING CYCLES AND BOUNDARIES

The relations between current debates concerning the changing role of higher education, and particularly the merits of public versus private, are complicated and controversial. In this context, the meanings attached to public and private are unclear, especially as applied to traditional universities. What privatization aspects do governments have in mind when public authorities seek to make public institutions behave like private companies in the market? What costs and benefits are created for governments, institutions, students, and other interested parties? What impact will privatization have upon traditional university values and contemporary roles and duties? Is privatization inevitable, irreversible, or even beneficial? The questions are numerous, legitimate, and unavoidable. Responses in the media concerning the question of whether universities are in crisis blame government funding cuts and privatization efforts, as evident in the following headlines: *Tenure Troubles; Breaking the Ivory Tower; Plans to Slash Arts; The Cash Crisis; Ignorant MPs Fiddle as Our Unis Burn;* and *Crisis in our Universities.* The Australian Senate report adds another critique of government reforms.

While the changes in the roles, expectations and conceptions of our public universities are complex; there is nothing inevitable or necessary about the way our universities have declined. Rather, the crisis reflects deliberate government policy choices about competition, markets, quasi-corporate governance structures and practices [that have led to the] de-professionalisation of academics, and [increasing reliance on private "impatient" capital]. (Democrats, Supplementary Report cited in Senate Standing Committee on Education, 2001, pp. 381, 384–385)

Government pressure to privatize in the once protected public university sector is sometimes critiqued for generating the worst of both worlds. This is often manifested in the confusion of applicability, apparent in the following quotes.

Universities are not private institutions producing predominantly private goods. Regardless of financing by government, universities are constituted by legislation, and produce a wide range of public and private goods, deriving their key functions in teaching and research. As such, the universities are part of the national infrastructure and major public responsibility. (Marginson, cited in Senate Standing Committee on Education, 2001, p. 99)

While Marginson relays that universities are public, the following quote relays the opposite premise.

The universities are private. Legally and economically, they belong to the private non-profit-making sector, private autonomous bodies, established by Parliament.... Universities are neither owned nor controlled by government. The government wants to have it both ways, to give universities all the burdens of the public sector with none of the advantages. (McNicol, 2001, p. 15)

Perhaps times are changing, and a new hybrid university model containing the best of both worlds is emerging?

If you want to see the future, look at universities. Broadly, it's the way the public sector will be organized and managed, odd though that sounds. In universities you're managing professionals who have relationships with community groups and with their own professions outside the university. They have a view of what they do that's bigger than the job of the day, teaching, building professionalism, and adding to the intellectual capital of the country. None of this is done within a traditional hierarchy. And that's where the public sector is heading. (McKew, 2001, p. 42)

Initially, this chapter explores the ambiguities and controversies concerning the public versus private debate, and its effect upon higher education. Additionally, this chapter examines qualitative evidence from the case studies regarding the impact of privatization, competition, and entrepreneurialism on the four universities, particularly noting the differences of impact and yet the similarities of responses. Lastly, this chapter addresses the implications of these findings, the inevitability and desirability of recent privatization efforts by government reformers.

CHANGING BORDERS OF PUBLIC AND PRIVATE

The last quarter of the twentieth century was indisputably the golden age of the private, with strong globalizing forces intertwining with broad public policy changes. These pushed inexorably towards new norms and structural reforms, often at the expense of public interest. Public policy reformers aimed to transform reality with specific directions, assumptions, and normative guidelines.

Private values were to be the guiding norms of policy initiatives and standards for judging success. The public sector was to be smaller and less trusted. Using private corporate models, reformers of public sector management deregulated by outsourcing, selling public assets, initiating markets or quasi-markets, reallocating competitive resources, and replacing bureaucratic or planned decision making and coordination. Traditional virtues of trusted and autonomous professionalism, rational hierarchy, social justice, and public service were to be replaced by private consumer interests, individualism, and entrepreneurial innovation.

These privatizing efforts have had a substantial effect on higher education, and as yet there is no sign of a slackening in reform efforts, although recently there have been indications that public policy priorities are altering. After the events of September 11, 2001, an unexpected sea change appears to have occurred, a movement away from privatization towards reevaluating the role of the public sector and the state.

Such a change should have been expected and predicted. Hirschman's (1982) theory of public policy generational cycles stipulates that generations alternate between public and private values. Excessive enthusiasm for one often leads to a countervailing movement, over time, to prioritizing the opposite pole. Thus, at least in Western countries, the mood has shifted from public activism in the 1930s and early 1940s; to private life and civic society preeminence in the 1950s; to renewed public and state activism in the late 1960s and early 1970s; then followed the cycle of rediscovering the individual, nonstate sphere. Perhaps last year's events in the United States will trigger a shift back to the public side. Nevertheless, the change in mood within the United States in less than one year is remarkable.

In 2000, during the United States' presidential campaign, George W. Bush stressed private sector, neoliberal themes such as tax cuts, smaller government in Washington, decentralization to state-level decision makers, and mistrust of big government bureaucracies. Yet after the September 11, 2001, terror attacks on the Pentagon and the World Trade Center Towers, the emphasis from Washington dramatically shifted, with Bush and advisers stressing the need for public trust and government action, pursuing the national, common interest. Even abroad, a change occurred from "going it alone," towards international cooperation and collaboration to fight terrorism.

For much of the frivolous 1990s, politics mattered less than business and communications, and the outside world barely rated a mention. Now, more than half the population thinks foreign affairs are "extremely important." In January, 2001, the figure was 17 percent. The war on terrorism has transformed politics by increasing the authority and prestige of national institutions. There has been a startling renewal of broader public confidence in government (*The Economist*, 2001b, p. 39).

The Economist also remarked that before September 11, 2001, when governments were intent on privatizing in the name of inevitability, they were shirking responsibility to make democratic choices between more or less, public or private virtues: "The crucial point is that international economic integration widens choices because it makes resources go further. Whenever governments use globalization to deny responsibility, democracy suffers another blow" (*The Economist*, 2001a, p. 30).

There are other signs indicating a change back to public resources; for example, a continuing anti-neoliberal, antiglobalization theme, including a growing interest in a modest, regulatory "Tobin Tax" on international, speculative financial transfers in many countries like France. In addition, key European leaders were the first to sign the Kyoto protocol on greenhouse warming, despite U.S. and Bush administration distaste. A further sign concerns the widespread popularity of center-left governments in the United Kingdom, France, Germany, much of the remaining Europe, Canada, and New Zealand. Finally, in higher education in Japan, Korea, China, Singapore, and numerous OECD countries, recent emphasis has been towards increasing public funding, without significantly increasing student fees. An indication of this is this recent, highly symbolic decision by Beijing University to reduce its entrepreneurial experiments designed to raise money in the private sector, as a result of renewed public, state financial generosity (Lawrence, 2001, p. 38).

However, it would be premature and foolish to deduce that the privatization and market competition era has ended. Recently, a WTO agreement pursued a new round of trade liberalization, including the People's Republic of China as a full member, showing that globalizing and neoliberal forces remain strong. What is becoming clearer is that neoliberal, globalizing changes and processes are more complex, uneven, and fluid than many apologists and opponents may have thought.

With hindsight, the different limits and complexities of privatization forces can be clearly understood. Feigenbaum, Henig, and Hamnett (1999) comment that there are four independent dimensions within the privatization policy process.

Table 3.1
Dimensions of Movement from Public to Private Forms of Policy

Dimension	Continuum: Public	Private	Illustration of Privatization
Financing	Government Pays/ Public Free	Individuals Pay	User Pays Fees
Delivery	Public Servants	Private Firms	Outsourcing
Accountability	Laws/Norms	Consumer Beware	Deregulation
Governance	Formal Procedures	Market/Management	Consumer Choice

Source: Feigenbaum, Henig, and Hamnett 1999: p. 10.

All four dimensions need not be introduced together in any particular policy sector. Moreover, this particular, complicated model is incomplete, not including the formal legal ownership or control dimension and the crucial questions of norms for implementation, including cost-cutting, efficiency practices, quality control, and performance evaluation. These are of particular interest in this book. A further categorization of privatization includes ownership dimensions, adding a qualitative and political aspect that is useful, for instance the different intentions or motives of government reformers undertaking privatization. These motives and goals can be categorized along an ascending scale of ambition and level of difficulty from pragmatic, to tactical, to strategic. The most ambitious forms of strategic privatization, for instance reducing government size and role permanently, changing public expectations, and political coalitions' ability to reverse reforms, are rare as they are extremely difficult to enact. Conversely, the most pragmatic, based on left and right government similar motives, such as saving money, adjusting to changing circumstances, or imitating significant reforms, are widespread and enduring. Meanwhile, tactical privatization is often a short-term, partisan, political move to attract voters, reward supporters, or differentiate platforms from those of opponents. For instance, in the strategic category there are reforms, such as asset sales of public housing, contracting out to favor private builders, deregulation to deligitimizing government oversight, and user fees to reduce the importance of public provision over time. (Feigenbaum et al., 1999)

UNIVERSITIES AND PRIVATIZATION:
NEW WINE IN NEWLY DESIGNED BOTTLES
BUT OLD PUBLIC CELLARS?

Universities have a curious and ambiguous role within this public and private reform debate. Some aspects of privatization and some limited goals have relevance; yet it is doubtful whether full-scale or strategic privatization is or could be practiced, even if government so desired. So far none have tried. However, Chipman (2000) suggests that there would be difficulty in privatizing universities: "To the best of my knowledge, no government in the world has privatized education. Yet the arguments for privatizing education are at least as strong as they are for privatizing airlines, telecommunications services, energy and water utilities, and hospitals. The reason the arguments have not prevailed is the belief that to try to sell that message of reform to an electorate in a democracy would be an act of political suicide" (p. 17).

Furthermore, higher education appears to have been a sector where public and private dimensions have coexisted, alternated, even hybridized. During the past few decades, the privatization push has been more pragmatic and tactical than strategic, it has been geared more to short-term political, electoral, and budgetary goals than to long-term structural reform, and has almost never involved asset sales or transfers from public ownership and control to full private hands. Interestingly, a system similar to the hypothetical "market socialism," once in vogue in Western European social democratic and Eastern European reform socialist circles, has been created by putting new market-oriented and corporate behaviors into old, public sector university bottles. Despite the legal and practical possibilities of fully selling off public universities, government ministers have universally preferred to retain both ownership and control of the higher education system and institutions, merely injecting new reforms for pragmatic, "re-engineering" reasons rather than starting afresh.

The likely consequences of privatization efforts depend upon a multiplicity of factors, especially the generosity of resources and the intelligence associated with reforms. Yet many public institutions fail due to poor management and lack of funding. Conversely, many notorious private institutions, for instance old, elite U.S. universities, maintain high levels of quality and redistribute educational opportunities to the intelligent poor through internal cross-subsidy scholarships. There are obvious risks associated with running public institutions that were previously well managed and funded. Yet privatization can be beneficial under certain conditions. This book explores many of these complexities and ambiguities.

Clearly the stakes are high. For government and public universities, pragmatic privatization, competition, and market entrepreneurialism may be justified under appropriate conditions. However, the costs of reform can be great if implemented poorly or by policy makers solely interested in saving money and hostile to university values such as quality and equity (Seddon & Marginson, 2001).

The need for further reform, making universities increasingly global, may appear difficult to understand in light of the long, remarkable history of traditional institutions, being exceptionally international and enduring compared to other forms of human organization (OECD, 1987). Very few cultural inventions of the European medieval period have survived without major interruptions or discontinuity in activities. Even as ideal types, universities have many different sizes, forms, and power configurations: public and private, static and dynamic, high quality and mediocre, anarchic and semi-authoritarian. There is no one, unique Procrustean bed where all universities can be forced to lie.

In contemporary times, privatization, marketization, and entrepreneurial enterprise have been notable features of public policy, increasing within the public sector, in all nation-states. New public management (NPM) reformers infer that universities can assume a private sector model if university service consumers, such as students and research users, are treated as customers. This assumption that public universities should have business-like practices evokes a clarification of the differences between private and public organizations. Are private sector successes applicable to the public sector? In addition, will classic university values, including trust and professional autonomy, be vanquished if private, corporate models and values are imposed, possibly without staff consultation? There are some generic processes of management common to all organizations, such as mission development, clarifying strategies, communicating policies, developing staff, or evaluating performances. However, there is no generic management model applicable to all organizations. During the 1980s and 1990s, generally speaking, the distinction between public and private blurred. Currently, the public sector includes many hybrid type organizations. In addition, universities are regarded as increasingly hybrid in nature (see Considine, 2001b). Moreover, higher education, including public institutions, has embodied competition, although often restrained, evident in the pursuit of prestige, the best students, and endowment gifts. Many private institutions, even in the United States, have been nonprofit, and have subordinated capitalist and competitive elements, instead promoting traditional university goals of academic freedom, autonomy, tenure, and collegiality in teaching, although expanding prestige, respect, and survival in the national and international higher education market.

In sum, similar trends are becoming more apparent in the higher education reform policies within Australia, Canada, the United States, the United Kingdom, Western Europe, and Eastern Asia (Albrow, 1993; Considine, 2001a,b; Friedman, 2000; Katzenstein, 1985; Korean Ministry of Education, 2001; Lijphart, 1984; Lowi, 2001; Scharpf, 1987; Scholte, 2000; Schwartz, 1994; Yoneyazawa & Yoshida, 2001). From the 1960s and 1970s to the 1980s and 1990s, there has been a dramatic shift from the previously vaunted OECD model of generous, government-funded, and planned higher education expansion and democratization policies, towards a new "ideal" that is austere, cost cutting, privately funded, market driven, with slower expansion and diversification programs. The effects of these changes upon the higher education system, universities, and staff may be dramatic or may be counterbalanced and modified, depending on varying historical, political, and cultural factors, as these case studies demonstrate.

CASE STUDIES: PRIVATIZATION, COMPETITION, ENTREPRENEURIALISM: ADVANTAGES AND DISADVANTAGES

During the past two decades, the key aspect of the globalizing reform agenda for higher education systems has been the systematic and relentless pursuit of privatized, competitive, and entrepreneurial behaviors within universities across three continents and, in particular, in all OECD countries. A variety of means have been used, including quasi-markets, competitive tendering, competitive performance evaluation and funding, outsourcing of public services, sale of public assets, and encouragement of new and old competitors. Many governments have sought a combination of lower costs, greater efficiency, flexibility, responsiveness, and openness to innovation. However, in currently competitive, public versus private systems, such as Japan and the United States, encouragement of existing private revenue-seeking entrepreneurial activities appears to be sufficient. Yet in public, formula-funded systems, like Australia and the United Kingdom, central authorities have created markets or quasi-markets, introducing private sector models of management and funding, and cutting or reducing existing funding which is redistributed by competitive bidding (Currie & Newson, 1998; DeAngelis, 1996; Marginson & Considine, 2000).

However, competition for funding, such as research funding, often heightens rivalry between universities and leads to internal friction between departments and among staff members. The premise is that heightened competition within the system will generate more productivity per unit. Essentially, within universities this push means that academics are asked, expected, or required to produce an increasing quantity of publications, to graduate more Ph.D. students, and to acquire more outside funding grants. Meanwhile, funding is increasingly allocated to a few key centers of excellence often characterized by larger, more concentrated research teams, especially involving international and interuniversity collaboration. Consequently, individual academics and less successful teams are forced to seek funding from various private sources, often involving private sector partnerships, to ensure the viability of large-scale or long-term research projects. In sum, the reputation, attractiveness, and endurance of universities is contingent upon academics adopting entrepreneurial behaviors.

Towards Privatization: Funding Cuts and Competitive Pressures

The four respective university respondents were asked different yet related questions regarding the implementation and effect of the private, competitive agenda. Avignon and Oslo, predominantly traditional public sector universities, were asked whether central authorities have cut existing budgets, while Twente and Boston College were asked whether management requested them to seek more funds from outside sources. A comparison reveals that *all* samples were affected by the globalizing competitive agenda. The responses, in percent, were largely affirmative; thus, there had been funding cuts or they had been asked to

Table 3.2
Competitive Funding Pressures? (percentages and numbers)

Questions: Are you being asked to seek more funding? Has the government cut your funding?

Universities	Yes	No/Unequal Effect	Don't Know	Total Responses
Avignon	73	25	2	100 (48)
Boston	76	24	0	100 (37)
Oslo	0	32	8	100 (38)
Twente	97	3	0	100 (31)

seek more funding elsewhere, with Oslo recording 61, Avignon with 73, Boston College with 76, and the largest response, Twente, recording 97. Nevertheless, there were some differences.

Avignon

The University of Avignon sample arguably contributed the most complex and contradictory responses, primarily due to its contemporary origins, recently consolidated campus, and transition from a local, municipal-aided institution to an expanding national university. Moreover, as in other continental systems, the funding arrangements of the university consist of a split budget with two major pools: a large, personnel salaries pool directly controlled by the capital, and a local, smaller pool under autonomous university control. Much research is funded separately by competitive public and private sources. With a traditional strong public sector and considerable staff and student union vitality, the full force of privatization, competition, or entrepreneurialism was not expected, even though it is beginning to emerge (Charle, 1994; DeAngelis, 1998; Musselin, 2001).

The various alterations to funding from different sources have contributed to the diverse responses from participants within this sample. For instance, over the past five years the ministry has increased funding for teaching, while local authorities have reduced funding for university personnel and other institutions have unevenly cut funding for research. Additionally, university costs have recently increased due to the provision and maintenance of new buildings and infrastructure and the loss of personnel. In sum, despite the ministry increasing the funding for smaller universities, many departments appear to be experiencing cutbacks and a subsequent need to gain funding from other sources. Two well-placed observers at Avignon capture some of these complexities.

No, there hasn't been a reduction in the minister's funding to the university, because we were already very low, and we are now starting to go up a little. I don't think that any of the universities in France have had their funding reduced at all, even when this should logically have been the case, due to fewer students, for example. But I think that the policy of the minister has not been to cut back on university funding. However, the local county and municipal authorities have put an end to their funding, as well as appointments. We had eighteen members of staff paid by them, working at the university two years ago, and they have all been removed, which has made a considerable difference. (Avignon, Senior, Male, Academic, Sciences)

No, for the last five or six years, the minister has considerably increased the credits [funding] of the university. In the past, greater credits had been exclusively allocated to the big universities; but four years ago, the presidents created what is known as le Groupe des Dix, which includes the ten smallest French universities that received the least credits. After having protested to the minister, this began to climb due to the minister's increased awareness of the importance of the role these little universities played. Before the 1984 reform, we had no real budget of our own, but we were dependent on the

University of Aix. Today we are proud of the status of our university, whereas in the past, we were ashamed. (Avignon, Senior, Male, Manager)

Oslo

Likewise, in Norway, government funding remains pivotal, with only one small, business-related private institution. Further, the government's budget remains steadfast due to huge oil reserves and wise investment of revenue by the state sector. Yet there has been a slight decrease of government funding for universities, and a slight push towards competitive and entrepreneurial practices. Nevertheless, more than France, Norway remains committed to public higher education. The following comment exhibits considerable insight into the contradictory, but logical nature of current Norwegian policy making in light of political traditions.

The government push of increasing competition has been largely upset by another important policy agenda mainly to coordinate its investments in higher education better. With the idea of Norway Net, each university specializes in a particular field, and that idea to some extent weakens competition. Norway Net is the idea of a rational division of labor where government can invest in the best departments, the best faculties around the country. This is perhaps one of the strange things about Norway over the past 5 to 10 years, a combination of attempts to put the market mechanisms to work, combined with typical social democratic planning in which everything is nicely and smoothly planned and delivered according to some overall national scheme—a traditional social democratic approach—let's plan it. (Oslo, Senior, Male, Academic, Social Sciences)

An overwhelming majority of responses indicated that funding had been cut. This was worrisome to many, even though cuts were uneven, thus not falling equally on all. Clearly, there is some principled solidarity; yet also there is typical parochialism and special pleading.

In Norway, we don't have a national policy, we have a regional policy [which at Oslo] does not favor us. The biggest university is being handicapped. Because Norwegians do not like cities, and everything that is in Oslo is not popular. Even among universities, Oslo is being disfavored. (Oslo, Senior, Male, Academic, Social Sciences)

The reduction in funding is largely irrelevant for me. I have a letter from the king that I am a professor. So to get rid of me you have to go to court. (Oslo, Senior, Male, Academic, Sciences)

Twente

In contrast, the Netherlands and the United States have notable reputations for policy directed at private and entrepreneurial innovation. In particular, the Netherlands embodies a genuine model combining neoliberal reforms and traditional social democratic welfare generosity. The United States has significant, prestigious private, often religious, colleges and universities, thus providing a competitive market for students. Therefore, we expected an acceptance of recent globalizing market trends in both countries (Clark, 1998; DeBats & Ward, 1999). When the University of Twente respondents were asked whether management had requested they gain external funding, 28 out of 31 agreed, with no significant differences between gender, rank or discipline.

Well, it is in general part of the job of every academic. (Twente, Junior, Male, Academic, Social Sciences)

I think that up until now the pressure has been more or less stable, but it will be getting more intense once the funding allocation is changed related to student enrollments. In the last few years, we had a decline in student enrollments; it just means there will be more pressure to get funds from elsewhere. (Twente, Junior, Male, Academic, Social Sciences)

Boston College

Similarly, in the United States a high percentage of responses were affirmative, indicating that academics were asked to gain outside funding. Some respondents thought of this as an encouragement rather than a pressure, and many regarded it as a way of life, an inherent part of the job necessary within the competitive American system.

There is a lot of pressure, but it is not a make or break type situation. I have heard that, at other universities, they do all but ring a bell at faculty meetings, that it's, "money, money, money." Here there is the expectation that you will be active in grantsmanship. Once you are active, there is a lot of reward for doing that. (Boston College, Junior, Female, Academic, Professional School)

This center will disappear unless we generate through direct or indirect funds the money to support the center. (Boston College, Senior, Male, Academic, Professional School)

We can't do any research unless we have money, so we apply for grants. Boston College has been absolutely superb at coming up with a least 30 percent, if not more like 50 percent of the funding, promising that if you bring in that amount of money, they will match it. (Boston College, Senior, Female, Academic, Sciences)

There is encouragement. I have always sought out grants for the things that I do. I have never been asked to do that. That is all self-initiated. (Boston College, Senior, Male, Academic, Professional School)

Consequences of Funding Cuts?

All university respondents were also asked about the consequences of reduced funding. The question concerned what changes their universities had made to gain outside resources or deal with reduced funding. The responses from Avignon and Oslo, which have experienced minor funding cuts, fell into three categories: those suggesting that the university gain resources from other sources;

those wanting the university to deal with reduced funding in alternate ways; and those who did not know. The responses identifying outside resources highlighted two sources: industry and private enterprises. However, these sources have limits.

Avignon

We try and establish research contracts with the private sector. But [for] teaching, we do not have any ways of increasing funding, and the research contracts only bring in extra money for laboratories. (Avignon, Senior, Male, Academic, Sciences)

Many respondents believed that funding for teaching should come from the ministry, and that this would be achieved by adopting vocational courses. However, these were not always successful. For instance, a tourism course was proposed in Avignon but was not supported by the Chamber of Commerce. Individual academics as heads of research laboratories seek funding mainly from industry. Other sources of funding include the European Union, different ministries, and the City of Avignon. However, all of these have potential dangers or limitations.

Research contracts from exterior sources are definitely worth exploring. But at the same time a little complicated, because they shouldn't interfere or dictate the content of research. So we have to be sensible. (Avignon, Senior, Male, Academic, Professional School)

The type of restructuring evident in American, Australian, British, and Canadian universities has not beset Avignon as yet. For instance, when asked about staff reductions, there was a consensus that this had not occurred. Academics had not been made redundant, been asked to retire early, or been given the golden handshake as in many Anglo-American countries. However, it was clear that there had not been an increase in staff either. Many responses suggested that the reduction in funding largely impaired secretarial staff funding, reduced the number of lectures, contributed to a restructuring of teaching, and increased their workloads.

We have tried to reorganize things and cut down on any superfluous items, but this is not sufficient and we are actually quite worried about making ends meet this year. I don't know how we're going to solve this problem. (Avignon, Junior, Female, Academic, Sciences)

Concerns about the financial situation of the university seem to be growing, yet a consistent university policy aimed at gaining outside funding is not manifest. Particularly interesting are those responses emphasizing the obstacles in French political culture, compared to the American or Australian situation.

The weak point we have here at the University of Avignon is that compared to big American or Australian universities, for example, we don't know how to go about looking for extra funding. (Avignon, Senior, Female, Manager, Administration)

This is not really a practice that is part of the mentality in our national education. Usually, the minister allocates credits and we have to make do with what we have. If we move away from this practice, this is going against the logic of the university and moving closer to the logic of an enterprise. (Avignon, Senior, Male, Manager, Administration)

In Avignon, reduced funding has resulted in the reduction of administrative staff, cutting some budget corners, and trying, often naively and inexpertly, to gain funding elsewhere, especially from research contracts. Nevertheless, many are hesitant and aware of how unfamiliar this brave new world of entrepreneurial activity can be.

Oslo

Likewise, at Oslo in Norway, funding cuts have resulted in a mixture of fee introduction where possible, subsidizing research with private money, abolishing posts or hiring freezes, working harder, and cutting subjects. In addition, to date, the reduction of existing staff has not been on the agenda.

This department has a long experience in being more entrepreneurial. But the other department here is a very traditional one, and they are critical [of us] because they think it is not what the university should be doing, [for example] offering a Master's course by fee. (Oslo, Senior, Female, Academic, Professional School)

We have some projects that are on a larger scale and need more funding; individual faculty members have been active in the market trying to get funds. (Oslo, Senior, Male, Academic, Social Sciences)

Because of the age of the faculty in some fields, many will retire, and then suddenly you have destroyed the whole field, because we cannot replace professors. (Oslo, Junior, Female, Academic, Sciences)

They are trying to rationalize; they are also seriously talking about cutting the Department of German. This is really drastic, cutting our cultural background. They haven't fired academics yet, but they are talking about it for the first time. This is sensational, because you have to be a criminal to be fired from your position. Until six years ago a professor was appointed by the King's Council and could never, ever be fired from their positions without a trial. (Oslo, Senior, Male, Academic, Professional School)

We also end up doing much more administrative work to enter [our] own finances now. There is no longer an administrative officer for that. We feel very frustrated that we get so much paperwork. (Oslo, Junior, Female, Academic, Sciences)

Increased Entrepreneurialism

The respondents were also asked whether their university was becoming more entrepreneurial at the institutional level and in mentality. Further, are outside resources being sought in the marketplace on a systematic basis? The answers were similar in most cases, with only a smattering of rejections from Avignon and Oslo. However, there were considerable qualifications, doubts, and hesitations within the positive responses from Avignon. In sum, the majority of responses indicated that all institutions were heading in a similar entrepreneurial direction. Table 3.3 reveals the range of responses, with those replying "Yes" ranging from 100 percent at Twente to only 38 percent at Avignon.

Avignon

In Avignon, despite public sector bureaucratic hegemony and the preference of most staff for a continued public/state dominant situation, when joining "Yes" and "Yes, But" categories, 87 percent of responses contend that entrepreneurial activity is increasing, perhaps only to survive funding costs. Of these responses, 49 percent qualified their answers, identifying this as an uneven process, with certain departments or individuals becoming more readily entrepreneurial due to their research area. The remaining 13 percent responded "No/Don't Know" to an increasing entrepreneurial university role, instead identifying this as being the search for knowledge, not money.

[It] is necessary because we cannot survive on ministerial funding alone. (Avignon, Senior, Male, Academic, Social Sciences)

Specific departments [with] a vocational dimension are becoming more entrepreneurial. (Avignon, Senior, Female, Academic, Professional School)

It is the big universities who get the most lucrative contracts. Here at Avignon, our modest size means that we are not a very prominent center of research. (Avignon, Senior, Female, Academic, Professional School)

There are people who take lots of initiatives to try to find money outside of that from the minister of education, but not in the literature department, rather from sciences, computing, and technology. These departments have more to do with business and commerce in general, and they have less difficulty than we do in finding money. (Avignon, Senior, Male, Academic, Social Sciences)

Table 3.3
Greater Entrepreneurialism? (percentages and numbers)

Question: Is your university becoming more entrepreneurial?

Universities	Yes	Yes, But	No/Don't Know	Total Responses
Avignon	38	49	13	100 (39)
Boston	82	15	3	100 (33)
Oslo	89	0	11	100 (35)
Twente	100	0	0	100 (20)

The following statements are from respondents who do not think the university is becoming more entrepreneurial, with many appearing not to want an entrepreneurial university, including at least one senior manager.

Essentially academics are not trained in this way of thinking. Their role is one of research, so this is not really part of their mentality. (Avignon, Junior, Male, Academic, Professional School)

The role of the university is first and foremost the search for knowledge and understanding, not a search for finances. (Avignon, Senior, Male, Academic, Social Sciences)

No. This kind of mentality is not part of the French culture. (Avignon, Senior, Female, Manager)

Oslo

Oslo embodies a public system more intimate and manageable than in France, with formula funding and planning more appreciated than in Avignon. Nevertheless, the majority of respondents perceive a push towards entrepreneurial values and behavior, and many view such change as beholding numerous disadvantages, with only a minority (11 percent) seeing benefits or the need for a balance.

There are certainly incentives to become more entrepreneurial. At the Research Council, an important source of research funding, there has been a general trend towards channeling increasing proportions of the funding through so-called research programs. The period when you could simply come up with a good application, submit it, and hope for the best is basically gone. The rules of the game have changed. (Oslo, Senior, Male, Academic, Social Sciences)

The Research Council now has strategic programs that you have to fit into; there also have been cuts, cuts, cuts. If you don't apply for these grants, it means no money, no Ph.D. students. So in many ways the university that was supposed to be free in terms of research is no longer. You can have your ideas, but nobody is going to give you money. (Oslo, Junior, Female, Academic, Sciences)

Yes and no, many of us are trying to resist this trend, and many realize that once we enter into that game, we will become dependent on external finances. (Oslo, Senior, Female, Academic, Social Sciences)

Twente

Within Twente responses unanimously affirmed that the university was becoming increasingly entrepreneurial, as expected due to its difficult beginnings and emergence into maturity as a model, self-defined, entrepreneurial university. Most indubitably accept this state, while others detect some disturbing aspects within entrepreneurialism.

Since we are already considered the most entrepreneurial university in the Netherlands, it would be difficult to become even more. Clearly, as in most systems, government funding is not increasing. We have to find money from the market. We do it well both in the social sciences and in engineering. There is a lot of contract research and setting up of companies. There is even the idea of making students become young entrepreneurs as well. (Twente, Senior, Male, Academic, Social Sciences)

People here have an assignment that is half teaching and half research. And it's more and more a development that they should get outside funding to cover their half-time research positions. The university cannot pay for the total salary of academics anymore. (Twente, Junior, Male, Academic, Professional School)

We all acknowledge that it is necessary to become more entrepreneurial, and at the same time we all hate it. (Twente, Junior, Male, Academic, Social Sciences)

Boston College

A similar response pattern to that of Twente was expected at Boston College, given its private, ultracompetitive status within the American academic marketplace (DeBats & Ward, 1999; Ménand, 2001). According to the respondents, Boston College is becoming increasingly entrepreneurial, especially in research. However, the process is uneven, varying between disciplines, being largely incorporated into accepted practice. Interestingly, there are an equal number of critical responses about the disadvantages as there are positive responses about the advantages. This shows considerable ambivalence and conflict within the United States system. Many scholars appear to be conservative and traditional, valuing familiar practice and structure. However, in actuality there is a high level of tension within the market realm.

There has been a concerted effort to hire more people who are more research-oriented, and therefore they are given more support by the university and encouraged to try to get their own support. (Boston College, Senior, Male, Academic, Professional School)

There's been just a modest move in that direction. Not a major change. (Boston College, Senior, Female, Manager, Professional School)

As we've moved up the food chain, we have become more entrepreneurial. (Boston College, Senior, Male, Academic, Professional School)

Advantages and Disadvantages of Entrepreneurialism

The respondents were asked what the advantages or disadvantages were of increasing university entrepreneurialism. Contrary to some expectations of almost total hostility in the public system and overwhelming acceptance in the competitive, entrepreneurial Dutch and American systems, the responses were divided between those perceiving advantages or disadvantages. However, some respondents postulated the need for a balance between public and private funding while others understood the situation as a dilemma or a necessity, unable to answer in terms of advantages or disadvantages.

The advantages identified are similar across four universities: increasing financial stability, university autonomy, competition, staff productivity, and proximity between staff, students, the market, and outside world.

I think the advantages will be that we would be more cosmopolitan and more into national networks. (Boston College, Junior. Female, Academic, Professional School)

Putting together a proposal is a reality check on ideas, even if you don't get the funding, if people [did] their job of reviewing [well], you have some good comments. (Boston College, Senior, Female, Academic, Sciences)

This would lead to more competitiveness and an increase in the work and productivity of the university. (Avignon, Junior, Male, Academic, Sciences)

This can make us far more motivated and can help us improve. (Avignon, Junior, Male, Academic, Professional School)

I don't see any inconveniences. This does not influence the teaching in a negative manner at all. On the contrary, this allows the university to open up to the outside world. (Avignon, Senior, Male, Manager, Administration)

Avignon

Many respondents in Avignon identified other advantages, such as commercial validation through collaboration with industry, increasing efficiency of university processes, and expanding freedom for academics. Many respondents made comparisons between the restricted French system and the openness of the Anglo-American system. In particular, one respondent viewed entrepreneurial logic as an advantage if grounded in the enterprise of European countries, excluding France. This comment signified a rare moment, deeming national, political culture and uniqueness as undesirable. However, many respondents who identified advantages also spoke of the disadvantages, suggesting an awareness of the limitations associated with solely adopting an entrepreneurial logic.

[I admire some of] the qualities of the Anglo-American systems, their freedom of movement, their freedom of contact, and their functioning like an enterprise despite remaining a public organization. They have an open-mindedness lacking in the French system. (Avignon, Senior, Male, Academic, Sciences)

I only see advantages in this, as long as this logic is based more on the European enterprise as opposed to a uniquely French one. The problem lies in the functioning of the French enterprise, which often functions in a very absolutist fashion, but for this to change, the whole French mentality would have to change. (Avignon, Senior, Male, Academic, Social Sciences)

A main disadvantage identified concerned the incompatibility of business with social/cultural values, or the public service with the private profit motive. A further disadvantage, strongly stressed by those in public sector dominant systems, was the threat to traditional university values.

The way we see things in France is that the university is a public service; therefore, this is not really compatible with the logic of an enterprise. (Avignon, Junior, Male, Academic, Professional School)

In addition, some respondents described the risk of losing freedom and creativity.

The ministerial funding is what allows us more innovation and creativity. We are more supple, we don't have to answer to anyone, and we have more freedom with this type of funding. If, however, we only have funding from private enterprises, this obliges us to have a more specific orientation; hence we lose out on liberty. We need sure, stable resources to ensure that sense of freedom. (Avignon, Senior, Male, Academic, Sciences)

The disadvantage would be dealing with money; you always run the risk of losing your freedom. I don't see many advantages of becoming entrepreneurial, opening to the world of business. (Avignon, Senior, Male, Academic, Social Sciences)

A further risk disclosed by some respondents involved the development of an unequal, differentiated system with increasing elitist universities, induced by the introduction of higher and varied fees; and many voiced concern about lowering standards and becoming similar to the American model. Of particular note are the precautions espoused by a self-described liberal.

I am a liberal, and so I am all for the shift towards the logic of an enterprise. However, there are precautions to be taken. So yes, if we can avoid waste, if it acts as a stimulant for our work; no, if it means eventually adopting the "American system," where the impression [is] that professors are dependent on their students and have to give good grades for fear of being denounced as "incompetent" teachers. (Avignon, Senior, Male, Academic, Professional School)

The good thing about the system in France is that the students pay exactly the same fees in all the universities. If we develop the logic of an enterprise, this will mean that fees will vary, so some of the universities [will be] more expensive and some will subsequently be considered more important than others, etc. This will be a handicap for the students. So we need to conserve our ties with the state, which I wouldn't describe as dependence but rather as a bond. (Avignon, Senior, Female, Academic, Sciences)

The following comment demonstrates the need for a balance between public and private financing.

I don't think that we should develop a logic that is 100 percent that of an enterprise. We should try and make a mixture of the two. The logic of an enterprise attaches far too much importance to financial profit. However, the positive aspect would be that academics would have to take a lot more initiatives. (Avignon, Senior, Male, Academic, Sciences)

Finally, some respondents could not contemplate the university operating like a business, while others believed becoming entrepreneurial was necessary but were unable to offer particular advantages or disadvantages. The idea of change has germinated; yet currently most have rejected it as undesirable or irrelevant.

Universities are public institutions, so in this respect, the question of whether or not we will develop the logic of an enterprise is not worth worrying about, because I don't yet see how this could become possible. The academics are at the heart of the university; they make up the foundation, that they are public servants means that for the moment, the university is going to remain a public institution. (Avignon, Junior, Male, Academic, Social Sciences)

Oslo

Most respondents at Oslo perceived an entrepreneurial stance as harmful to traditional university values; for instance, losing basic research and freedom to conduct curiosity-based research. However, many take for granted that teaching will remain immune from such commercial pressure.

It can ruin the academic, traditional values that universities have. (Oslo, Senior, Female, Academic, Professional School)

I don't think it will continue to be a university. We could not participate in international scientific dialogues any more. So much of this [new, applied, funded] research is short-term and very conservative. In basic research you are concerned about things where the users are not even born yet. (Oslo, Junior, Male, Academic, Sciences)

We spend so much time writing proposals, copying them, and trying to get money that we neglect our basic university duties. (Oslo, Junior, Female, Academic, Sciences)

I am very against the idea of the university's becoming more entrepreneurial. For these new strategic programs from the Research Council, you need teams, and preferably they should come from all over the world. If you have a black, handicapped, Sami woman as your collaborator, you are more likely to get a grant. (Oslo, Senior, Female, Academic, Social Sciences)

Twente

Likewise at Twente, most emphasize numerous drawbacks of entrepreneurial policy, including short-termism, loss of creativity, loss of freedom, and inequality.

You have to apply too often to get money, and in general, the chance you will get funded is only a few percent, like a kind of lottery. (Twente, Junior, Male, Academic, Social Sciences)

If you want to study subjects that are not industry-related, then it is difficult to get money. And the projects are usually short-term. (Twente, Senior, Male, Academic, Sciences)

There can be a bit of tension between the kind of additional money that you have to bring in and the time you actually would prefer to have, a bit more short periods for reflection and writing. People always feel they have to do it on weekends and holidays, so there is never enough time. (Twente, Senior, Male, Academic, Professional School)

In contrast, some explained the advantages.

You have to be alert to what's going on in industry in your subject and be on top, so it's good to keep your research a little more applied. You can also develop fundamental questions from applied research. (Twente, Senior, Male, Academic, Sciences)

I find that students usually like to work at things that are real, and if you have contacts with industry that makes it possible. (Twente, Junior, Female, Academic, Professional School)

The advantage is gaining greater academic freedom. If we can get funds outside of government funding, it gives us more financial autonomy. (Twente, Senior, Male, Manager)

Boston College

Respondents at Boston College had similarly mixed views.

Not in my area. No business out there really wants to look at funding my kind of research. (Boston College, Junior, Female, Academic, Social Sciences)

You can become a slave to somebody else's ideas. (Boston College, Senior, Male, Academic, Professional School)

It is an enormous amount of time just doing the forms. There is just not enough research money out there. (Boston College, Junior, Female, Academic, Professional School)

There is the potential for conflict of interest, for the faculty member to be loyal not to the institution and not to academic science, but to the corporation. (Boston College, Senior, Male, Academic, Sciences)

Here is something that does irk me. More space has been made for research, and it has been taken out of teaching space. So when push comes to shove, teaching loses at the expense of research. (Boston College, Junior, Male, Academic, Sciences)

The modulation and sophistication of these responses is significant, especially considering the exceptional institutional loyalty, which often presupposes considerable marketing and entrepreneurial effort to survive. These responses suggest considerable room for constructive, critical dialogue.

Increased Competition

An important aspect of entrepreneurial logic is competition, which arguably improves the quality of organizations by driving out bad products and elevating good products. Public institutions may become inactive due to lack of competition prompting improvements and expansion. In many countries, ministers of education are introducing competition into public schools and universities to improve the quality of educational institutions. These ministers influence public institutions to overcome competitive scarcity by incentives, thus steering from a distance, yet without having to directly control or provide more funding.

The respondents were asked whether the minister has introduced measures to make universities more competitive with each other. Table 3.4 reveals the variety and complexity of answers received, particularly the cross cutting of descriptive and normative answers, and high degree of disagreement as to what is happening. The pattern of responses for this question is quite distinct from the patterns for previous questions. There are substantial conflicts of opinion between case study samples, though rarely along the traditional cleavage lines of gender, age, or disciplinary specialty. Many respondents distinguish between a classic, acceptable, research-based rivalry to attract the best students, and a recent, controversial, market economic competition for basic funding and survival.

In Oslo and Avignon, older, established forms of competition are regarded by many (almost half) as normal and natural, and the recent form of entrepreneurial competition is rejected by most, perceived as largely irrelevant. In contrast, Boston College and Twente have experienced competitive pressures and generally regard them as positive. However, Boston College responses were not hostile to competition, whereas a strong minority of Twente responses conveyed less enthusiasm to mild hostility, as if saying "Yes" to entrepreneurialism, but "No" to full competition. This perhaps befits a recent public sector convert to reform or a Dutch traditional preference for publicly agreed accommodation, rather than risking full competition and creative destruction. The following quotes concern the traditional, natural, competitive pressures.

Avignon

The minister has not had to introduce competition, because it is a natural phenomenon among the universities. (Avignon, Senior, Male, Academic, Social Sciences)

This idea of competition is something that the establishment of French universities refuses [although it] still exists. But it is not organized or even encouraged by the state. To survive, the smaller universities have to excel in one or two specific areas. Avignon, for example, excels in communication, computerization, and drama. (Avignon, Senior, Male, Manager)

Table 3.4
More Competitive? (percentages and numbers)

Question: Is your university becoming more competitive?

Universities	Yes Good/Need More	Already	Don't Know	No Good/Yes Bad	Total Reponses
Avignon	12	43	17	28	100 (42)
Boston	82	12	0	6	100 (34)
Oslo	18	42	15	24	99 (33)
Twente	42	29	0	29	100 (31)

There is no competition between the universities in the public sector and the private organizations. There are very few Catholic universities in France, and there is a spirit of cooperation between the two. However, there is more competition between the regional and national universities. For example, Avignon, as a reasonably poor industrial region, cannot compete with universities in towns like Marseilles, Lyon, or Nice—the universities are much bigger. (Avignon, Senior, Male, Manager)

Oslo

Similarly in Oslo, there is a normal level of competition, especially in research.

In my field [molecular biology], which is very international, one wouldn't dream of anything other than trying to publish in the best international journals. There is no Norwegian or Anglo biology. (Oslo, Junior, Female, Academic, Sciences)

Twente

At Twente, the competitive spirit has been internalized by many.

I think that it's self-propelling. There's no pressure. (Twente, Senior, Male, Academic, Sciences)

No, I wouldn't say that the dean or the department has put pressure on academics. This pressure is inherent in the system. (Twente, Senior, Male, Academic, Social Sciences)

If you don't feel the pressure, then you don't belong here. So there is no reason for anybody to talk about it, even the dean. So the mentality is such that everybody works hard and competes. It is not an issue. (Twente, Senior, Male, Manager)

Boston College

At Boston College, the system appears to be equally accepted by the majority.

This university very much wants to become a nationally prominent research university, but they are not all aware of the financial support that's needed in faculty loans, research assistance, and administering grants. (Boston College, Senior, Male, Academic, Professional School)

I don't know whether pressure is necessary. I think everybody loves it. They couldn't be held back. (Boston College, Junior, Male, Academic, Sciences)

Disadvantages of Competition

Those expressing a negative view of competition advocated that it was either unfortunately being introduced or fortunately not being introduced. Interestingly, many respondents justified their answers by using comparisons with other systems, often having elaborate reasons for their stances, not always benefiting their local or national systems.

Avignon

I don't think that competition between the French universities is part of the minister's perspective. Here in France we are very attached to the idea of the university as having a national character. (Avignon, Senior, Male, Academic, Sciences)

Oslo

This rating of universities is a very Anglo-American way of thinking. It is not a Scandinavian way. (Oslo, Senior, Male, Academic, Social Sciences)

Twente

In the last 10 to 20 years in the Netherlands [there] is much more pressure on academics to publish, and so we have changed from a German environment to an American environment. So it is now "publish or perish" and the quality is not looked at enough. And now you have to publish in the right type of journals. Dutch publications don't count anymore. You have to publish in English and in international journals. (Twente, Junior, Male, Academic, Social Science)

Quite a lot [of pressure]. The whole system puts quite some pressure on academics to be competitive. (Twente, Senior, Male, Academic, Professional School)

It seems there is not much interest in the central roles of teaching and research. There is more interest in getting money and developing a corporate image. Change for change's sake. (Twente, Senior, Male, Academic, Professional School)

It's a crazy enterprise, as simple as that. The whole idea of managing science is just so narrow-minded. We are just a drop in the ocean. The locus of control is not here. You have to follow where the field is going, and trying to manage that from here is hopeless. It is much better to have personal quality control rather than at the level of programs. It's paperwork, bureaucratic, a waste of time. Efficiency is not the strongest point in the university. (Twente, Senior, Male, Academic, Professional School)

Boston College

Even at Boston College, there is some modest, informed dissent that competitive pressures are always useful.

We bring in new people who have excellent records and give them reduced teaching loads. I am torn about this kind of thing. The people who are doing the loads of courses have much less time to write. There is always this growing gap. (Boston College, Senior, Male, Academic, Professional School)

When respondents suggest that competition will improve a system, they often assume that institutions are on a level footing. However, the above comment indicates that this is almost never the case, with unequal advantages available to certain institutions or individuals. For instance, when universities compete for

funding from industry, those located closer to the rich industrial or high-tech regions are advantaged. Generally, the larger the institution the more chance it has
to compete in any arena, due to economies of scale and ability to put more money
towards advertising or marketing. In addition, the subjects taught in universities
shift standing. For instance, universities teaching vocational subjects and like areas
fitting within the market are advantaged over others distant from the market,
such as nursing, education, classics, languages, philosophy, and social sciences.

Advantages of Competition

In contrast, some respondents explained the advantages of greater competitive pressures, especially within public institutions, illustrating the openness of
many academics to certain reform efforts, but resistance to wholesale restructuring. Those in favor of competition wanted to introduce the logic of enterprises, make research more competitive, and make the university more job
oriented. The following comments include respondents from faculties where
competition is often difficult.

Avignon

No, the minister has introduced very few measures, and as far as I'm concerned, too few,
because this would help change the traditional mindsets of [those] over the age of 55.
The role of the university has evolved, so I don't see why they shouldn't evolve with it.
(Avignon, Junior, Male, Academic, Professional School)

Competitiveness can be a way of motivating and improving the universities. (Avignon,
Junior, Male, Academic, Social Sciences)

It would be better to maintain the universities as public institutions, [but] with more financial means, more punch, dynamism, [and] entrepreneurialism. Instead of the university being run by a group of tired old men, [I'd] rather have a group of young people
30 and 40 years old, who have the desire to go forward and are not behind the times.
(Avignon, Senior, Male, Academic, Sciences)

Oslo

In Oslo, some respondents indicated that greater competition would be wel-
come, but only if introduced by a government that understood what it was doing.

I think of advantages not just for the people who are earning extra money, but also for
teaching and consultative work, perhaps the knowledge will work better in some of these
applied projects than those small pieces in the so-called international journals that no
one reads. (Oslo, Senior, Female, Academic, Social Sciences)

Well, I think the advantages are that we become closer to what is happening in society
and in the professions. I think that is a good thing. (Oslo, Senior, Male, Academic, Professional School)

Norwegians think they are best in everything. I don't think they have [an idea]. For instance, if you compare Norway with Switzerland, which is about the size of Norway, about 2.8 percent of their gross national product goes into research and development. Switzerland has 20 Nobel prizes in physics, chemistry, and medicine. So, I don't think this government understands what competition is. (Oslo, Senior, Male, Academic, Sciences)

I don't think the government is advanced enough to understand these issues. In private industry they talk about advanced owners, and I don't think the government is an advanced owner in Norway. That is part of the problem. (Oslo, Junior, Male, Academic, Sciences)

In Twente and Boston College, many respondents feel the competitive pressures and find them beneficial.

Twente

You have to be competitive to survive. There was a time when you could sit down and think for 20 years and then come up with the final publication that will change the world. It doesn't work like that nowadays. It's teamwork, [and it's competitive], and you have to get a certain rate of publications. (Twente, Senior, Male, Manager)

Boston College

Yes, absolutely. It is through things like bringing in new people who have excellent records and giving them lots of benefits. Giving them big salaries, drastically reducing their loads and showcasing them as the ideal. Like, "See how nice their life is. Yours could be just as nice if you were as productive." (Boston College, Senior, Male, Academic, Professional School)

The answer is definitely yes, and it is shown in the criteria for tenure. The process for evaluating people for tenure has gotten a lot more oriented towards people's research and publications. (Boston College, Senior, Male, Academic, Professional School)

DISCUSSION

In all four universities included in this study, academic and management responses overwhelmingly indicated a changed climate from that which prevailed in the postwar period of high growth in student numbers that was publicly funded. To varying degrees, all the interviews pointed to several similar recent trends.

- There has been some reduction in governmental funding evident in the cuts to public and private institutions (the funding cuts for Boston College are in the area of reduced federal research grants).
- There is greater competition and encouragement for entrepreneurial enterprise, especially for recruiting students and giving public or private research contracts.

- There is an increasingly insistent and public requirement both to be more collaborative in sharing scarce resources and to pursue more money-generating activities

It is clear from the findings and the literature that varying levels of competition and privatization are undertaken by various interested groups for differing motives. Many European university systems have been less likely to pursue full privatization or competition agendas for a combination of reasons. These may include greater public toleration of higher taxation, preferences for high-level quality public service, a greater degree of public resistance to extreme laissez-faire forms of capitalist competition, and greater union or interest group mobilization for the public services. Only in the Netherlands as evidenced at Twente are practices and attitudes favorable to significant private sector and competitive reforms, while elsewhere such changes are partial, pragmatic, and subject to immediate modifications if they fail to work.

However, significantly, in the wholly private, nonprofit, Jesuit Boston College, there is support for many practices that are not inspired by private, corporate, capitalist models. For instance, widespread tenure, consultation with teaching departments over work practices and content, academic autonomy and freedom, professional judgment concerning the utility of new technology, cross-subsidization of students by need, and support for academic fields by criteria of academic excellence and coherence.

In the European universities, the traditional values and practices are even stronger. None has introduced full fees for students, sold public assets to private enterprise, or allowed public institutions to come under total ministerial control. In addition, formula funding for teaching and some research predominates, rather than competitive market bidding, and performance indicators are rarely or unsystematically introduced. Nevertheless, there have been considerable efforts to decentralize, creating greater autonomy and responsibility at institutional levels. Perhaps a greater degree of central government control precludes the need to introduce privatization or competition from outside the public sector. In contrast, Anglo-Saxon government systems long ago created buffer bodies and autonomous universities, which they finance but are not supposed to normatively influence or control. Anglo-Saxon reformers, unable to simply use government fiat, had a greater need to use private sector sledgehammers to attain their goals, such as reducing public expenses and responsibilities.

Clearly, a recent trend towards private and entrepreneurial procedures, following business and corporate models, in running institutions is not necessarily against local wishes. A hybrid situation results when the public sector is reformed but nonetheless remains in public ownership. While some private universities emerge and may be encouraged, they remain minorities often requiring official protection. Up to this time, there have been no cases of selling entire public universities as ongoing enterprises into private hands, yet nearly all systems have or allow new private, nonprofit, and for-profit universities to exist and compete with public universities.

Why are governments reluctant to sell or privatize universities, as they do with other services? Is it due to fear of political backlash, or due to possible union resistance by staff and students? Whatever the reason, it leads to a paradox that reform in a competitive, user pays, cost-cutting direction must take place within public institutions, requiring many staff members to be reengineered. Many staffers believe in the old public service procedures. They believe in trust, professionalism, autonomy, academic freedom, and free education for its own sake. Thus, the forced changes become inherently difficult and divisive.

Much of the so-called best practices within the private sector, such as TQM—businesslike, benchmarking activities—derive from diverse businesses, and are often out of date in reality by the time they are fashionable with academics. Many entrepreneurs are cutting their hierarchies when universities are making theirs bigger and more expensive. They are trying for consensual, devolved, cooperative, egalitarian relations, when universities are reinventing the managerial wheel. They are becoming more diverse as universities become more uniform. They gave up plans and manpower projections, just when universities are doing both.

There is considerable evidence that many of the old university values persist in all four case studies, including Boston College and the entrepreneurial Twente. However, even at Oslo and Avignon, many staffers believe in some changes related to privatization, such as diverse private funding, efficiency and effectiveness, and increased competitiveness in research.

CONCLUSION

The privatizing challenge facing universities is apparent. Firstly, it seems reasonable to argue that enterprise practices need to be strengthened if universities are to confidently face the future, especially in traditional continental systems. In Avignon, Oslo, and Twente until recently, the traditional continental model of authority distribution was characterized by a weak central-level dependence on formula funding from central bureaucracies. This severely limited the capacity of universities to adapt and respond when government ministers were unwilling to supply adequate funding or trust academia. Secondly, the academic heartland, where traditional values of teaching and research are firmly rooted, needs to continue contributing substantially to institutional decision making; especially given that valuable information concerning money-making opportunities in the market is found in the lower levels of the organization. Therefore, if governments and institutional leaders require successful universities, they need to give professionals ample rewards, room to maneuver, and involvement in decision making.

Like Rome when it conquered Gaul, the force of globalization in higher education certainly exists and has created a new world context for ongoing debate and contest. As in Rome, globalization may eventually carry all before it, though for how long and at what price? Traditional conceptions of university purpose and value, and the strong French, Norwegian, and Dutch models of public service appear to keep the present-day Romans at bay, at least for now, perhaps forever. If the recent mood since September 11, 2001, which has re-created a trust in public authorities, displaces the previously fashionable wave of privatization and worship of the market, a shift back towards the state may be currently underway. Clearly, the findings presented within this chapter show the strengths of different historical and local cultures, which may resist the forces leading towards homogenization and uniformity.

The last word belongs to an insightful French respondent, who argues cogently for an intelligent, mixed balance of principles.

With this [French] system, all three terms [managerial, bureaucratic, collegial] are applicable. We have both the best and the worst of these things. It is a very good system in that it leaves room for innovation and creativity, but at the same time there is the monitoring by the minister, but from a distance, and I think that is an excellent balance, like the status of academics in France. They are free to do as they please, but at the same time they are constantly evaluated for the advancement of their careers. This allows them the possibility to carry out their best work, [but in some cases, also their worst]. But for the most part this liberty leads to better conditions for the academics to work under. (Avignon, Senior, Male, Academic, Sciences)

Chapter 4

University Governance

Three classic models of university governance are generally distinguished: the American, the British, and the Continental models (Clark, 1983). These enable an understanding of the traditional forms of academic organization and management. However, since the 1980s and 1990s, these models have begun to disintegrate (Dill, 2000). Throughout the world national governments launched reform policies, stimulated by international agencies such as the World Bank and the OECD, accompanied by new policy instruments that have since impacted academic organizations.

It appears that universities around the world are confronting similar circumstances and are increasingly considering similar kinds of organizational design. In addition, it seems that differences between higher education systems are lessening due to political and economic developments. Goedegebuure, Kaiser, et al. (1994) suggest that these differences will continue diminishing in the years ahead as kindred forces, including competition, national level deregulation, and entrepreneurialism, push towards higher education system similarity. Since the mid-1980s, national governments have encouraged a strengthening of institutional management by changing the composition of institutional governing bodies, streamlining decision-making within universities, providing greater power and authority to institutional executives, and altering the role of democratic senates and councils from decision making and control-oriented to advice-oriented (Goedegebuure et al., 1994).

Government ministers and university administrators regard the traditional models of university governance, such as the British and the Continental model, in which collegial decision making plays an important role, as obsolete and unfit for the rapidly changing environment. Consequently, many universities began to adopt corporate-like strategies and structures in order to manage (Bauer, Askling, Marton, & Marton, 1999). The key aspects of these competitive strategies encompassed responsiveness, adaptability, and flexibility, which created new lines of authority within universities. For instance, a frequently encountered design involves a strengthening of executive leadership at the central and middle levels of universities, and in many countries collegial decision-making structures were slightly or substantially redefined (see Trow, 1994, for a distinction between soft and hard managerialism). Additionally, in many cases corporate managerialism and line management replaced systems of elected executives and affected the powers of senates and academic councils.

Without a doubt these developments within universities created new tensions. Some, mainly executives and administrators, welcomed the changes as means to increase their power, while others, mainly academics and students, remained silent or voiced resistance to the changes. These academics and students felt that external agencies and university managers were shifting the balance of power, thereby removing the authority and opportunities of academics and students to participate in strategic decision making. They argued that such a shift might have risky implications for the future viability of universities. Nonetheless, universities are inherently bottom-heavy. This implies, firstly, that academics and students are in a position to question the legitimacy of institutional policies, which may seriously delay policy implementation or even paralyze university decision making. Secondly, it implies that academics and to a lesser extent students hold essential information for meaningful decision making. According to Dill and Peterson Helm (1988), a main feature of universities is that academics possess the essential expertise necessary to evaluate the feasibility of strategic proposals. Hence, due to the key position of academics in accomplishing university goals, bypassing them may affect the level of information input for policy making and the implementation of policy decisions.

Clearly, developing an optimal model of university governance will be challenging. On the one hand, executive powers within the university need strengthening to respond to external pressures, particularly within traditional Continental systems where university authority distribution is characterized by a weak central level, which severely limits the capacity of universities to adapt and respond to change. On the other hand, the academic heartland, where traditional teaching and research values are firmly rooted, needs to survive and continue to substantially contribute to institutional decision making, particularly as valuable information concerning the markets is found in the lower levels of the organization. If the aim of governments and institutional leaders is to be successful, universities must consider allowing professionals ample room to maneuver and participate in strategic decision making. The future performance of universities depends upon the ability to blend traditional academic values with new managerial values.

This begs a question concerning the nature of ingredients for a successful blend. This requires a description of the institutional structures, backgrounds, and changes over previous decades. A comparable change of climate, such as the rise of globalizing practices with an overwhelming emphasis on managerialism, may distinctly impact on the blend. Moreover, it is likely that varying backgrounds may perceive the same phenomenon differently even if, for example, they are all called Continental systems.

Initially, this chapter addresses the concept of governance, a complex concept used frequently, often having different meanings for different people focusing on different dimensions. Following, this chapter addresses university governance in France, the Netherlands, and Norway, where all have had a Continental mode of authority distribution within their higher education systems. However, because "the university is one expression of a nation's historic memory, and no country's history is the same as its neighbors'" (Neave & van Vught, 1991, pp. x–xi), it is not surprising that structures, practices, and procedures within universities are of a wide variety across national higher education systems. A description and analysis of university governance in the United States is not included, as there is no national system. Instead, each private university has its own governance structure and each state has its governance system for all its public universities. Nevertheless, increasing managerialism, discussed later in this chapter, is a prevailing trend within many U.S. universities, particularly in Boston College, where the faculty senate was abolished during the 1970s and senior administrators hold most of the financial and academic power. While many academic decisions are made at the departmental level, major policy decisions for the direction of the university are made by a handful of people at its apex. Finally, this chapter presents the case studies of Avignon, Oslo, Twente, and Boston, the latter exemplifying a governance structure that originated from a vastly different background. This prompts a question as to whether there are similarities or striking differences between the American and European cases. However, the key question is whether managerialism, which we regard as a globalizing practice, has led to increasing homogeneity in institutional governance.

GOVERNANCE: MODES OF
AUTHORITY DISTRIBUTION

All systems of power or decision making can be divided into levels of organization. The levels within higher education systems are often arbitrary[1] and interdependent, yet a shift in the balance of power at one level will have consequences for other levels. According to Neave (1988a), a rationalization and wholesale redistribution of functions between governments and institutions has varying consequences for the delicate power balances within universities. De Groof, Neave, and Svec (1998) argue that changes to intrauniversity arrangements are by-products of new forms of state-university relations. In sum, changed patterns between the superstructure and the middle structure affect the understructure. Clark (1983) provides a further analysis of authority distributions between levels.

Vertical Profiles

Clark (1983) presents the rudiments of three national combinations of authority distribution: the Continental, the American, and the British models. Though somewhat dated and oversimplified, these models provide an understanding of a complex issue, namely institutional governance. In the Continental model authority is distributed traditionally in a combination of faculty guild and state bureaucracy. Guild authority involves individual professors having a domain where they control subordinates. These professors then combine as a body of equals to exercise control over a larger domain. These persons are simultaneously autocrats and colleagues. The administrative or bureaucratic authority is located in the superstructure level, often including national governments. This composition of authority primarily expresses the interests of full-time professors and officials located in state bureaucracies. Generally within this system, professors control the lower levels and state officials control the higher levels; however, this may not necessarily be with respect to all issues. For instance, state bureaucracies may appoint new chairholders while professors may heavily influence national-level decision making, as will be shown in the French case.

In its ideal type, weak autonomous authority at the university level and within constituent faculties characterizes the Continental model. The powerful professors did not want professional university-level administrators. They preferred to elect deans and rectors as amateur administrators on short appointments and easy recall. The state bureaucracy had its own personnel on the business side of the organization in a classic hierarchy and its own representatives acting as watchdogs. In this pattern, bureaucracy and oligarchy were not interested in creating an autonomous third force in the middle. The institutional level was regarded as the "middleman," relaying information. Clark (1983) describes the rudiments of the Continental model authority distribution: "Thus, in vertical profile, the traditional Continental distribution of authority has placed authority at the bottom, in guild forms; secondarily at the top, in ministerial bureaucracy that accommodates to the faculty guilds; and has only weakly provided for authority at middle levels of the system, in the form of institutional administration or trusteeship" (p. 127). Clark noted that during the late 1970s and early 1980s the already weak middle level, consisting of the institutional level and its faculties, became increasingly weak as higher education systems expanded. In the 1990s, significant changes to this level took place in several Continental structures (Bauer et al., 1999; de Boer & Huisman, 1999; Henkel, 2000).

The traditional British model involved a combination of faculty guilds that were modestly influenced by trustees and administrators at the institutional level. In this model universities were autonomous institutions and not placed directly under a governmental bureau. Professors remained powerful even when most funding came from the national government through the buffer of the University Grants Committee. Put succinctly in Clark's (1983) pithy words: "Thus, in vertical profile, the British mode has placed strong authority at the bottom, in guild forms, but has emphasized the collegial over the personal approach more so than the Continental systems. It has given some strength to middle levels of coordination, providing a modest degree of administrative leadership and allowing for the participation of lay trustees as well as collective faculty rule. Governmental bureaus traditionally had little power" (p. 128). During the 1960s and 1970s, this British ideal type began changing through the gradual strengthening of national-level authorities. During the 1980s and 1990s, reforms fundamentally changed the authority distributions within the system, as reflected in Halsey's (1982) book, *The Decline of the Donnish Dominion*.

The American model involved a combination of faculty forms with institutional trusteeship and administration. However, compared to the British ideal type, in the American model faculty rule was weaker and the influence of trustees and administrators was stronger. Trustees were given the opportunity to assign administrative staff to run the institution and the administrators were given considerable autonomy. Contrary to the Continental and British models, full professors did not become the building blocks of the organization. The universities were more bureaucratic than their European and British counterparts, due to the greater influence of professional administrators. In this model the bureaucracy was localized, and state bureaucracies had little or no influence. As Clark (1983) noted: "Thus, in vertical profile, the American academic structure developed a strong middle, in the form of institutional administration and trustees. Second, authority grew at the lower levels of the department and multidepartment college or school, in a blend of guild and bureaucratic forms. Weakest, in comparative perspective, have been the governmental levels" (p. 130).

These three types of authority distribution focus on vertical relationships; that is, relationships between levels of the organization within the system. These are important, as argued previously, since changes of functions and roles at one level affect balances of power at other levels within the system. However, what about power balances within any one level, for instance the horizontal profiles? De Boer and Denters (1999) developed a classification scheme consisting of four dimensions, derived from normative theories of institutional design. One of these dimensions, the vertical dimension, overlaps with the approach used by Clark and will not be addressed. One further dimension, the "democracy versus guardianship" dimension, will be discussed in a subsequent section. The remainder of this section addresses the other two dimensions dealing with horizontal distributions of power.

Horizontal Profiles I

When considering the constitutional design of a university, it is important to decide whether there should be a separation of powers. Arguments favoring a separation suggest that a monopoly of power may easily lead to abuses and that findings reached by joint decision making are more generally accepted. Within this vision consultation and participation improve the effectiveness of decision making. However, others argue that a concentration of power may be helpful in higher education for protecting scholarships, building distinctive enterprises, or activating an immobilized system. In this respect, concentrated powers are able to respond quickly, avoiding the cumbersome procedures associated with joint decision making. Yet, according to Clark (1983), a concentration of power does not work well for long as it soon freezes an organization around the views of just a few.

There are two theoretical options for a horizontal distribution of power. Parliamentary government, based on a fusion of powers, is a form of governance where executive authority emerges from and is responsible to legislative authority (Lijphart, 1984). Alternatively, presidential government, based on a separation of powers, produces a high degree of independence between the executive authority and the legislative powers.

These options may manifest themselves in a number of different ways. Firstly, within the parliamentary system the executive is elected or appointed by the legislature, whereas within the presidential system the executive is elected by the people or selected by another principal. In a university setting, a parliamentary system may decide that the representative university council, the classical faculty, or the representative senate will elect or appoint a rector, who is accountable to and may be dismissed by that body. Conversely, in a presidential system, in a university context, the president is able to act independently from the council or senate. In this system the powers of the president and the council or senate are clearly separated.

A further contrast between parliamentary and presidential systems concerns the membership of the governing bodies. In principle, a system embodying a separation of powers implies independence of the executive and legislature, and hence that one person cannot simultaneously serve in both, namely the incompatibility rule. A fusion of powers implies that one person may simultaneously serve in the executive and legislature (monism). In several countries, parliamentary systems do have an incompatibility rule (dualism). Therefore, it is possible to subdivide the class of parliamentary systems, vis-à-vis that between monistic and dualistic. According to this theory, parliamentary systems may differ in the degree of executive independence, for instance a relatively high degree of independence is associated with dualism and a relatively low degree of independence is associated with monism.

In a university setting, dualism, as defined here, means that the rector and other members of the executive board cannot be members of the senate or the university council. In a strict sense it may even be argued that the rector cannot chair the council meetings. Alternatively, in monistic systems members of the university council or senate may be members of the executive.

Both systems have strengths and weaknesses. For instance, in parliamentary systems there is the problem of executive stability. In the case of university governance when the legislature or the university council or senate uses its right to dismiss the executive, the rector, the functioning of the rectory is often seriously undermined and may result in severe damage to the university, especially to strategic, long-term issues. Conversely, in presidential systems there is the potential problem of deadlock, which occurs when the executive and legislature are unwilling to compromise. Constitutional provisions may be necessary to overcome the deadlock; however, in the absence of such provisions, deadlocks may paralyze the university.

In all three respects, the difference between presidential and parliamentarian systems is the difference between one based on a clear separation of powers and one based on a fusion of powers. Presidential and parliamentarian systems are two distinct alternatives for a monocentric system with concentrated powers. Thus, three types of authority distribution in a horizontal profile can be discerned: concentration of powers, fusion of powers, and separation of powers.

The above discussion bequeaths four alternative models for horizontal authority distribution within universities at the institutional level. Analogously, similar models can be applied to other levels within the university. These four models are:

Concentration of powers (monocentrism). Implies an almighty ruler at the apex of the university. Such a rector or president holds the executive and legislative powers. At the faculty level all powers are vested in the dean.

Monistic fusion of powers. Implies that the senate or council has power to select and dismiss the executives and hold these officeholders accountable. Moreover, the executives remain members of the legislature.

Dualistic fusion of powers. Implies that the senate or council has power to select or elect and dismiss the executives and hold officeholders accountable. However, the rector cannot be a council or senate member simultaneously.

Separation of powers. Implies a clear separation of powers between the rectory and representative council or senate. Both bodies are able to operate more or less independently from one another.

Horizontal Profiles II

The consideration of institutional design regarding university governance is further complicated by the distinction between "monocephalic" (one head) and "bicephalic" (two heads) structures (Neave, 1988b, p. 111). These refer to the locus of executive powers. There are two types of qualifications that may be relevant for university leadership: specialized knowledge in an academic discipline or general knowledge of the art of governing. In debates on university governance it is generally accepted that the former type of qualification provides entitlement to participation in executive matters. In monocephalic systems this has resulted in a unified structure whereby the head of the university is the head of the academic and administrative hierarchy. However, in bicephalic systems the role of the administrative hierarchy is more prominent, whereby the rector or equivalent is the head of the academic hierarchy, which is run parallel to an independent administrative hierarchy.

This dual structure can be found in most Continental higher education systems and has a long history in university governance (Neave, 1988b). An important reason for a separate administrative chain of command alongside the academic hierarchy is the desire of national governments to ensure a certain degree of continuity and to provide some guarantee that the university is managed in accordance with public laws. Therefore, the apex of the administrative hierarchy is typically appointed by the state and variously titled as kanzler, curator, secretary-general, or director.

GOVERNANCE: WHO IS ENTITLED TO RULE?

A further dimension derived from the classification scheme of de Boer and Denters (1999) refers to the concept of democracy. The notion of democracy is highly ambiguous and is used by virtually everyone to refer to a system that is characterized as "rule by the people," whereby ultimate political authority is vested in the people.

This immediately raises the question: who are the people that are entitled to rule? A common answer is based on the principle of affected interests, which states that every adult affected by a collective decision should have a say in making that decision be it direct or through representation (Dahl, 1989). If this deceptively simple criterion is applied to the context of universities, it becomes unclear whose interests are at stake in university decision making.

It is evident that various democratic systems may be based on radically different definitions of the people. For pragmatic purposes, systems will be defined as democratic provided they allow academic staff, nonacademic staff, and students to participate in decision making. Here decision making assumes a broad sense, meaning that it is not limited to only making decisions but also refers to processes, such as making recommendations, agenda setting, developing plans, and setting guidelines. A democratic university system implies that academics, nonacademics, and students are qualified[2] to participate either directly or indirectly by choosing representatives in this broad context of decision making that affects their fate (Dahl, 1989). Therefore, nobody from the university population is excluded from making major decisions. This principle of inclusion is highly distinctive. This inclusive concept of democracy conflicts with the practices of collegiality (Bess, 1992; Chapman, 1983). Generally, collegial governance systems refer to joint decision making and shared authority among academics and senior administrators, excluding nonacademic staff, students, and other potentially interested constituencies.

Throughout the centuries, the concept of democracy has met severe criticisms. Many opponents forcefully reject democracy, stressing that not everyone is equipped with the expertise and knowledge that is required to govern. They argue that political power should be entrusted to a minority of persons who are specially qualified to govern based on their superior knowledge and virtue. During the late 1960s and 1970s, heated debates frequently expressed these types of arguments whereby opponents of the democratic university contended that senior academics had the specialized knowledge and experience to govern the university, at least regarding academic affairs.

These highly qualified rulers are often referred to as the guardians. Advocates of guardian rule argued for the hierarchical subjection of ordinary community members to the rule of a few enlightened rulers. Essential to guardianship is the assumption that people are incompetent or are insufficiently competent to govern themselves. Consequently, the fundamental distinction between democracy and guardianship concerns the question: who is qualified to govern?

In the Western world, the 1970s are generally regarded as the heyday of university democracy. In several European countries, university governance was democratized, allowing equal representation of the constituent groups in all university bodies (Daalder & Shils, 1982). However, if the more exacting definition of democracy is applied in practice, throughout history true university democracy has been rare. Usually, decision-making rights have been vested in or have gravitated to those informed or learned in relevant ways, or who were believed to be at any rate.

What type of expertise is needed to make university decisions? For instance, in the organizational context of a university, there are at least two bases for legitimate claims to enlightenment. Firstly, being a scholar or an expert in a particular academic field, referred to as professional authority. Secondly, having a set of skills related to the "art of governing" or managerial authority. The entire notion of academic self-governance has rested upon the claim that scholarship is the primary source of authority within universities, if only because no other source is as firmly rooted in the very essence of universities. For ages, academic communities have argued about the legitimacy of these competing sources of authority. Even though both perspectives may be successfully combined, they tend to create potential tensions because in professional organizations the professionals and administrators seek dominance over the strategic domain (Bacharach, Bamberger & Conley, 1991). The distinction between these two sources of authority is important for understanding university governance. The balance of power within the university is related to the choice of who is qualified to rule, and the kind of expertise considered necessary to successfully run a university.

The distinction between the concept of democracy and the concept of guardianship manifests itself in radically different systems of selecting rulers. In contemporary democracies, the people typically elect those who are to govern. Except for some short-lived experiments in direct democracy, academic democracy has been synonymous with representative democracy. In an academic democracy, as a minimum condition everyone in the university community is given the right to vote in elections of representatives who will undertake major decision making. An alternative type of governance is guardianship, whereby officeholders are appointed on the basis of their competence, referring to a combination of professional expertise and/or managerial expertise. In addition, it refers to a system where officers hold positions in an ex officio capacity, such as in traditional senates consisting of only full professors.

However, the distinction between electing and appointing decision makers is quite complicated. Firstly, there may be mixed systems of governance regarding this dimension. Within one university some decision-making bodies consist of guardianships, for example an executive board, while other bodies consist of elected representatives, for example a university council. Secondly, as Neave (1988b) shows, elections may differ from one place to another and are usually related to the constituencies that are allowed to vote. For instance, should students only vote for student representatives or should they also be allowed to vote for nonstudent representatives? Moreover, there are several options regarding different voting systems. The process of appointing officeholders is also sometimes complicated, both formally and in practice. How should a system be named when rectors are appointed by the national government after consulting the democratic elected university council or when such councils have the right to nominate? Who does actually make such a decision when it is an unwritten rule that nominated persons will be appointed?

The concepts of democracy and guardianship provide useful insights into university governance structures, even though they contain pitfalls. The following section applies this theoretical discussion to the university governance models in France, the Netherlands, and Norway.

STRUCTURES IN UNIVERSITIES IN THREE COUNTRIES

France

It is common knowledge that French higher education has a long history, and that this rich and turbulent history has left deep marks on higher education. At the end of the twentieth century the higher education system, compared to other systems, is still quite centralized and has a diversified structure, which originated in the French Revolution and Napoleonic era.

During the French Revolution, corporations, including universities of the Ancient Régime, were abolished.[3] Around 1808 Napoleon established a single, unified organization, the Université Impériale, for all public education in France. This was subdivided into 16 academies or regional administrative units and later increased to 23. Under the Université Impériale former universities were not restored. Instead, Napoleon designated faculties as the basic entities of higher education. Five faculties were established: theology, law, medicine, letters, and science. These were expected to deliver graduates for highly trained doctors, administrators, and so on for the stability and welfare of the country. This classification of faculties remained unchanged until 1968.

Broadly speaking, in the nineteenth century the faculties were administered by the Ministry of Public Instruction, yet functioned separately from each other. At the end of the nineteenth century, the national government gave the faculties a certain autonomy by granting them the opportunity to create councils and assemblies for self-government, allowing them to select deans, and giving them their own budgets (van de Graaff & Furth, 1978b). In the same era universities were restored as organizational units whereby each university had a council, chaired by a rector, and primarily composed of deans and other faculty representatives. However, the faculties were already deeply embedded, consequently the re-creation of the university had little unifying effect (van de Graaff & Furth, 1978b).

Inspired by or in response to experiences in Germany and due to the increasing need for technologically trained people, new institutions were created that focused on research and specialized professional training. These institutes were established parallel to the existing faculties that were considered to be too rigid to keep up with the demands of "modern" times, and were given formal status within the higher education system. More recent system "intruders" are the University Institutes of Technology (UITs), which are administratively independent from the faculties.

In contrast to many countries, research was conducted outside the faculties. In France, teaching and research have never been connected as the Humboldtian ideal type suggests (Merrien & Musselin, 1999). Traditionally, most research was conducted or at least initiated by institutes such as the National Center for Scientific Research (CNRS). However, these institutes influenced research within faculties by means of various kinds of facilities such as loans, services, and equipment. Furthermore, most researchers who are part of these national research institutions are located and frequently teach courses within universities. Nowadays, the discourse on the separation of education and research in France is more of a myth that does not exist in reality.

Thus, the French system is enormously fragmented into diverse sectors with specialized functions, mainly for historical reasons (see Kaiser, 2001, for a detailed analysis of the system). According to van de Graaff and Furth (1978b), "research was primarily the responsibility of central research institutions, whereas training in the traditional professions was given in the faculties, and various administrative and technical cadres were recruited through the grandes écoles" (p. 50). Another striking feature of the fragmented French system is that public universities have never been an institution for the upper class only (Merrien & Musselin, 1999).

France is a typical example of the distribution of authority that Clark (1983) named the Continental mode. The dominant powers are the professionals within the faculties and the national government. Until at least 1968, the two powerful pillars were the state bureaucracy and the faculty guild. At the institutional level, the university itself hardly participated in the governance game (Merrien & Musselin, 1999).

French higher education is usually stereotyped for its administrative centralism. Many important issues are ultimately settled in the Parisian cabinet or bureaucracy. However, there is much administrative fragmentation, as lines of authorities run vertically within bureaucratic sectors. The minister and the directorate of higher education mainly exercise the extensive powers of the national government and have formal authority over all university matters. Issues related to university governance structures, curricula, degree requirements, and procedures for faculty appointments are determined by the national administration. However, full professors exercise considerable influence upon high-level decision making, as they dominate the two main national advisory bodies for higher education and the numerous standing committees (van de Graaff & Furth, 1978b). Frequently, academics are visitors to the ministry, asking for resources, as well as experts or leaders of national programs.

For most of the twentieth century, three organizational levels within universities could be distinguished: the chair, the faculty, and the university itself. Only full-time professors had full rights to participate in faculty, university, or national decision-making bodies. In contrast to the German full professors who had access to and control over substantial research funds, the French professor "seldom possessed research resources by virtue of occupying a chair" (van de Graaff & Furth, 1978, p. 54). Some research money, relatively small amounts from the national government, were controlled by the faculties. Their most powerful privilege was a rather unlimited freedom to use their time and organize their work, a situation characterized as a typical French combination of "administrative rigidity and anarchistic liberty within a framework of regulations" (Raymond Aron, cited in van de Graaff & Furth, 1978b, p. 54).

The second level concerned the faculties that were governed almost exclusively by professors. Each faculty had a council consisting of full professors. In addition, there was an assembly composed of professors, senior lecturers, and a small number of junior staff as an advisory voice. Under this regime the council was the more powerful of the two. The dean, who was a professor, served a three-year period that was normally renewed; however, many deans remained in office for a long period. They were powerful people, especially in the Paris region. According to van de Graaff and Furth (1978b), they were regarded as an integral part of the centralized administrative system.

The third level, the central or university level, had little power. The only institutional body, namely the university council, was extremely weak (van de Graaff & Furth, 1978b). The weakness of this council was caused partly by the lack of an elected professor as its chair and a symbolic head of the institution. Consequently, the faculties, the deans, and the national government handled most important issues.

Before 1968, universities contained groups of faculties. The deans within these faculties held power: "Underneath them, the departments or the other formal structures had no power and no budgets. Above them, the rector, a state civil servant, was the president of the university council and had only a symbolic role of representation" (Prost cited in Merrien & Musselin, 1999, p. 223). Within the faculties, decision making was collegial or strictly made among professional peers.

A turning point in French higher education occurred in 1968. After the widespread student protests and riots in May, the newly appointed minister of education, Edgar Faure, launched a new bill that was passed by parliament in November. This reform act, the Orientation Act for Higher Education, had three objectives: the promotion of interdisciplinary cooperation, the broadening of participation, and the decentralization or strengthening of university autonomy (Merrien & Musselin, 1999; Mignot Gerard, 2000). The following section focuses on the second and third objectives.

The 1968 Act detailed guidelines for the composition, functions, and responsibilities of the various decision-making bodies to be established at the universities. These newly formed councils consisted of representatives from all groups, including senior and junior teaching staff, research staff, students, nonacademic staff, and lay members representing the public.[4] A typical university council of 80 members is composed of 20 senior teaching staff, 12 junior staff, 4 researchers, 25 students, 5 nonacademics, and 14 lay members. The collegial mode of governance prevailing before 1968 was transformed into a form of representative democracy. However, in practice academic staff and especially senior staff tended to dominate the meetings. Moreover, research matters belonged to the jurisdiction of a separate, scientific council consisting of academic staff alone, the majority being senior members.

The Orientation Act of 1968 introduced a presidential system aimed at strengthening the central level of the university. The university council elected the university president, usually a professor within the council, for a period of five years. The president was assisted by a secretary-general, an administrative staff, and by one or more vice presidents elected from among the academic staff. The main problem facing the president, especially during these turbulent times, was governing a heterogeneous collection of faculties that once had substantial powers. Initially there were some misinterpretations regarding the relationship between the president and the university council. According to the minister, the president was not accountable to the council, implying that universities should be run by a *régime présidentiel* rather than *régime d'assemblée*. During the 1970s, the system of representative government within universities confronted several problems. The representative bodies became "theatres of ideological and political fights, elections were frequently boycotted, discussions lasted for hours, and presidential proposals were systematically blocked by motions" (Mignot Gerard, 2000, p. 5).

Twenty years later Merrien and Musselin (1999) drew a more equivocal conclusion arguing on the one hand that French universities were finally becoming more autonomous and on the other hand that:

The renewal of French universities through the improvement of their governance capacity heavily depends on institutions, norms and social behaviors inherited form the past and that strongly constrain the existing leeway for action. Many disadvantages have to be overcome. French universities have to face the state as well as the academic corporation, and they have to find a niche in the higher education marketplace. The pull of these three forces has complicated and slowed the pace of university development in France. (p. 221)

During the 1980s internal decision making within French universities entered calmer waters. Decision making remained weak and ideological debates subdued. In 1984, the Savary Act was passed by national parliament and aimed to strengthen the autonomy of universities and coherence at the institutional level. The 1984 framework was not a radical change but more or less in keeping with the main ideas of the late 1960s. Moreover, the university governing bodies remained the president and the two university councils (the *Conseil d'Administration* and the *Conseil Scientifique*). A third advisory body was introduced, the *Conseil des Études et de la Vie Universitaire* (CEVU) and soon after attracted criticism. Some believed that the participatory mode of governance enabled too many opportunities to politicize debates, while others believed that it prevented effective and strong leadership, maintaining fuzzy balances of power among the main players.

In the late 1980s and early 1990s, French universities faced a new policy that affected their governance. This "contractual policy" was not aimed at university reform, yet ironically it introduced some profound and successful changes to the French university governance model (Mignot Gérard, 2000). According to Merrien and Musselin (1999) it was not the contracts but the policy objectives that were essential, including increasing internal institutional dynamics, strengthening the president's role, and modifying the state-university relationship. This contractual policy clearly stated, among other things, that universities needed to strengthen and update their management tools to prepare strategic documents for negotiation processes with the ministry. It became necessary and possible at the institutional level to consider decisions that would not have appeared on the agenda in earlier times. In these contractual processes presidents discovered they could do more than simply represent their institution. Moreover, "presidents were the *only* legitimate interlocutors for the ministry and the not-to-be-by-passed relays between the universities and the central administration" [italics added] (Merrien & Musselin, 1999, p. 230). Increasingly, presidents appear to have taken the opportunity to exercise their powers.

This section concludes with an enumerative description of the state-of-the-art French university governance bodies at the end of the twentieth century:

The governing board, *Conseil d'Administration*, determines policy, votes on the budget, approves the accounts, distributes posts, approves agreements and conventions signed by the university president; this central decision-making body consists of 30 to 60 members and approves all proposed decisions of other bodies.

The scientific council, *Conseil Scientifique,* proposes guidelines for research policy to the governing board and is consulted on initial and further education programs, research programs, contracts, and on plans to create or change to the diplomas given by the institution.

The council for university studies and university life, *Conseil des Études et de la Vie Universitaire,* proposes guidelines on initial and further education to the governing board, prepares measures for student guidance, university social life, student living and study conditions, libraries, and documentation centers and may examine requests for new branches of study.

These three councils are composed of elected representatives from teaching staff, research staff, students, the administrative, technical, ancillary and service staff, and individuals from outside the university. The advisory councils consist of 20 to 40 members.

All members within the three councils elect the university president for a term of five years, and reelection is not permitted. The president directs the university, presides over councils, orders expenditure and income, has authority over all staff, nominates examining boards, and is responsible for the orderly running of the establishment. The president may appoint vice presidents for certain management fields, although sometimes vice presidents are elected after being nominated by the president, and they regularly chair meetings within certain councils. The presidential team may be regarded as the executive board within the university.

The secretary-general is nominated by the president and appointed by the minister, and directs the general management of the institution under the authority of the president. The position involves elements of a political and administrative nature.

At the faculty level (UFR) the administrative structure includes:

The dean (*directeur*) who is elected by the faculty council, of which s/he is a member, for a term of five years.

The faculty council that consists of chosen representatives of academic staff, nonacademic staff, students, and external people, which defines the teaching and research programs.

The Netherlands

Dutch universities differ in age, size, history, and mission. The first university established was the University of Leiden (1575) and the last was the University of Maastricht (1976). Some universities are comprehensive and classical, such as the University of Leiden, Groningen, or Utrecht, while others have technological disciplines, such as Delft, Eindhoven, or Twente. There are three denominational universities, Nijmegen, Brabant, and the Free University of Amsterdam. These are private institutions but are publicly funded, and are consequently regarded as public institutions. In the Netherlands there are a total of 13 universities that have been separate legal entities since 1960.

Prior to the 1970s, a striking feature of the governance structure within Dutch universities was its bicephalic nature.[5] Authorities of academic and nonacademic affairs were clearly separated in different bodies. This type of university governance is an example of the Continental model of authority distribution outlined by Clark (1983). At the apex of the administrative hierarchy the board of curators (*college van curatoren*) was responsible for upholding laws and regulations, the administration of the university finances, and for personnel policies. They represented the state bureaucracy. They hired and fired junior academics, student counselors, and other employees, and contributed nominations for the full and associate professor positions after consulting the faculty and the *college van rector en assessoren* ("executive board") for day-to-day management. The other pillar in the bicephalic structure was the senate that consisted of all full professors. The senate embodied academic self-governance.

During the 1960s, higher education participation expanded in the Netherlands and was accompanied by growing concern regarding the effectiveness and efficiency of traditional forms of university governance, for instance the senate. However, these concerns were overshadowed by demands for democratic participation of junior academics, staff, and students in university decision making, as was occurring in France and Norway. This democratic movement deeply influenced the new Act of University Governance, *Wet op de Universitaire Bestuurshervorming* (WUB), passed by parliament in 1970.

The most striking feature of the 1970 Act was the emphasis upon external and internal democratization, though there were other objectives, including effectiveness and efficiency. The WUB abolished the senate and the *college van curatoren* ("boards of guardians" or "boards of curators") and created a system of functional representation through university and faculty councils. Academics (professors and other academic staff), nonacademics, and students were given the right to elect representatives to these legislative bodies. In addition, a limited number of lay members representing the general public were appointed to the council from outside the university. Council members were required to serve for at least a period of two years, except for students required to serve for only one year. The council meetings were public. A council member elected by other members became the chair of the university council, which considered budgetary matters, institutional plans, annual reports, general academic procedures, and the internal regulations and rules. Though numbers have varied over the years,[6] generally the elected seats were held by a minimum of one third academics, a maximum of one third nonacademics, and a maximum of one third students.

The *college van bestuur* (CvB) carried out the executive function. This chief executive board originally consisted of five members, later reduced to three, including the *rector magnificus*. The national government appointed three of these members, including the rector, and the university council elected the other two members. The board of deans and the university council submitted nominations to the minister, and the executive board performed the tasks of the former *college van curatoren* and assumed responsibility for the university administrative hierarchy. The board of deans consisted of faculty deans and was chaired by the *rector magnificus*. Its powers were mainly advisory in the areas of teaching and research, and its chief function, apart from an important role in nominating the *rector magnificus,* was the granting of doctoral degrees (see de Boer, Denters, & Goedegebuure, 1998, for a detailed description of the other levels in the university).

In the mid-1990s, several interrelated problems regarding the prevailing governance system were identified by an ad hoc committee chaired by the minister of education, culture, and science. These problems were: 1) the inadequacy of the governance structure pertaining to the organization of teaching; 2) the lack of clarity regarding responsibilities (in collective decision making, individuals did not seem to accept personal responsibility); 3) the scattering of authority; 4) the bicephalic structure, particularly at the faculty level; 5) the strong orientation towards research at the expense of teaching, which may negatively impact on teaching quality; and 6) the inadequacy and incoherence of communication between the various organizational levels.

In 1997, the Dutch parliament passed a new bill on university governance. In the explanatory memorandum attached to the bill, the minister of education, culture, and sciences stated that a modernization of the governance structure within universities was a prerequisite for improving the quality of primary processes, such as teaching and research. The reforms promoted efficiency and effectiveness in university decision making, and were in line with the overall governmental steering strategy that aimed to enhance institutional autonomy. This provided opportunities for universities to become increasingly adaptive and flexible in a turbulent environment.

The introduction of the Act Modernizing University's Governance Structures, *Modernisering Universitaire Bestuursorganisatie* (MUB), indicated substantial change.[7] The MUB abolished the system of "co-determination" by board and council and the system of power fusion. Most powers regarding academic and nonacademic affairs were attributed to the executive positions at central and faculty level. In addition, the structure became less decentralized in several ways; for instance the abolition of the organization third layer—that is, the powerful *vakgroepen* ("departments"), one or more chairs, including other academics in the same disciplinary area.

At the central level, the main bodies within the new structure include the supervisory board (*raad van toezicht*), the executive board (*college van bestuur*), and the university council. The supervisory board consists of five persons appointed by and accountable to the minister. The supervisory board receives and endorses the most important university plans, such as strategic plans and budget plans, and arbitrates disputes between the executive board and the university council. The executive board consists of a maximum of three people, including the *rector magnificus,* appointed by the supervisory board. The executive board has significantly greater powers than the old governance structure equivalent. The university council no longer has decision-making powers, including budget approval. The university council is chiefly a representative, advisory body with some additional powers, for instance the right to comment upon institutional rules, regulations, and important policy documents such as the strategic plan.[8]

At the faculty level the new Act favors single-headed authority in the form of a deanship, though universities are permitted to retain a smaller faculty board as the executive body. However, the dean and the faculty board have more powers than in the previous governance system. The university executive board appoints the deans, who may be drawn from inside or outside the university or faculty. As at the central level, faculty councils have had their powers reduced and have become largely advisory bodies. The Act details that half of the faculty council members must be students. In addition, students participate in the education committee. The faculty council size varies from 3 to over 20 members.

For the first time since 1997, Dutch universities have a monocephalic structure. The new institutions comprise a system where executive and legislative powers are concentrated (monocentric). Compared to the past, the academic community has little say in final decisions. All members of the crucial governing bodies, *raad van toezicht* ("supervisory board"), *college van bestuur* ("executive board"), and *decaan* ("dean"), are appointed by the body above it. Thus a new hierarchical management system based on appointments replaced the old, democratic system, inclusive of all interested groups based on elections.

Norway

Compared to other European countries, the Norwegian university sector is young. The first university, the *Universitas Regia Fredericiana*, later named the University of Oslo, was founded in 1811. The second university, the University of Bergen, was established in 1946. Two other universities, the University of Trondheim and the University of Tromso, were founded in 1968. The university sector consists of six specialized institutions with university status in fields such as business administration and agricultural sciences.

Norwegian higher education is traditionally a public affair. The ministry of education and science has overall responsibility for higher education and research. However, for many years there was no general law governing all institutions, instead most universities and institutions with university status had separate laws. It was not until 1989 that institutions came under the umbrella of one legal authority.

Until the 1980s Norwegian higher education was an example of the Continental model of authority distribution elucidated by Clark (1983). Central state authorities used detailed regulations in determining the framework for universities. Concurrently universities clearly needed and had considerable academic autonomy, for instance professors had substantial power and freedom regarding teaching and research (Midgaard, 1982).

A further salient feature of Norwegian university governance is the relatively long tradition of participation. Since the beginning of the twentieth century there has been a general tendency to broaden participation in university government. For many decades students and academics were represented within universities in a form accepted by these groups themselves (Midgaard, 1982).

This section outlines the main changes over the final decades of the twentieth century regarding university governance and management, focusing largely on Oslo. There are substantial differences between Norwegian universities due to the lack of a comprehensive higher education law stipulating university governance and the fact that two of the four universities had to start from scratch. In the 1960s university governance was reassessed, not as a direct result of the 1968 events, as in the Netherlands, though the spirit of democracy was a primal impetus. The reform processes began with the establishment of the Organization Committee in 1967, and were further fueled by the events in 1968 concerning the lack of "democracy" in institutional governance. After years of discussion, experiments, and incremental adaptations the new act was adopted in 1976, and was put into effect on January 1, 1977. In sum, the reform validated a three-level university structure (central level, faculties, and departments), and a broadened composition of the collegiate bodies substituting representation with elections (Midgaard, 1982).

When describing the decision-making processes between 1967 and 1976, Midgaard (1982) concludes that central-level authorities gave universities ample opportunity to handle the situation locally; however, the national government did not completely stand aside, but interfered a few times. Yet for a country and higher education system with a strong tradition of state regulation, government interference was surprisingly modest. In the 1970s the universities themselves dealt with the pressures to reform their governance (Bleiklie, 1996; Midgaard, 1982). A further change occurred in 1989 when parliament passed an Act affecting the four universities and the six university-level colleges. This Act strengthened institutional autonomy by shifting decision-making authority for many issues from the government to the institutions.

The 1996 Act provided a common framework for the governance and management structure of universities, colleges with university status, and non-university-level state colleges. This contributed two major changes to the former steering principles, including increasing emphasis on stronger academic and administrative leadership of institutions and a definite division of responsibility between academic and administrative leaders. Dimmen and Kyvik (1998) describe the first change as initiating managerialism, by granting the central board and rector more power and authority, giving elected deans and chairs stronger academic leadership roles, and giving the administrative director a stronger formal role in institution management and greater regulative authority over all administrative levels. Dimmen and Kyvik describe the second change as divided leadership, by developing a tangible boundary between academic and administrative activities. At the end of the 1990s, all higher education institutions had a divided governing structure at the central, faculty, and department level and the academic leaders had less administrative power and were developing a more political role. In addition, two to four external members had to hold a seat in the central board, which initially bestowed much skepticism, but was later assessed as "constructive" (Larsen, 2001).

The 1996 Act, like the 1989 Act, decreed that institutions were to be governed by a central board and a university council. The university council determined the size and composition of the board, which consists of 9 to 13 members including the rector, pro-rector, two to five academic staff, one or two technical and administrative staff, two or three students, and two to four external members. Academic staff or a combination of academic staff and students must form the majority. Staff members are elected for a term of three years and students for a term of one year. Separate elections are held for academic staff and technical and administrative staff, while the ministry, upon nomination, appoints the external members. The university council assumes an advisory role, having at least 15 members including staff and students, and is required to manage long-term planning, guidelines for resource use, budgets and other financial matters, development and coordination of courses, and major organization change.

The highest governing body, the central board, is required to develop strategies for teaching, research, and other academic activities, and is responsible for financial matters and the annual financial statement. This central board is responsible for ensuring that the internal organization of activities are appropriate, cost effective, and in accordance with authority rules. It proposes the annual budget and is required to report the results of its activities.

The second organizational layer is the faculties and the third layer is the departments. Both layers include executive boards and their authority stems from the institution and not the government. The three layers have a hierarchical relationship, with the central-level board determining the size and composition of the faculty and department-level boards, which must have an academic staff majority and may have external members. The 1996 Act, like its predecessors, stipulates that academic leaders, including rectors, deans, and department heads, are elected. The rector is the chair of the board, has supreme responsibility for institution activities, and legally represents the institution. The deans and department heads have similar roles within their levels.

The elected leaders are not superior to the administrative leaders within their level. The administrative director appointed by the central board heads the administrative side of the institution and has the authority to instruct and direct all administrative personnel. During the last 10 to 15 years, administrative director positions have been established at the faculty and department levels, though not all departments have one, and they are accountable to the central director. In this sense the university is regarded as one entity rather than a collection of faculties. The administrative director is accountable to the minister and is responsible for preparing proposals for governing body meetings and ensuring they are implemented according to existing legal rules and practices. Norwegian institutions obviously have bicephalic structures where academic and nonacademic affairs are separated. This is one of the major differences between the Norwegian and Dutch governance models. The abolition of the dual structure was one of the main objectives of the Dutch university reforms.

According to Dimmen and Kyvik (1998), the most important additions to the Norwegian 1996 Act are:

The work and responsibilities of the central board (the executive) have been expanded at the expense of the council domain.

The 1996 Act regulates the various steering bodies hierarchically under the board to a general administrative model of delegation.

The board went from two to four external members.

The role of the administrative director as head of the institution was strengthened.

The responsibility for implementing resolutions and decisions shifted from the rector, deans, and department heads to the administration. Elected academic leaders are not administrative leaders, but they are representatives from the internal political decision-making system, distinct from the administrative hierarchy, and are required to adopt a more political role.

INTERMEZZO: A TENTATIVE CONCLUSION

These reports on Continental university governance demonstrate that similar changes occurred in all three countries during the same periods, and with significant impacts on university governance. Democratization movements in the late 1960s and early 1970s and managerial ideologies in the 1990s influenced university governance. Additionally, in the 1990s, a tendency to strengthen the executive role is evident in all three countries. Nevertheless, considerable differences also exist and persist. How should the decreasing powers of the French deans and the increasing power of the Dutch deans be compared? How should the establishment of a unified structure in the Netherlands be compared with the separation of academic and administrative roles in Norway? How should the Norwegian election of academic leaders be compared with the Dutch appointment of academic leaders?

A central issue within this book concerns whether globalizing practices have led to increased homogeneity. Have globalizing practices, as discussed in Chapter 1, contributed to the evolution of similar university governance structures? It is too soon to draw a firm conclusion. It is possible that differences in the governance structures of institutions, considering their different backgrounds, cultures, and size, have become smaller and have moved in the same direction. However, the brief description of the formal university structure evolution indicates that there are still substantial differences in these three countries. One may ponder how people inside universities experience the governance structures and changes. Do they have similar observations, perceptions, and feelings?

EMPIRICAL DESCRIPTION: INSTITUTIONAL GOVERNANCE

Managerialism is a broad, vague ideology and it is beyond the scope of this chapter to describe in depth this multifaceted ideology (see Pollitt, 1990). Rather, with respect to university governance, we focus on a few elements that characterize the managerial approach.[9] These elements emphasize executive leadership at the expense of the professional role in decision making; instrumental rationality stressing the three Es (economy, efficiency, and effectiveness); and top-down structures, such as centralization and hierarchy. Have these "managerialism" elements entered the daily governing practices in Avignon, Boston, Oslo, and Twente? Have there been changes to the operations of these universities? For instance, what is the role of academics in decision making? Has this role changed due to globalizing practices?

The Rise of Managerialism?

In Twente, an overwhelming majority of respondents said that there had been a shift towards managerialism and particularly the centralization of decision making. Approximately half of the respondents think this is a positive shift, while the other half have objections.

A few respondents had different perceptions, for instance some mentioned that the university is collegial, one said it is bureaucratic, and some believed that managerial and democratic features are blending. However, we need to remember the distinction between formal structures and regulations, and the mixture of formal and unwritten rules in practice, which are aptly depicted in the following quotes.

In theory we have become more managerial, but in practice we haven't. I think it would be fairly difficult to say that we have actually gone to a more managerial mode. It has been intended, but it has not been achieved. (Twente, Senior, Male, Academic, Social Sciences)

In a formal sense there is more line management but in practice I think the decision-making system remains highly collegial. (Twente, Senior, Male, Manager)

In Twente a shift has occurred towards "soft managerialism" (Trow, 1994) with the emphasis on collegial decision making at the lower levels of the organization. The Twente respondents indicate that there is considerable autonomy at the "shop floor," even though the deans and the central executive board have more power than before 1997. Clearly, since 1997 a more hierarchical structure has developed within the University of Twente and a more top-down rule for some strategic decisions—a point on which respondents are almost unanimous. Other structural governance aspects, such as "more businesslike," "more transparent," and "more bureaucratic" are rarely mentioned. Only three respondents believe that there have been few or no changes. Twente once had a rather decentralized structure, implying that a change more or less "automatically" means more centralization.

At the faculty level a split occurs between respondents who argue that deans now have more power and those who argue that middle-level decision making is still consultative. It is hard to draw conclusions from this result as the two answers are not, per se, at odds. There is no doubt that deans formally have more powers, but it is not evident how they use these powers, which according to at least half of the respondents is at times in a more consultative style.

Now it is a top-down management. Certainly for the faculties it has changed a lot. Now the dean has all the powers. (Twente, Junior, Male, Academic, Sciences)

Nowadays it's centrally managed. It used to be reasonably democratic, but it has changed. (Twente, Senior, Female, Academic, Sciences)

It's transformed itself a little bit now to become more centralized, because we need to have more steering power at the central level in order to guide the institution as a totality in the right direction. (Twente, Senior, Male, Manager)

The official way it is organized is the hierarchical way. But unofficially, the dean is a very open-minded and very approachable person. (Twente, Senior, Male, Academic, Professional School)

The changes aren't as dramatic as they look. You can only operate on a consensus basis, certainly in the Netherlands. It's still collegial or consensus decision-making, but let's say it has gone somewhat in the direction of more hierarchy. Some more central management has been installed. (Twente, Junior, Male, Academic, Social Sciences)

The Twente case is interesting as the interviews were held during a period of transition, and the individuals who were largely in similar positions under the previous administration frequently held the new positions. These individuals tended to carry over many of the old rules and their old habits, which may have hampered innovative efforts and reinstated features of the previous regime. Over time the reform process outcomes may look strangely similar to the practices innovators wanted to eliminate (Lanzara, 1998). It will be very interesting to see what happens with the next generation of deans. The following quotes illustrate this point.

Well, for my daily work it doesn't matter at all, because the dean we have now was the dean before. So he has changed very little in terms of organization. (Twente, Junior, Male, Academic, Sciences)

I mean they [deans] have been appointed by the executive board, but on the basis of a recommendation from the faculties, and most of them actually were the deans that were already in position at the time, so they still very much reflect the old traditions and the old values. Certainly they are not strong managers so to speak. (Twente, Senior, Male, Academic, Social Sciences)

As in Twente, a majority of Oslo respondents perceive a shift in university governance towards "managerialism," and sometimes mixed with bureaucratic or collegial elements. Fewer than a quarter of respondents describe Oslo as "bureaucratic" and only a few describe it as a collegially run institution. Collegiality is regarded as something good, while bureaucracy tends to evoke negative connotations. The assessment of managerialism is split unevenly as in Twente, with approximately half expressing negative perceptions, approximately a quarter expressing positive perceptions and approximately a quarter expressing mixed feelings.

In Oslo, the most frequently mentioned changes in governance at the institutional level concern increased bureaucracy and smaller governing bodies with external representation. In this context, the Norwegian respondents refer to bureaucracy as increased control, emphasizing transparency and accountability, and strengthening central steering capacity and centralizing power, meaning that the rector, deans, and heads of departments have more responsibility. The aim of creating smaller governing bodies at each level is to streamline and hasten decision making. By and large these changes are not appreciated for several reasons.

I left the university 25 years ago and it was governed by researchers, and I came back to a university governed by bureaucrats. (Oslo, Senior, Male, Academic, Professional School)

The central administration has been strengthened. (Oslo, Senior, Male, Academic, Professional School)

[There] were large bodies [with broad representation] at all three levels and endless discussion in many cases. But things were really discussed. There were so many represented in these councils that it was possible to have a feeling of what was going on. You had sufficient information, papers, background notes, memos and so on. Now these councils have been abolished, and we are left only with smaller steering groups. (Oslo, Senior, Male, Academic, Professional School)

The most dramatic thing, at least symbolically, is that we have external representatives on the board. It was seen as threatening our independence. (Oslo, Senior, Male, Academic, Professional School)

At the lower levels in Oslo the main responses to governance changes regard increased power for the deans and heads of departments, the need to economize due to budget cuts, and to a lesser extent the restructuring of faculties and departments into larger units. Despite the trend toward managerialism and increased bureaucratization, the Oslo academic culture of democracy and collegiality remains strong. Managerialism and bureaucracy may have changed the role and freedom of academics to some extent, but at the end of the 1990s they have not fully undermined the academics. This is well illustrated by the following quote.

There is a managerial culture, the administrative culture, and the academic culture. And I would still think that by and large the academic culture prevails. I think in the central administration there is some move towards professional managerialism, but once you move out of that building you would still see the other culture prevailing. The academic culture is very, very strong. (Oslo, Senior, Male, Academic, Social Sciences)

The situation in Avignon differs from Oslo and Twente, as respondents assert that managerialism[10] has not as yet entered the institution's governance structures. In addition, only a few Avignon respondents suggest that there has been a shift towards a managerial approach. Others perceive collegiality as the main feature, particularly within the university lower levels, while approximately one third of respondents perceive the bureaucracy as the main logic of organization. Several times respondents refer to the governance structure as blending collegial, bureaucratic, and/or managerial elements. Bureaucracy is mainly related to increased formalization due to university growth, which in turn places existing informal decision-making structures under pressure. The following quotes indicate these diverse points of view.

Such a university [the "old one"] could be managed informally and the larger size made it necessary to have this drive toward managerialism. I'm not so sure the term "managerialism" applies here. Let us say bureaucratic and more formal. (Avignon, Senior, Female, Academic, Professional School)

I don't think that we have the logic of an enterprise at all. I don't believe that there has been a shift towards managerialism at all. What struck me, coming from an enterprise into the university, is the greater amount of internal democracy. (Avignon, Senior, Male, Academic, Professional School)

I would say that the university functions according to a mixture of both bureaucracy and the logic of an enterprise. (Avignon, Senior, Male, Academic, Social Sciences)

I would say that the university has more of a bureaucratic logic, mainly because of the streamlining of decision making. (Avignon, Senior, Male, Academic, Sciences)

I would describe the administration more as having a collegiate logic—the decisions in the university are taken in a collective fashion—not like in an enterprise where the power lies in the hands of one individual. (Avignon, Senior, Male, Manager)

In Avignon the general mood is more upbeat compared to Oslo and Twente. In Avignon approximately half of the respondents feel there have been minimal changes in recent years, while other respondents mention some changes. However, most of these changes are not related to governance and management structures as such. The most often-mentioned change is the arrival of new leadership, and other mentioned changes include the new premises, better equipment, and new and renovated buildings. These are not governance changes, but nevertheless they can impact on the university operations. New presidents and new deans often introduce their own style. New premises at one location and the regrouping of faculties increase the chances for interaction, though the larger size of the new institution may be a countervailing constraint. A few positive changes include increasing transparency, solidarity, and responsibility. Those who perceive negative changes refer to greater financial restraint, fewer resources, and the loss of informality and a sense of greater impersonality.

I don't think there have been any fundamental changes in the way in which the university is governed. I would say that there has been more of a change towards modernizing the university, with the move to the new buildings, the new president, and new executive committees. So it is not really the manner in which the university functions which has changed, but rather its surroundings and the people involved. (Avignon, Junior, Female, Academic, Sciences)

In comparison, Boston College differs completely. There has not been a shift towards managerialism in recent times as most elements of managerialism began to take effect in the early 1970s. Boston College respondents describe their university as being "centrally managed" at the institutional level and according to one respondent it is an extreme example of central management. There does not appear to be much resentment regarding this top-down kind of governing, even though there is no faculty senate. In other words, academics do not have much of a voice at the institutional level. Nevertheless, most faculty feel that the university is well run and that the amount of faculty involvement at lower levels is sufficient to maintain a good university.

Basically decision making is more centralized here than in many other places. And that's worked well for us. And that comes out of our particular history. (Boston College, Senior, Male, Manager)

I would describe it as a benign dictatorship. (Boston College, Junior, Female, Academic, Social Sciences)

They run a tight ship here. It's centrally managed. We don't have a faculty senate. I think that they select a few faculty who are well rewarded and with whom they basically consult. (Boston College, Senior, Female, Academic, Social Sciences)

The majority of respondents state that there were few or no changes to Boston governance structures in the last five years. Most respondents are considerably pleased with the existing managerial structure. Despite this top-down structure for university-wide decisions, at the departmental level decisions are more collegially made. Nearly all respondents say that departments are either collegially and/or democratically[11] run, as stated by one extreme respondent:

We vote on everything, and things we don't vote on, we won't vote on because we're striving for consensus. (Boston College, Senior, Male, Academic, Social Sciences)

It is not surprising that respondents within collegially run departments have no complaints about the existing structure, as they do not feel constrained by the central administration. If people continue to feel that the university is well governed, they will tolerate the appointment of their leaders and a highly centrally managed university. For instance the following respondent favors more faculty participation, but he can see that the present arrangement has benefited him.

Yes, I would like more faculty involvement, but the system does work. I would say the level of alienation here is relatively low. I may just be saying that because I have been treated well by the place. (Boston College, Senior, Male, Academic, Professional School)

In sum, the managerialism ideology has begun to take root in the structure of all three European universities, but in differing degrees. Twente is probably the clearest case, whereas the situation in Avignon is doubtful. Moreover, there appear to be differences between the levels in the universities. At the "shop floor" it is mostly "business as usual," that is, collegial or democratic type decision making. However, managerial tendencies cannot be denied and are mostly visible at the institutional level. In contrast, Boston College has become increasingly managerial over the past three decades; yet there is little opposition to this trend of disenfranchising academics because they simply appear to lack the time or motivation to become more involved in university-wide decisions.

Academics in Decision Making

Approximately half of the Twente respondents believe that the role of academics in decision making has changed over the past five years. This is a remarkably low number considering the new 1997 Act and the perceived shift towards managerialism. Many regard the changes as not dramatic, and rather perceive them as modest.

Most of the respondents who perceive changes to academic roles indicate that their role has generally been diminished, but not necessarily in a negative way.[12] The positive outcomes refer to increased transparency, efficiency, and less gratuitous interference with detailed decision making. The negative outcomes refer to the loss of collegiality, potential power concentration, and greater difficulty in being involved and well informed.

I'm not so sure about that, I must say. I think we are all too busy to notice actually the big difference. There is a difference, but I must say I didn't notice any difference actually. (Twente, Senior, Male, Academic, Sciences)

In the old system you were always cognizant about what was going on. You were involved, you knew the details, and you knew the topics that were on the agenda. Now more and more you find there was a topic and you didn't realize it. It had never been announced. (Twente, Senior, Male, Academic, Professional School)

Most of the Oslo respondents stipulate that the academic role in decision making has changed during the past few years, and most believe that academics now have a smaller role; however this does not imply that they are sidelined. Approximately one quarter perceive no significant changes.

The majority of those perceiving changes assess them as negative, including greater accountability, increased workloads, more power for the administrative staff, less teaching time, and lowered standards. A few respondents also mentioned a lowered degree of academic involvement. Those perceiving the changes as positive refer to the benefits of increased efficiency and greater accountability.

The common wisdom is that the power of professors has been reduced and the administration has gained. I think that is true, as a tendency, but it hasn't had that much effect yet. Because tradition is very strong and professors at this university have had a great deal of autonomy; they do exactly as they please. (Oslo, Senior, Male, Academic, Professional School)

Clearly one of the side effects, if you like, of greater autonomy and more accountability is more administrative work. So we have generally seen an expansion in the resources used to measure various kinds of academic performance. For the academics this means an increase in planning, reporting, and increased administrative obligations. (Oslo, Senior, Male, Academic, Social Sciences)

Earlier we didn't have to write a yearly report to the head of department telling what has been going on, how much we have published, but now we have to. But that is something that I think is OK, to write a yearly report, because you also have to be accountable to yourself. (Oslo, Senior, Female, Academic, Professional School)

In the previous subsection it was indicated that the Avignon respondents perceived fewer changes in their governing structures than Oslo and Twente respondents. Therefore, it is not surprising that Avignon respondents also perceive that the academic role in decision making has changed less. Approximately one third of the respondents perceive absolutely no change. Many of those who perceive some change express positive feelings, including increased openness, collegiality, and information exchange. Negative feelings regarding the role of academics involve less freedom or academic autonomy and the imposition of reforms upon academics. The following quotes illustrate the variety of responses.

Well, I don't think it changes our lives much in relation to our teaching. We do what we like. (Avignon, Senior, Female, Academic, Social Sciences)

Not fundamentally, no but it is true that we are now a lot closer to the administration offices, and so we have a far easier, far more direct contact with the administrative services then we did before. (Avignon, Senior, Male, Academic, Sciences)

Well, I would say that we feel so much more directly involved now, we feel more concerned, because we are far more aware of what goes on here, of how things work. (Avignon, Senior, Female, Academic, Sciences)

Well, now there are a lot more people who are aware of what is going on at the university, and we have not only become more conscious of the problems in the administrative departments, but also of any problems generally speaking, and even of the financial situation of the university. So there is an increased collective consciousness of the university's functioning and problems throughout the university, and especially within the academics. (Avignon, Senior, Male, Academic, Social Sciences)

Everything regarding finances is being taken progressively out of our hands, and I get the impression that we have less and less freedom of movement to carry out our projects. (Avignon, Junior, Male, Academic, Professional School)

The Selection of Academic Leaders

The remainder of this section will analyze whether "managerialism" has had a direct impact on democratic decision making within these universities. This concrete point refers to the concept of democracy vis-à-vis the concept of guardianship. One distinction between these two concepts concerns the system used to select rulers. In democratic structures leaders are elected by a voting system involving all members, whereas in guardianship structures leaders are appointed. During the past three decades of the twentieth century, democratic university structures took root in several countries; however, before the end of the twentieth century these appeared to be in decline. In several countries, managerial ideologies appear to have put pressure on democratic and collegial structures.

What can be said about the concepts of democracy and guardianship in the four case studies? In Avignon and Oslo, leaders, such as the rector, deans, and department heads, are elected while in Boston and Twente these key positions are appointed. In all four cases respondents were asked to express their opinions regarding the opportunity to elect academic leaders.[13] Nearly all respondents in Avignon and Oslo were in favor of democratically elected leadership, while in Boston nearly all respondents were against elections, and in Twente respondents were divided, with some preferring to elect or at least feel sympathetic towards democracy and most not preferring elections.

These outcomes suggest that many respondents prefer the traditional methods for selecting leaders, unless some clear disadvantages are perceived. Obviously change is not appreciated or given much thought. In the Twente case, evidence of change appeared to lead to split or mixed opinions, perhaps largely due to the recent changes to mechanisms for selecting leaders. During times of transition, patterns in opinion appear to be less uniform.

Boston College has a strong tradition of appointing leaders and the majority of the respondents do not appear to have problems with this selection mechanism. Respondents do not want a change to the selection system and have not even considered democratic elections of academic leaders, as illustrated by the following answers.

I am totally unfamiliar with that process. It doesn't appeal to me. (Boston College, Senior, Male, Academic, Professional School)

Oh gosh. It seems so remote I can't even imagine it. (Boston College, Junior, Female, Academic, Social Sciences)

Quite honestly the idea is so foreign to me that I find it hard to even contemplate how that would occur. (Boston College, Senior, Male, Academic, Social Sciences)

Moreover, several respondents believe that appointing leaders works well, or conversely that a democratic system may not operate well within the context of U.S. universities. According to several respondents, the U.S. research universities appear to perform well compared to the European equivalents, and consequently a change to the system for selecting leaders is neither necessary nor desirable. Managerial expertise, that is, knowledge about the art of governing, is necessary and one should not take the risk by allowing members to decide who these persons should be. Faculty members do not seem to have sufficient capacities to pick leaders. According to the respondents, they do not fully understand what it requires to run "big corporations."

Ghastly idea. The problem in an elected system is that the most popular person will usually be the one to be elected. And the most popular person may not have the management skills to do the job. (Boston College, Senior, Male, Manager)

I think American universities are giant corporations and actually you need somebody who isn't just an old machine-style politician who just has a lot of support from various sections within the university. I think you need someone who can hire and fire. (Boston College, Junior, Female, Academic, Social Sciences)

I would be afraid, I think, that the democratic process would lead to a result that might keep the majority of the people happy but I don't think that it would necessarily be the best way to develop the university. So I feel comfortable with the mechanisms that we have for choosing people. (Boston College, Senior, Male, Academic, Sciences)

There are a few respondents in Boston who believe that electing presidents and deans would be a positive change, creating closer and better connections between faculty members and a better understanding of the processes and practices of the institution. Yet others maintain their doubts, perceiving negative and positive aspects, or distinguishing between theory and practice.

Like, my gut reaction is to say "yes," but my practical reaction is to say "no." (Boston College, Junior, Female, Academic, Professional School)

Avignon and Oslo have a completely different tradition and background. These universities elect their leaders[14] and are keen to conserve this university tradition. Democracy is normatively appealing to them, involving intrinsic values traditionally held by society. The democratic nature of the French and Norwegian societies *at large* is regarded as a reason to retain democracy *inside* universities. These arguments are not used in the cases of Boston College and Twente,[15] although the United States and the Netherlands are known as liberal, democratic countries. It is hard to find a plausible explanation for the fact that in some democratic countries, democratic values are taken for granted in organizational structures of universities, while in other democratic countries those values are not taken for granted. A possible explanation may be that the degree of (perceived) marketization within a higher education system impacts on the preferences in institutional governance. There may be feelings that the "market" and "democracy" do not fit well together in higher education and that there is more marketization in the United States and the Netherlands compared to Norway and France. A further possible explanation could be that preferences regarding democratic values in university governance are linked to opinions concerning the roles and functions universities are supposed to fulfill in society.

The way of life originating from the French Revolution plays a role in the French responses, and a similar lack of imagination witnessed in Boston College is frequently mentioned as a reason for maintaining existing procedures. This is evident in the following answers regarding the question about the preference to keep the value of democratically electing the rector, deans, and heads of departments at the University of Avignon.

It goes without saying. We didn't go through the whole French Revolution and cut off the heads of our kings only to end up today with a system where the former president chooses the next one. Heavens, no—this is absolutely unthinkable! (Avignon, Senior, Male, Academic, Sciences)

This is the only system we know, and quite honestly this is the only one I can imagine. (Avignon, Junior, Female, Academic, Sciences)

Other reasons frequently mentioned refer to a better choice of leaders, greater solidarity among academic staff and leaders, the development of a sense of responsibility, and mutual trust and respect for each other. Moreover, in the Oslo case it is argued that having different candidates running for president adds to and stimulates internal discussions. It invites people to become informed and involved. A further interesting reason submitted by one Norwegian respondent provides a very clear answer to one of the classical questions in theories on democracy: "Who is entitled to determine who is qualified to rule?"

I think it is important to have an election because we who work here are more capable of saying who will be the best for the university than an external committee appointing someone. (Oslo, Junior, Female, Academic, Sciences)

Twente provides the most interesting and complicated case, as it has no tradition of electing its leaders directly.[16] However, until 1997 the whole governance structure was characterized as democratic, as the various factions of the university community had the opportunity to elect representatives for university and faculty councils, which were the supreme decision-making bodies for some time. Moreover, these representative bodies had a voice in the selection of the leaders. Thus, it is fair to say that democracy was the dominant concept in Twente until 1997, even though academic leaders were not directly elected (de Boer & Denters, 1999). This is not very different from the French situation, where elected representatives choose the president and the deans. However, since

1997 the guardian concept prevailed and the rector, deans, and other executives are appointed. Nomination rights and the like are no longer formally in the hands of councils with elected representatives. What are the opinions of those within a structure that was previously perceived as democratic but has recently changed towards guardianship?

There are 9 out of 31 respondents who do not prefer to elect the rector and the deans, whereas 22 respondents would like to have a "kind of democracy," that is, to have a democracy without direct elections for rectors and deans. Those in favor of elected leadership use similar arguments as their French and Norwegian colleagues, suggesting that universities are professional organizations that are impossible to manage without some kind of democracy. Expertise concerning the information for decision making and support for the implementation of policies is essential and requires involvement. Elections may contribute to that, or to put it a little differently:

I think for the best functioning of the academic environment it would be good to have academic staff to have a say in the ways the university is being managed. And the electoral process may be a very good mechanism for that. (Twente, Senior, Male, Academic, Social Sciences)

Like the other three cases, the Twente case shows that traditions have a considerable impact on opinions regarding the issue under scrutiny. Here it seems to be the experiences with previous structures and procedures that are considered to be important, at least according to the majority of the respondents.

What about the nearly one third of the respondents who declared themselves openly against elected leadership? They gave several reasons: elections might politicize internal decision making further, which is perceived as obviously wrong as also mentioned in the Boston case, and without elections decision making would be more efficient. One respondent mentioned that elections are not indigenous to the Netherlands and, consequently, they should not be introduced. Finally, the most expressed reason that was unique to Twente was that very few people are eager to fulfill those leadership positions, and therefore meaningful elections would be difficult. The following quotes indicate some of these objections to electing leaders.

We do not have that system [of elected leaders] and I do not see a need to introduce it. We have democratic elections for the councils but not for the dean or for the rector. I don't see it. That's not a tradition also in the Netherlands. (Twente, Senior, Male, Manager)

It's not such a question of electing; it is more a question of getting a person who is mad enough or idiot enough to do it! (Twente, Senior, Male, Manager, Sciences)

Universities and faculties need professional managers and not people who do that just for four years because they're elected, and they know they will be back in their group of peers afterwards and it will be someone else's turn. We need people who can be managers, you know, individuals who understand finance, human resource management, and all those external relations and strategies. (Twente, Junior, Female, Academic, Social Sciences)

There would be a risk of even more politicized internal relations than otherwise. (Twente, Senior, Male, Academic, Professional School)

I would like to see people appointed, because then there is a clear-cut line of command. The previous law when everything was democratic was simply too much. (Twente, Junior, Male, Academic, Sciences)

In reality, the differences between elected and appointed leaders are probably not as great as they seem to be on paper. The mechanism of appointing leaders does not fully exclude the involvement of various university actors. Sometimes the process may be collegial and the final decision is only a matter of rubber-stamping. Take for example some quotes from Boston College and Twente, where the executives are appointed instead of elected.

I think the way we do it at Boston College is interesting. There is a faculty search committee that's assisting the academic vice president. So I view that as a representative form. My new dean will not be appointed, he is going to be really the result of a representative process and of a multidimensional, larger committee. I know a number of the people on that committee so I trust their judgment. (Boston College, Senior, Male, Academic, Social Sciences)

I don't think the present situation is that bad. It may look undemocratic, but, of course, there is a whole circus behind the façade. It's more from top to bottom today, but it doesn't exclude bottom-up processes, not at all. (Twente, Junior, Male, Academic, Social Sciences)

In terms of the way it actually functions, it still has rather democratic elements in it. Our dean was more or less put forward by the faculty to central management, and then they accepted him as dean. In the formal way it might not be too democratic. But in the actual functioning of it, it still has democratic elements. (Twente, Junior, Male, Academic, Social Sciences)

In sum, managerialism as a globalizing practice has had little impact on the opinions of respondents regarding the mechanisms for selecting academic leaders. By and large, respondents think that traditions should continue. However, the Twente case is somewhat confusing. There the influence of the university community in selecting their leaders has decreased, though there never was a tradition of having elected executives, but opinions differ as to whether this has been a shift for the worse or the better. Most of the Twente respondents appear to prefer to stick to their tradition of being involved in the process of appointments without the necessity of electing leaders.

CONCLUSIONS

Managerialism is one of the characteristic globalizing practices in higher education. According to the literature in the field, this globalizing practice appears to have an increasing impact on institutional governance. In fact, it is widely suggested that managerial ideologies have helped to establish broadly similar kinds of institutional regimes. Strengthened executive leadership, for instance, is supposed to be one of these consequences. However, at least two counterarguments can be put forward. The first deals with the different histories and backgrounds of the universities around the globe. As we described in this chapter, there are significant differences between the universities under scrutiny, if only for historical reasons. Governance structures appear to be path dependent. Why should these different institutions automatically mold their internal structures in the same direction when they are exposed to managerialism? The second counterargument concerns the differences between formal change and its accompanying rhetoric on the one hand, and day-to-day practice on the other. Managerialism may be the talk of the town in many countries and within many universities, but has it really changed daily policy making and management?

The case studies of the four universities clearly show a difference between formal rules and daily practice, or between imposed changes and day-to-day business. There is a tendency to strengthen executive leadership, or to centralize certain aspects of decision making, but this has not automatically changed the academics' role in decision making. It is also questionable how deep the changes have penetrated the university. At the "shop floor" level, only moderate changes, if any, were perceived.

A related conclusion drawn from both the country reports and the four case studies concerns the importance of traditions within universities. The way it was is the way most like it to continue. Managerialism appears to have entered the universities to some extent, but when it comes to the very practical point of selecting leaders, the overwhelming majority of the respondents in all four universities are inclined to maintain their established procedures. Tradition, at Boston College and Twente, balances consultation with appointment to gain greater central effectiveness; at Avignon and Oslo, it means elections are still sacrosanct and academics prefer their involvement in decision making at the cost of some greater central control of academic processes. Managerialism has had an impact on Boston and Twente to some degree but little impact on Avignon and Oslo. One explanation for the reduced impact may be that new concepts are being implemented by people who are used to the old rules and customs.

At the end of the day, it depends on how one looks at these kinds of phenomena and their effects. Suppose for argument's sake that we have a red, yellow, and blue university structure exposed to the very same black development. We can at least draw two conclusions regarding the action of black on the three other colors. The first one is that each university's color will change. Moreover, it will change in the same direction: all universities developing darker colors. The second conclusion to be drawn, however, is that the universities continue to have different colors! Red and black do not yield the same color as the yellow and black mixture. The ultimate color depends, of course, on the precise composition of the mixture of colors. This analogy can be used to interpret the findings of our study (of course, if you were to add enough black the other colors will disappear—and that is the fear of those who see the threat of managerialism to traditional values in universities).

First we showed that the institutional governance structures significantly differ (different colors). The case studies indicate that according to the nearly one hundred European respondents, managerialism—meaning strengthened executive leadership, instrumental rationality and centralization in universities—has begun to take root in all three European universities (mixing the colors with black). Managerialism was already strong at Boston College and it strengthened its roots over the last three decades. The intensity of the managerial ideology and its impact, however, differs from one university to another (a little more black is spotted at some places and is nowhere totally dominant). In the end it is clear that the four universities still have many differences in their governing styles and structures. Adding one single color has not (yet) resulted worldwide in one gray institutional structure for universities.

NOTES

1. Clark (1983) and van de Graaff and Furth (1978a) classify six levels of organization in higher education systems: the institute or department, the faculty or school or college, the university, the regional boards or statewide coordinating bodies, the state government, and the national government. Becher and Kogan (1992) discern four levels of organization: the individual, the basic unit, the institution, and the central authority. Clark (1983, pp. 109–110) discerns three levels of organization: the understructure or department and faculty level; the middle structure or the university; and the superstructure or the multicampus organization, the state government, and the national government.

2. A further question is whether all were considered equally qualified to be represented.

3. The French Revolution suppressed all that were organized as corporations. This directly concerned the universities and the faculties within, because they were functioning as local corporations. However, there were some exceptions (see Kaiser, 2001), for instance existing schools such as the École des Mines were not threatened.

4. UER councils did not need to have outside members.

5. Local situations may differ. There were two exceptions regarding the bicephalic structure: the Agricultural University of Wageningen and the University of Twente each had a monocephalic structure and where some curators and senate members were united into one executive body.

6. In practice there were great differences due to, among other things, an electoral threshold and student boycotts in the early 1970s (Daalder, 1982).

7. The magnitude of change in practice is debatable. In some respects the MUB was more or less a codification of an already existing practice (de Boer, Denters, & Goedegebuure, 1998).

8. The MUB offers two options regarding the university council. The first entails a divided system of representation consisting of separate advisory bodies for employees (academic and nonacademic) and students. The second entails a unified body consisting of representatives from employees (50 percent) and students (50 percent). To date five universities have installed a divided system and eight universities have chosen a unified body. The councils vary in size from 9 to 21 members in divided councils and 16 to 24 members in university councils.

9. There is much, mainly Anglo-Saxon, literature on managerialism or new public management, where the various types of managerialism are differentiated and analyzed (de Boer & Huisman, 1999; Exworthy & Halford, 1999; Hughes, 1994; Marginson & Considine, 2000).

10. In the French interviews managerialism was referred to as "the logic of the enterprise."

11. The respondents express little or no difference between collegial and democratic forms of governance, which appear to be used as synonyms.

12. One respondent believed the role of academics was growing, but this refers to a different phenomenon, namely that there will be more executives with academic backgrounds.

13. The question posed in Avignon and Oslo was: "Would you like to keep the value of democratically electing the rector, deans, and heads of departments?" In Twente the question was: "Would you like to see democratic elections of rectors, deans, and department chairs in the future?" In Boston the question was: "Do you think it would be of value to democratically elect your department chairs, deans, or the president?"

14. In Avignon the (elected) members of the three councils indirectly elect the president.

15. Though there is an exception in Twente with one response indicating that:

Democracy is good for the country, why is it not good for a university? (Twente, Senior, Academic, Sciences).

16. Until 1997, the faculty council, consisting of elected representatives, selected the dean. The rector magnificus was appointed by the minister on the basis of a nomination made by the deans, after having received the choice of the university council.

Chapter 5

Accountability

Accountability plays an important role in higher education. In a number of countries accountability is institutionalized and commonly accepted, in others it is a recent phenomenon, and in others it is a contested issue on the higher education agenda. Some analysts think that governments and other stakeholders do not have the right to make academics formally account for their performance. To support their view most of these analysts refer to the concepts of academic freedom and professional autonomy. Others believe that the increasing attention to public, measurable, accountability is the logical consequence of a recent balance involving a government retreat from closely monitoring higher education and an increase in institutional autonomy. Moreover, others are preoccupied with issues related to the intended and unintended consequences of the growing attention to accountability. Given this concern many interesting questions arise regarding accountability. Why is accountability part of higher education systems? How does it work in general? How do national and institutional contexts impact on accountability mechanisms? How do views on accountability change over time?

The purpose of this chapter is fivefold. First, it sets out a framework for the analysis of the phenomenon of accountability. Second, it examines the relationship between accountability and globalization. Third, it describes and analyzes changing views on accountability and the mechanisms used at the national (policy) level in Norway, the Netherlands, the United States, and France. Fourth, it provides insight into the views and opinions of respondents within the four universities. Finally, it reflects on the findings.

THEORETICAL EXPLORATION

A Framework for Analyzing Accountability

In elaborating on the concept of accountability, we largely draw on two authors. The first author, Romzek, is rooted in the public administration discipline and solidly discusses accountability in the broad context of the public sector. The second author, Trow, is rooted in the sociology of higher education and specifically focuses on accountability from a higher education perspective. Despite their different backgrounds the authors agree to a considerable extent upon the definition of accountability. Accountability is the "answerability for performance" (Romzek, 2000, p. 22) or "the obligation to report to others, to explain, to justify, to answer questions about how resources have been used, and to what effect" (Trow, 1996, p. 310). Both authors supplement these definitions with the question: Who is to be held accountable, for what, to whom, and through what means? Trow (1996) also questions the consequences (see Wagner, 1989, for a similar approach, and Kogan, 1986, for a slightly different method).

Romzek (2000) offers the most comprehensive framework for analyzing types of accountability. This is particularly helpful for our analysis as it may enable us to place accountability in a broader perspective and then narrow this to a specific higher education sector. She distinguishes two dimensions: the degree of autonomy and the source of expectations and/or control. The first dimension ranges from low to high autonomy, and the second dimension runs from internal to external sources of expectation. Table 5.1 presents a matrix of the interrelationships of the two dimensions.

Table 5.1

Types of Accountability and Accompanying Value Emphases and Behavioral Expectations

		Source of Expectations and/or Control	
		Internal	External
Degree of Autonomy	Low	Hierarchical Value: Efficiency Expectation: Obedience to Directives	Legal Value: Rule of Law Expectation: Compliance with Mandates
	High	Professional Value: Expertise Expectation: Deference to Judgment and Expertise	Political Value: Responsiveness Expectation: Responsiveness to Stakeholders

Source: Romzek 2000: 24, 29.

Hierarchical accountability relationships are based on close supervision of individuals who have low work autonomy and face internal controls. The underlying relationship is that of supervisor-subordinate. In a higher education context one could think of the laboratory assistant being accountable to his/her chief concerning compliance to the institution safety or environmental requirements.

Legal accountability relationships involve detailed external oversight of performance for compliance with established performance mandates, such as legislative and constitutional structures. This form of accountability is typically reactive. In contrast to hierarchical accountability, legal accountability relationships are between two relatively autonomous actors. For example, a governmental bylaw on the annual financial reporting system requires a university to provide the Ministry of Education with an account of its profits and expenses.

Professional and political accountability systems reflect situations,

where the individual or agency has substantially more discretion to pursue relevant tasks than under legal or hierarchical types. And the review standards, when they are invoked, are much broader. The difference between professional and political accountability is the *source* of the standard for performance.... Professional accountability systems are reflected in work arrangements that afford high degrees of autonomy to individuals who base their decision-making on internalized norms of appropriate practice. (Romzek, 2000; pp. 25–26)

In an academic context one could think of a researcher accounting for his/her choice regarding the research methodology in a report, paper, or article. It is a typical feature of the academic profession to explain and if necessary argue for such choices.

Political accountability relationships afford managers the discretion or choice to be responsive to the concerns of key interest groups, such as elected officials, clientele groups, and the general public. For example, higher education institutions are generally answerable to the public regarding their activities and how they benefit society. This form of accountability can be implemented by informing the public in layman's language on specific research projects or explicitly reporting to regional groups if the university adopts regional functions.

The distinction between forms of accountability with a low or high level of autonomy and the accompanying examples show that accountability models with a high level of autonomy are less tangible than those with a low level. In addition, a high level of accountability is often either characterized by taken-for-granted, nonexplicit rules based on norms and values, for instance professional accountability, or by a configuration of representatives and their power positions, for instance political accountability.

Trow (1996) distinguishes external versus internal accountability—which coincides with a dimension from Romzek—and also distinguishes legal and financial versus academic accountability, which can be interpreted as a specification of professional accountability for higher education matters. Trow (1996) adds to Romzek's framework by more explicitly pointing to the functions of accountability and more specifically focusing on the higher education context. Regarding the functions, he first maintains that accountability is a constraint on arbitrary power, thereby discouraging fraud and manipulation and strengthening the legitimacy of institutions that are obligated to report to appropriate groups. Second, accountability is claimed to sustain or raise the quality of performance by forcing those involved to critically examine their operations and to subject them to critical review from outside. Third, accountability can be used as a regulatory device through the kind of reports and the explicit and implicit criteria to be met by the reporting institutions.

Finally, Romzek and Trow do not explicitly deal with the level of accountability. Trow mentions reporting, explaining, and justifying elements of accountability but does not elaborate. Leithwood, Edge, and Jantzi (1999) distinguish three forms of accountability ranging from low-level accountability to high-level accountability: descriptive, explanatory, and justifiable accountability. The first describes a factual event in a qualitative or quantitative way, the second obliges those accountable to explain and give reasons for the event, the third forces those involved to justify the event. This distinction seems particularly relevant when discussing the increase or decrease of accountability.

Globalization and Accountability

It would be an unduly restricted view to regard globalization as the procurer of accountability. Globalization is linked to other trends that together have impacted the conceptualization of accountability and the types of accountability mechanisms used in various systems. Accountability is prominent on many higher education agendas for the following interrelated reasons:

Changing relationships between governments and universities: There was a relatively strong bond between government and higher education institutions through funding, legislation, and planning mechanisms. However, governments have retreated and opened the arena for greater autonomy and free market mechanisms (Gornitzka et al., 1999). In this context, Neave's (1988a, 1998) analysis of developments in Western Europe is revealing. He points to the striking change from *ex ante* governmental control by legislation and procedures to *ex post* justification by quality assurance and accountability measures. This development was particularly visible in Western Europe in the 1980s and in Central and Eastern Europe in the 1990s. The situation is quite different in the United States. It has combined public policies and market mechanisms throughout its higher education history, but particularly since the 1970s. It logically follows that accountability mechanisms change as interest groups change. This does not imply that accountability in higher education is an entirely new phenomenon, but rather that its appearance has altered. In particular, accountability before the fact is replaced by accountability after the fact.

Efficiency and value for money: A related yet autonomous development is the growing trend of governments to document value for money. This is partly due to the massification of higher education around the world pressuring governmental and public sector budgets. Elite higher education at fairly autonomous institutions was fine with those responsible at national levels; however, with increasing student numbers the cry for efficiency and effectiveness became louder. This is also partly due to members within society, for instance parents and taxpayers, challenging the presumed quality of higher education. The critical public and governmental viewpoints have heightened the attention paid to aspects of accountability. According to Trow (1996), accountability has replaced trust. During the past decade in many countries, a specific element of the value for money issue has shifted from considering higher education as a public or quasi-public good towards considering higher education as a more private good. Within this context debates occurred regarding the introduction of tuition fees and student grant systems or interest-bearing loans. Understandably such debates have impacted the accountability issue. Students confronted with increased private costs for higher education may be more critical of the services delivered in exchange.

Internationalization and globalization of higher education: National borders were once evident; however today, globalization of the economy, that is, the free flow of goods, services, ideas, and people, has blurred these boundaries. Globalization has facilitated the entrance of foreign higher education institutions and business organizations into national arenas and has blurred the previously homogeneous cultural and normative expectations concerning the nature and future of higher education. This cultural change, which may only be a gradual long-term change, raises questions related to accountability. Should foreign institutions be treated in a similar manner to national institutions or should they be treated differently according to their position, possibilities, and duties within the higher education landscape? Additionally, should foreign institutions be accountable to the government in their home country or to the government in the country where they preside? In this context the current but very preliminary debates regarding the inclusion of education in the General Agreement on Trades and Services (GATS) are also relevant (see Altbach, 2001; Cohen, 1999/2000). What if higher education is included in the WTO agreement—does this imply that such global arrangements supersede national or supranational, for instance European, agreements on accountability?

Information and communication technology developments: The increasing technological possibilities particularly in the context of information and communication technology have hastened internationalization and globalization processes. This adds to the previous point in two ways: 1) the actual location of a higher education institution becomes less relevant as technologies allow institutions to work globally and easily across national boundaries, and 2) questions regarding legal and political control over less tangible or virtual institutions become more urgent and complex.

In sum, various interrelated trends, imperatively including globalization, have affected or will affect higher education. We expect that accountability will continue to have an impact upon universities, but its precise impact is difficult to predict for at least three reasons. First, as previously mentioned, accountability is affected by globalization and other trends; second, the impact may be dependent on the configuration and power positions of interested parties in specific contexts; and third, accountability has its own dynamics.

Romzek (2000) considers these dynamics and comments that some forms of accountability are primary and others underutilized, depending upon the context whereby accountability mechanisms and procedures are applied. The shift from *ex ante* to *ex post* control as described by Neave (1998) is exemplary of this dynamic. During the 1960s and 1970s, primary attention was allocated to regulation and checks before the implementation of changes, whereas since the 1980s primary attention has been allocated to post-accountability.

Moreover, accountability expectations can conflict and the combination of these may have unintended consequences. For example, an academic within a higher education institution may be confronted with quality requirements concerning teaching duties from the hierarchical levels within the institution and from an external accreditation agency. It would be a sound strategy for the institution to bring its internal requirements in line or at least not to be at odds with the external requirements, but it is possible there will be some friction between the two. Dill (1999) shows the unintended consequences of the alignment of different accountability expectations. A U.K. university adopted an internal quality review process that mirrored the national external quality assessment mechanisms. Dill (1999) argues that this may encourage a "culture of compliance" that might substitute for more effective processes designed to improve teaching and learning.

In addition, one type of accountability relationship can trigger a further type. In case the higher education institution does not have formalized requirements regarding the quality of courses to be delivered by staff, then the implementation of accreditation procedures may trigger the institution to formalize these requirements. An example from the United States illustrates the general idea of "triggering." Following the implementation of the GI Bill in the 1940s, providing funds directly to students rather than to universities and colleges, the U.S. government was confronted with the question of how to ensure that students would spend taxpayer money at institutions of efficient quality. Instead of regulations and national standard setting, the government opted for a less stringent mechanism, namely self-governing accreditation (Myers, Frankel, Reed, & Waugaman, 1998).

ACCOUNTABILITY IN NATIONAL CONTEXTS

Accountability has different guises within different countries. In the United States accountability is an institutionalized phenomenon, whereas in Western Europe accountability only recently gained momentum and is discussed at national and institutional levels. Furthermore, the term accountability is very common within the United States, whereas in most European higher education systems this concept has not assumed a dominant role or rather is existent but often hidden in terms like "getting insight into performance," "assuring quality," and "showing credibility." Before presenting our findings, we describe the developments of accountability with a brief comment on its relationship to globalization in the four national contexts.

Norway

During the 1970s and the early 1980s university governance was democratized, education and research became more socially relevant, and universities were given greater autonomy (Bleiklie, Høstaker, & Vabø, 2000; Smeby & Stensaker, 1999). During the latter half of the 1980s quality became the main policy issue. The Hernes Commission (NOU 1988)wanted more graduates and wanted universities to ensure their quality at an internationally acceptable level.

Government changes in the 1980s stressed the economic importance of higher education. Prior to this higher education was largely considered a welfare benefit. For instance, in the 1960s and 1970s attention to the regional position of higher education institutions was understandable. However, in the 1980s the Hernes Commission predominantly considered higher education as a long-term strategic tool in the international economic competition and wanted universities to focus on efficiency and quality (Bleiklie et al., 2000). Similarly, Aamodt (1990) maintains that since the mid-1980s there was a growing political interest in higher education as a knowledge-based industry that would contribute to Norway's future economic growth. This shift relates to a general government philosophy that anticipated globalization processes.

It would be a fallacy to reduce the changing view on higher education to developments of economic globalization only. The 1988 OECD review and European integration clearly demonstrate that developments were related as much to regionalization at the European level, and were not purely economic developments (Tjeldvoll, 1992). The OECD (1988) review, like the Hernes Commission, discussed issues such as cooperation and task differentiation among higher education institutions. At the end of the 1980s, the government implemented a number of recommendations from the Hernes Commission; for example, *Network Norway*, directed at facilitating an integrated, cooperative network among the higher education institutions, stimulating student mobility, encouraging institutional specialization and cooperation, and promoting "research academies" or graduate schools.

Analogous to the general view of higher education as an international economic tool, a new planning system was implemented. This new planning instrument, "activity planning" (*virksomhetsplanlegging*), not only concerned higher education but all public sector agencies in Norway. This new system was based on new public management ideas (Pollitt, 1993, chap. 4) previously incorporated in government documents. It focused on management by objectives and *ex post* evaluation or performance control of outcomes (Larsen & Gornitzka, 1995). Due to the changing views of higher education, the government emphasized increasing student numbers and greater efficiency of student and research "production." It was assumed that an efficiency increase could be achieved by setting performance indicators, formulating production goals, mobilizing resources by means of incentive systems, and strengthening the administrative powers of the university (Bleiklie et al., 2000). One consequence of this was that academic performance was redefined in measurable and quantifiable terms. Nonetheless, the ideological change towards strong leadership should not be equated straightaway with entrepreneurialism and market-oriented corporate businesses. Bleiklie et al. (2000) argue that new public management did not replace traditional governance patterns but was to some extent integrated into the existing patterns of governance.

Activity planning implies that the university was to develop general and specific goals at different levels of the organization. The general goal was considered to be fairly stable over time, whereas objectives at lower levels of the organization could be more flexible, evaluated, and adjusted regularly. At Norwegian universities, the idea of activity planning was not welcomed (Bleiklie et al., 2000). At the University of Oslo the policy was regarded as an attempt to control academic activities and was at odds with the idea of academic freedom. Bleiklie et al. concluded that activity planning had moderate consequences and was experienced by academics as merely a ritual with hardly any harmful effects.

A few years after activity planning was introduced, the government initiated a national evaluation system for higher education. The two policy initiatives were unrelated, although the evaluation system gave valuable input to the activity planning processes. This quality assurance system was first administered on an experimental basis by an independent research institute and was later institutionalized. The methods and procedures, for instance self-evaluations, external visits, reports, and follow-up conferences, were developed jointly by the government and the research institute. The ministry appointed the external evaluation team, but the higher education institutions involved could suggest evaluators. The responsibility for quality assurance was handed over to the Network Norway Council in 1998, an advisory board to the ministry (Smeby & Stensaker, 1999). The most significant effect relates to institutional culture. The institutions involved reported that they learned to evaluate themselves. In addition, many departments used the quality assurance system to position themselves vis-à-vis the ministry. The ministry did not use the outcomes to steer higher education. Observers have concluded that the power balance between institutions and the state was not dramatically altered; instead there are reasons to believe that the intended mechanisms of accountability have been turned into opportunities by the higher education institutions (Stensaker, 1997). The quality assessments were adjusted to the already strong bottom-up traditions inherent in the higher education system.

In Norway, particularly, new public management ideas and the country's position in the European political landscape, that is, part of Europe but not of the EC, seemed to have been triggers for paying attention to accountability. The government intended to introduce accountability mechanisms, such as activity planning and quality assurance; however, concurrently the government decentralized a number of activities, thus giving way to greater institutional autonomy. Throughout the 1990s the relationship between the state and institutions was relatively stable. During the implementation process, the accountability policies were stripped of their thorns and in practice were less effectual than foreseen by the government.

The Netherlands

As in many Western European countries, a shift in steering philosophy became visible in the 1980s and 1990s in the Netherlands. This trend can be described as one from state control to state supervision (Neave & van Vught, 1991). However, a closer look at what actually was intended and took place yields a more differentiated picture.

Traditionally, the role of government in higher education in the Netherlands, as in many other welfare states, was rather dominant. The government considered education as a citizen's right, and it was the government's duty to stand for the quality of this quasi-collective good. This principle was laid down in the Dutch Constitution, and the government fulfilled its tasks by developing regulations and controlling, mostly ex ante, educational processes, funding principles, and the governance of institutions. Nevertheless, in higher education academics had considerable leeway when it came to the content and the form of education.

The 1985 white paper, Higher Education Autonomy and Quality (HOAK), was a breakthrough regarding the government's views on higher education. The white paper promised that the government would step back and that higher education institutions would be granted more autonomy. We take this policy paper as a starting point for discussing the most important developments since the mid-1980s. An analysis of the actual policy changes implemented in the period after the white paper shows that the government was duplicitous (Maassen & van Vught, 1988; van Vught, 1997).

On the one hand, higher education institutions received more freedom regarding the spending of government budgets, the administrative and financial control over the buildings, the appointment and management of staff, and to an extent the organization of their governance structure. On the other hand, government was less eager to grant substantial freedom to implement new study programs (Huisman & Jenniskens, 1994). The 1985 white paper proposed to leave the organization of the supply of places to the higher education institutions. During the late 1980s and early 1990s Parliament discussed the legislation, and this proposal received much criticism. A majority in Parliament feared an explosion of new programs, a phenomenon to some extent already visible in the higher professional education sector that was already granted greater autonomy in this area. The growth of the supply would threaten the macroefficiency of the higher education system. The minister was forced to change the regulations and install a national committee to watch over the efficiency of the supply of programs. From 1993 this committee judged annually whether institutional proposals for new programs would harm the macroefficiency of the higher education system. During its almost 10 years of existence the regulations regarding the supply of programs and the national committee charged with guarding its macroefficiency met considerable criticism and resistance by the higher education institutions. In the near future, accreditation mechanisms will be implemented that will make, according to the minister, control over the supply of programs less obvious and relevant. However, Parliament again forced the minister to make explicit his role regarding the efficiency of the supply in the new regulations on accreditation.

A further important element in the 1985 white paper related to quality assurance. Similar to the proposed policy instruments regarding the supply of programs, the government decided to make the institutions themselves primarily responsible for maintaining the quality of education. The view of the government was that the institutions should regularly carry out internal evaluations at different levels of the institution. In addition, government would charge the Higher Education Inspectorate to carry out independent evaluations. The use of quantitative performance indicators was suggested to gain insight into the quality of the various institutional processes. Peer review by independent external evaluators would complete the set of quality assurance mechanisms. When there was concern about the quality of a certain program, the government would send out an official warning. If the quality did not improve over a certain period of time, the government could stop funding the program. From these proposals, it became clear that the government would still be visible in the quality assurance process, but that the focus shifted from *ex ante* measures controlling quality and setting the rules and procedures in detail to *ex post* evaluations of quality.

While discussing the policy proposal with those directly involved in the implementation of the policies, a number of elements proved to be untenable in the eyes of the buffer organizations and the individual higher education institutions. During the period of consultation and concretization of the proposals, the content was changed significantly. The most important changes included a much less prominent role for the Higher Education Inspectorate, the buffer organization was allocated the coordination of the quality assurance systems, and performance indicators were eliminated.

The idea of accountability as a globalizing practice is most readily seen in the focus on competition within Dutch higher education and particularly the challenge of competing in the European and world economies. Dutch higher education institutions were expected to take up this challenge and, according to the most recent rhetoric, constitute a "tableland with peaks." Empirical research on the quality assurance systems shows that it was more or less accepted in Dutch higher education. Frederiks, Westerheijden, and Weusthof (1994) conclude on the basis of a survey that, "The level of satisfaction with the implementation of the Dutch quality management system within the institutions is fairly high" (p. 167). A number of years later Hoppe-Jeliazkova and Westerheijden (2000) conclude that the recommendations of the visitation committees are taken seriously and followed up by institutional action at the program level. However, in institutions where the quality assurance system is highly developed a "sufficient" score does not stimulate further educational improvement.

In conclusion, the Dutch higher education system received more autonomy in a number of areas. This general trend requires two qualifications. First, government is still in charge regarding a number of aspects of higher education and research. Second, in some areas it is not so much a question of more or less autonomy but of shifting responsibilities and accountability mechanisms. The government has shifted its attention from *ex ante* control by means of regulations and procedures to *ex post* control. The most noteworthy development in practice relates to the introduction of a national quality assurance system for the universities. The original intentions of the government seemed far reaching, but consequential to the Dutch corporatist model of policy making and implementation, the actual policies in practice turned out to be more modest.

The United States

Given the size of the U.S. higher education system and the considerable differences between states regarding the composition of the system and policy initiatives, it is not feasible to describe in detail the interrelationship between globalization and accountability. Hence, this section is confined to addressing general trends, particularly in the last decade. In addition, developments regarding accountability, for example, changes in the state regulations, primarily and directly affect public institutions. Given that Boston College is a private university, the impact of developments in accountability is presumed to differ from those at public institutions. In fact, accountability mechanisms at Boston College are initiated or maintained by the university administration and its board of trustees.

The concern for accountability is not a recent phenomenon in U.S. higher education. Accountability by means of accreditation mechanisms has been part of higher education practice for a century and has taken different forms over time. Folger (1977) noted that accountability has taken a new meaning in the 1970s. Meeting fiscal standards is less important. The focus of concern is whether social institutions in general are effective and use resources efficiently. The change in meaning can be traced back to the feeling that public confidence has declined with respect to public institutions.

It is interesting to note that whereas the majority of researchers argue that public confidence has decreased, Trow (1996) mentions some indications that point in the opposite direction, implying that trust has increased or at least not declined. It casts doubt on the boldness of the arguments contending a lack of confidence in public institutions. A further element of the debate is the assumption that the call for accountability logically implies a decrease in institutional or academic autonomy. Here, Altbach (1997) provides some input "against the current." He states that, particularly in the areas of curriculum, degree requirements, and the teaching and learning process, "Most academics retain the sense of autonomy that has characterized higher education for a century"

(p. 14). In addition, Dill (1998) warns higher education researchers against falling victim to professional interests, confusing individual and/or collective academic concerns with general public concerns.

The real or presumed public lack of confidence in government institutions has made politicians and government administrators more attentive to the effectiveness and efficiency of their services. Thus, in higher education different measures were taken to improve accountability mostly by internally focused mechanisms, for example by performance budgeting, performance audits, and program reviews.

Neal (1995) indicates that accountability had a different tone in the 1990s when compared to the 1980s. Internally focused assessment strategies were replaced by concern with productivity and efficiency and voluntary action was superseded by mandatory participation in external accountability processes. Dill (1997) aptly describes the developments in the 1990s of quality and accountability policies, paying attention to the dynamic interrelations between evolutions at the level of the federal government, state governments, accreditation organizations, and institutions. At the federal level, the 1992 reauthorization of the Higher Education Act implied the creation of State Postsecondary Review Entities (SPREs). The SPREs were to develop performance standards for the institutions regarding graduation rates, withdrawal rates, and thresholds for performance. Although the Higher Education Act was softened in 1994 with less federal interference at the state level, it seemed likely that at the state and regional levels the development of standards would flourish. In addition, at the state level, policies changed from quality improvement to accountability, for instance requiring performance indicators (Dill, 1997). In 1994 the higher education community formed a National Policy Board on Higher Education Institutional Accreditation (NPB) that led to a proposal to create a new accrediting agency a year later. This response was partly yielded by the fear that the existing accreditation practices would be threatened by government regulation following the 1992 Higher Education Act. The NPB plans proved to be a failure. In 1996 the establishment of the Council for Higher Education Accreditation (CHEA) was accepted as an organization providing information services and preserving nongovernmental accreditation. At the institutional level the new competitive environment, following fiscal realities, provided incentives to use assessment information to improve teaching and learning performance and productivity.

Alexander (2000) elaborates upon the changing tone of the accountability debate by stating that there is an emerging societal requirement in the 1990s to be more responsive to governmental demands for increased performance, but also to national economic needs. Regarding these needs, specific reference is made to augmenting learning skills and to the improvement of worker abilities. In short, government shifted its focus to the enhancement of economic productivity in a competitive and global environment. Part of the societal requirement arose in the change from an elite to a mass higher education system and the limitations of public expenditure. In a similar vein, Honan and Teferra (2001) argue that the rising costs of higher education, a consequence of the growth of the system, led to a demand for more value and improved service. Government, therefore, has a considerable interest because of its "utilitarian compulsion," in making higher education more efficient. In particular, the government is interested in assessing and comparing performances of institutions. Alexander (2000) states that "[S]uch government initiatives devised to seek greater efficiencies by employment of evaluative techniques to assess and compare the performance of colleges and universities constitutes the current thrust of the 'accountability movement' in higher education" (p. 413).

The present use of accountability measures in the United States clearly has two effects: an improving one and a punishing one. The Measuring Up 2000 project (Callan, Doyle, & Finney, 2001) uses performance indicators relating to preparation, participation, affordability, completion, and benefits to benchmark the states. It is presented as an attempt to improve internally oriented assessment strategies and thus stimulate and assist institutions as well as the states and the nation in maintaining and enhancing educational opportunities in a rapidly changing world. At the same time the report can be interpreted as a management information tool, because it gives national- and state-level policy makers some insight into how effective and efficient the institutions are, and policy makers might develop strategies to "punish" less effective and efficient organizations or practices.

The two interpretations of the consequences of accountability clearly demarcate the uneasy feelings many practitioners in higher education have regarding accountability. This may explain the views of many involved in higher education that accountability is much more present than a decade ago. The National Center for Postsecondary Improvement (NCPI, 2000) reports that many universities feel that they have become more accountable in the last five years towards interest groups. Public institutions report a higher level of accountability than private, liberal arts institutions. Following the Carnegie classification, in particular, research/doctoral and comprehensive institutions reported increasing accountability to more factions in society.

Regarding the developments in the United States, the face of accountability has changed through time. Broadly speaking, from mostly internally oriented responsiveness aimed at improvement, the focus changed towards explicit external justification. The reasons for the change lie significantly in the fact that the costs of higher education have grown enormously with consequences for the national and state budgets and the external groups' perception that higher education is not delivering value for money. The changes have started dynamics that have not yet settled down. Regarding the link between globalization and accountability, the use of performance indicators to assess institutions in a competitive ranking that determines funding could be considered a globalizing practice, but the writers mentioned did not explicitly refer to such links.

France

The 1968 *Loi Faure* granted the universities more autonomy than they had previously. They were granted legal individuality and administrative, financial, and educational independence. However, the overall arrangements were still rather centralized (Guin, 1990). In 1984, the Loi Savary united all higher education institutions in one framework. The idea behind the act was to let higher education be more flexible to respond to local, regional, and national needs. This implied that the government was acting less operationally and more strategically. Nevertheless, the state still had important responsibilities regarding the drawing up of curricula, the certification of diplomas, and the allocation of posts (Kaiser, 2001). In addition, despite the government's intentions to draw up new statutes for the universities, Guin argues that in the second half of the 1980s political resistance and turmoil, for instance changes of government and the period of *cohabitation*, created a kind of vacuum for real changes in the universities.

Decentralization and other changes, such as regionalization, took place at a faster pace in the 1990s. Regional councils became more important because they received part of the administrative and executive power. Regarding accountability, two important changes took place. First, the idea of contracting (*contrats d'établissement*) was introduced in the beginning of the 1990s. Chevaillier (1998) argues that the ideas for contracting in higher education stem from a general notion that central planning was not considered to be effective any longer, and the attractiveness of the "management by objectives" doctrine was visible in a number of French public sector agencies. Contracting meant the disengagement of government from the daily administrative practices of the universities and the obligation of the institutions to draw up a mission statement. A four-year contract describes the activities the university will carry out, what additional resources are needed, and how the institutions will monitor the outcomes. The choice of activities is largely based on an internal institutional audit. The details of the contracts have changed over the years, but the basic principles still hold (Abecassis, 1994). The contracts applied to only a small percentage of the total budget of the university and the evaluation of the contract did not involve redistribution of funds between universities but remained faithful to the "spirit of dialogue" and the development of trust. Furthermore, the contracts had no legal value and thus lacked sanctions when the commitments were not met (Musselin, 1997).

A second development regarding accountability relates to a national evaluation system that was implemented during the 1980s. The attention paid to evaluation at that time was part of a general development to strengthen evaluation efforts in the public sector. For higher education, another element played an important role. The government at the time intended to increase student numbers as much as 100 percent. The government was concurrently aware, anticipating this unprecedented growth, that a change was needed in organizing control over the system: "The basic assumption that central government could uphold the legal fiction of homogeneity of provisions across the nation was thus called into question by the sheer scale of the enterprise" (Neave, 1994, p. 72). By the end of the 1980s one third of the universities were evaluated on a voluntary basis by the *Comité National d'Evaluation* (CNE), an organization set up in 1985. The CNE evaluated the policies and governance of institutions instead of actual study or research programs, and it did not evaluate individual academics (Staropoli, 1996). Although the CNE efforts were serious, most evaluations were descriptive and hardly critical, but constructive as befits a voluntary scheme (Guin, 1990). Some analyses point out that indeed a culture of evaluation was introduced in higher education. However, given the fact that the evaluations were without obligations, the impact was minimal in the short run.

At present, the CNE seems to have a limited role in higher education accountability. The CNE nowadays evaluates institutions according to their missions. An institution is supposed to write a self-evaluation, and the CNE organizes an expert peer review. The intermediate results are confidential reports from this expert group. The final result is a series of public conclusions and recommendations, followed by a meeting after 18 months to measure the impact of the evaluation on the functioning of the institution. The total duration of an evaluation is about one year. The report is sent to the university community, governmental departments, and the press.[1] The fact that the CNE does not play a role in evaluating contracting between government and the institutions may be an indication of its present, relatively weak position; however, all universities agreed to be evaluated.

Despite the tendencies towards decentralization and increasing autonomy, several analysts (Chevaillier, 1998; Musselin, 1997; OECD, 1996) point out that the weight of a long tradition of centralism still exists. Also, until recently, France has been very reluctant to implement or expand market type mechanisms in higher education (Kaiser, et al., 1999).

In conclusion, the French higher education system is still largely steered from the central level, despite some developments towards deregulation and decentralization. The efforts of the government to implement formal accountability mechanisms have not been accepted wholeheartedly and turned out to focus mainly on monitoring developments in higher education. The quality assurance through the CNE is voluntary and has few consequences for the institution involved, other than prestige and a university's reputation.

Preliminary Conclusions

The relationships between accountability and globalization in the different countries are as follows:

Globalization and other general trends in higher education, for instance changing government involvement, market mechanisms, and so on, have a collective impact on accountability policies and mechanisms.

The relationship between accountability and globalization is particularly visible in policies that stress the importance of higher education in its competitive role, that is, supporting the nation in the global economy. This challenges national and state governments to keep a close watch on the effectiveness and efficiency of higher education institutions and make them more accountable.

Given the complexity of the interrelationships between globalization and other trends on the one hand, and accountability on the other, these relationships are to a considerable extent shaped by specific national contexts and change through time.

These preliminary conclusions are rather similar to those of Leithwood et al. (1999) regarding accountability in education in general: "The current preoccupation with educational accountability appears to have begun in most developed countries in the 1960s, acquiring significant new energy during the mid-to-late 1980s. The reasons for these calls for greater accountability, furthermore, are to be found in the wider economic, political, and social context of which schools are a part. These contexts are not uniform across all countries" (p. 11). It is clear from the four countries studied that accountability policies that stress a competitive and economic role for universities are more apparent in the United States and the Netherlands, less so in Norway, and almost nonexistent in France.

ACCOUNTABILITY IN INSTITUTIONAL CONTEXTS

Below we take a further step in our investigation of accountability by looking at levels within the four universities discussed so far. In fact, this is the most interesting level, for here we will discover the impact that the national debates and policies actually have on daily practices and on the views of academics and administrators.

Accountability Measures in Force at University, Program and Department Level

Here we asked respondents to mention the accountability measures, for example research indices, quality reviews and teaching evaluations, that have been introduced by the government to monitor universities and their programs and departments. The University of Avignon seems least occupied with accountability requirements from or through the responsible minister or government. A small number (16 percent) of responses indicated that there is no control or monitoring in place and a little less than one third (29 percent) of the responses stated that there is no change or only debates taking place on the issue of accountability. In sum, almost half of the responses stated that there was a lack of accountability mechanisms or a lack of change other than changes to student numbers that are monitored regularly as a traditional form of accountability.

I would say that the structures of evaluation haven't really changed much. As for your examples, I am not really convinced that the minister takes much notice of the pass rates; however the percentage of students enrolled, yes, evidently. But the only thing that this is used for is so that the minister can establish a budgetary notation to allocate credits to the university; but after this has been done, we are the ones who decide what we are going to do with the funds and whether or not we are going to cut certain courses or keep them. So the minister in a way rids himself of this responsibility. Otherwise I would say that in this area, nothing has really changed. There has been a change in the minister's discourse, a change of methods, but not a change in the procedures of evaluation. (Avignon, Junior, Male, Academic, Professional School)

About half (47 percent) of the responses indicated that accountability exists "out there" but that no immediate effect was noticeable. Most of the elements of accountability, for instance monitoring of student choice, pass rates, required qualifications of academics, and performance-related funding for small parts of the university budget, seemed relatively harmless. Whereas the general tendency in the responses was that accountability mechanisms were not necessary, a few responses mentioned that there should be some external scrutiny from the government.

Boston College could be positioned at the other end of the spectrum. It must be stressed that although the university, being private, is not monitored by the state legislature, 74 percent of the responses indicated that accountability is all around the place, mainly by external reviews. Nevertheless, a number of responses indicated that external reviews were a fairly recent monitoring device, introduced to improve the performance of some departments and used to reward others. External reviews were closely related to preparatory activities at the institutional level.

The university puts together an evaluation for the department as a whole. There are sticks and carrots with respect to monitoring. The university has just come out with an award for teaching for faculty with a little cash prize of $4,000, not much. It's more recognition than a monetary reward. Our performance is measured individually but also departmental-wise. In the university's opinion are we allocating too many resources to the graduate program versus undergraduate? Do we have enough electives on the books? (Boston College, Senior, Male, Academic, Social Sciences)

In addition to the external review mechanisms, 15 percent of the responses explicitly named the internal scrutiny of class sizes and other elements of the educational process. The attention paid to accountability does not always mean that respondents are seriously "bothered" by accountability.

The academic vice president and deans do not seem to monitor departments all that directly. There is an annual report that's put in, but I don't know exactly what happens to it. It goes up to the dean, and I have never had any feedback. (Boston College, Senior, Male, Academic, Professional School)

Most of the responses in this category, however, accepted external reviews and stated that these are helpful for improving their programs and procedures. Also, a number of responses inform us that there are departments that are hardly evaluated or held accountable. In addition to the accountability measures described above, some responses relate to university rankings. This should not be literally taken as a direct accountability measure, for external organizations use university data to monitor and rank institutions, indirectly implying that the university could be asked to explain or justify its performance vis-à-vis its regulatory bodies.

The University of Twente and the University of Oslo took middle positions between Boston College and the University of Avignon. At Twente almost all respondents refer to external reviews of different aspects, teaching and research separately, by national visiting committees. The compulsory participation in these quality assurance processes implies that each study program for education and each department/faculty for research write self-evaluations, and that a peer review committee visits the program to eventually come up with recommendations.

The university is fairly well set up in terms of quality assurance procedures and accountability procedures. The faculties are reviewed twice yearly, and all that is done in terms of performance indicators, reviews, students evaluations—everything you can imagine. (Twente, Senior, Male, Academic, Social Sciences)

A number of responses mentioned the funding mechanisms that partly take into account the performance of the university based on the number of graduates at the Master's level, time to complete a degree, and number of Ph.D.s granted. A small number of the responses related to the internal monitoring practices of the university, partly as a preparation for the national quality assurance system, and partly as a preparation for obtaining accreditation. At the time of the survey, this was a voluntary activity, soon to become part of the obligatory accreditation mechanisms.

At the University of Oslo, most responses (75 percent) reported the role of completion rates in accountability procedures and the annual productivity forms. A minority of responses (9 percent) mentioned the discipline reviews. It was clear from responses that completion rates and annual productivity reporting practices did not lead to severe consequences in terms of the budget, as these indicators determine only a small part of the budget.

Completion rates of students were introduced several years ago by the government, so part of the funding is related to credit points. It is still not a major element, but it is there. Research indices are still rather primitive. It is essentially a question of publications and the number of doctoral candidates we produce. It's not sophisticated, and so far it is not specifically linked to the budgets or any reward or punishment. Quality reviews are done not on an extensive, regular basis, but the government asks the Research Council to conduct periodic reviews on the state of a discipline. It is done on a national basis. And teaching evaluations, again there has been a consistent push I would say from the ministry, even supported by prizes for those who do this the way the former minister would like it to be done. So yes, again there are really no heavy sanctions for those who don't use these evaluations. The pressure so far has been essentially to use course evaluations on a regular and a fairly systematic basis. The results of the evaluations have few consequences for those involved. As yet, there is no mechanism for translating the results of these reviews into decisions about budgets. (Oslo, Senior, Male, Academic, Social Sciences)

There is a push to pay attention to quality monitoring and quality reviews, but there are no mechanisms for translating the results of the reviews into decisions about budgets. Also, given the fact that many interviewed were not aware of all the mechanisms in place to monitor their activities, the accountability practices seem rather ceremonial, without threatening elements for the university's or its departments' survival.

Accountability Measures in Force at the Individual Level

Although there is some overlap in the responses regarding the organizational and the individual level, we discuss the latter separately from the former.

At the University of Oslo, teaching evaluations (43 percent of the responses) and annual reports (40 percent of the responses) are mentioned as accountability mechanisms at the individual level.

We have, of course, now an increased amount of reporting: that you record your plans for teaching for the term, then after each term, then after each year, you report what you have been doing. How much teaching you have done. What kind of research you have carried out. Also all sorts of publications and things like that. This is new to the university. It is not something that happened in that format earlier on. And the head will have a conversation with each member of the staff once a year. (Oslo, Senior, Male, Academic, Professional School)

Eleven percent of the responses related to the international reviews of their research. A small amount of responses regarded university prizes and dialogue meetings between central administration and the faculties as other monitoring mechanisms.

There is a lot of evaluation, and that's new. We didn't have that at all many years ago, and of course, I think that it is quite useful. We have had international committees evaluating our research. And as to teaching, this institute has been doing that for a longer time than other institutes. The student organization picks out a couple of different teaching units every semester to evaluate. Together with the teacher in charge they choose the questions, and one of the students is given some money to do the statistics. I think it works quite well. (Oslo, Senior, Female, Academic, Sciences)

The latter can easily be interpreted as "soft" monitoring, that is, discussing problems and raising possible solutions; the former is more difficult to directly connect to accountability. One should interpret the mention of prizes, however, as a mechanism through which individuals are not so much held accountable as rewarded on the basis of a comparison of their merits or achievements.

At Boston College, 62 percent of the responses referred to the annual reviews, built on the evaluation of each individual's teaching, research, and community service.

Everybody has to submit an annual report. In collaboration, the department chair, dean, and associate dean scrutinize that annual report. So we look at the publications, the teaching evaluations, and the service. And the assumption is that everybody will be given a small raise, and then on top of that somewhere between 1 and maybe up to 2 percent in merit pay can be added to that depending on judgment. So the faculty are aware that they are expected to be productive. I think the criteria for productivity are fairly well known. We tend to rely on some quantitative measures across the board, and the chair can add the voice that looks at quality as well. (Boston College, Senior, Male, Academic, Professional School)

A minority of responses (13 percent) mentioned mentoring programs and peer teaching evaluations, and another 13 percent mentioned tenure review. With respect to the latter, those without tenure go through the tenuring process, as has always happened traditionally, and those who are going for promotion to full professor are scrutinized in great detail.

At the University of Twente, four direct methods of monitoring the performance of academics were mentioned. Over one third (35 percent) of the responses reported that annual individual reviews were used without sanctions; 28 percent of the responses mentioned teaching surveys; 20 percent mentioned annual reports from the department chair; and 11 percent of the responses identified annual reviews with bonuses or task reassignments.

We have some system of personal interviews every year linked to the annual report. There may be some sort of task reassignment, and some departments don't seem to have any system. This is a major policy issue that the board of the university wants to deal with, and it is in favor of a systematic approach of academic management by the dean and the department chairs. This would enable departmental chairs or group leaders to implement a system of interviews every half a year and link these to assignment of tasks and results of the tasks, looking back and looking forward. (Twente, Senior, Male, Manager)

The first method was criticized for its lack of usefulness; that is, it did not result in salary increments or even promotion if it was not signaled by the academic, and the annual review meetings were not used for discussing career development. Regarding the teaching surveys, respondents indicate that these were mostly applied to first-year courses and that the focus was to a larger extent on the courses and the program rather than on the individual academic participating in the program.

At the University of Avignon, the pattern was similar to that of accountability at the organizational level: 21 percent relate that there was no evaluation of academics, and another 9 percent that this was a good thing, given the subjectivity of such evaluations. Another 19 percent reported that there are discussions on this issue. In sum this implies that almost half of the responses mentioned the lack of formal accountability at the individual level.

For the moment, there are none at all, but I know that there is talk of establishing accountability measures during the new reform. And that these measures will include student evaluation courses. This has been planned for sometime this year, but for the moment, nothing has materialized. (Avignon, Senior, Male, Academic, Sciences)

The remaining responses ranged from formulating obstacles for the implementation and use of such accountability mechanisms (12 percent), to expressing the usefulness of indirect and/or informal evaluations (16 percent), or to stating the necessity of implementing individual accountability measures (17 percent).

How Effective Are These Measures?

Here we asked the respondents to react to the question of whether the accountability mechanisms in place were effective in either monitoring quality or improving the quality of teaching and research within the university. Do accountability measures improve the quality of teaching and research?

Almost half (44 percent) of the responses at the University of Oslo indicated that accountability measures do not improve the quality.

In lots of instances, you can see that this has been a major source of stress and resulted in somewhat unproductive adjustments. When you reward a specific kind of activity and not something else, which may be equally important, you can see unintended consequences. (Oslo, Senior, Male, Academic, Social Sciences)

An approximately similar percentage (47 percent) thought that they improved quality, though a fair proportion of this percentage added comments to their positive reaction. Examples of comments include that the improvements of the quality were mainly a result of internal motivation or that it was necessary to encourage but not to punish staff to improve quality. There were a few responses (8 percent) suggesting that they were not sure about the impact or found it difficult to know.

At Boston College the responses were in general more negative than positive. About 56 percent of the responses stated that the measures were not effective.

The annual review in which the dean sends you a letter about your strengths and weaknesses, I don't get a sense that this is used to improve the quality of teaching or research. I have never heard of people acting on these things. I don't have a sense that this method has been used to create new ways or better ways to teach. (Boston College, Junior, Female, Academic, Professional School)

They described the kind of evaluation that they thought would be more effective. It appears that most want more formative rather than summative evaluations, more collaborative and peer-review types of evaluations and more one-on-one feedback, in a developmental, supportive atmosphere. A few respondents felt that the current mechanisms were not harsh enough. Also, some commented on the fact that formal mechanisms were not as important as having a culture in which teaching was taken seriously. About 44 percent of the responses saw the current mechanisms as effective. They felt that the teaching surveys gave good feedback and the rewards and sanctions may make people more productive, and also that the tenuring and promotion processes helped to focus attention on teaching and research. No one felt that the salary increments were enough to really change behavior, but receiving a negative increment or even just an average increment would signal disapproval of performance and may effect a change. Teaching and research awards were also seen as beneficial. Only one response (2 percent) indicated that trying to judge the effectiveness of these measures was really too difficult.

At the University of Twente there is a more positive picture of the impact of accountability measures. Slightly over half (54 percent) of the responses indicated that the measures were effective.

Yes, I think they do have positive influences in the long run. I've been working at the university for 20 years, and in the beginning there were few monitoring activities in research or in teaching. And now I would say that these monitoring activities have improved the quality of teaching and research. (Twente, Junior, Male, Academic, Social Sciences)

A little over one third (38 percent) of the responses showed that there were doubts about the effectiveness of accountability measures. The comments made were about the lack of effectiveness of the current mechanisms, because they did not think that these mechanisms really changed the motivation to research, and they believed that there might be other mechanisms that could have greater impact.

It is a difficult question to answer, because the quality of education has for sure improved in the last decade and research the same. But I'm not sure if the major impact of this improvement is due to the measures we have been discussing or pressure from outside, such as international competition for funding, national competition for students and so on. (Twente, Senior, Male, Manager)

A few responses in this category also doubted whether the quality of research or the effectiveness of teaching could be assessed. A small number (8 percent) of the responses explicitly indicated that the mechanisms in force needed to be changed. They suggest introducing more collaborative, nonindividual measures, peer review, and more formative evaluation.

Given the lack of accountability mechanisms at the University of Avignon, people responded to the general question of whether these measures could potentially be effective in improving the quality of teaching and research in their university. About one fifth (22 percent) of the responses implied a positive response. The arguments were that the university needed to be more efficient and open-minded to the scrutiny of external demands. Over half (56 percent) of the responses were doubtful, but in a positive sense. They added to their positive view that internal motivations were also necessary, and that there was a risk if assessment would only take into account quantitative indicators. In this category of responses, there were also academics and administrators indicating that it would be difficult to develop accountability mechanisms. Some arguments related to the choice of criteria.

I believe that the academics should have the responsibility for evaluating their own work, it is part of their job. But it is difficult to know exactly which mechanisms should be put into place to make sure that this procedure is put to use effectively, and that it actually does become part and parcel of their role in the university. (Avignon, Junior, Female, Academic, Professional School)

A minority of responses (14 percent) indicated that accountability would not improve academic performance.

More or Less Evaluation Needed?

Implicitly or explicitly in the responses to the survey questions above, the academics and administrators already revealed the desire for or resistance to more evaluation. We asked the respondents whether they would like to see more evaluations and more monitoring of both academics and organizational units, or whether the current amount was just about right.

At the University of Avignon, the respondents were quite hesitant about the need for more evaluation. The majority of the responses (64 percent) could be placed in the categories "Yes, but" and "It will be difficult," or they showed ambivalence in other ways. In particular, they mentioned the existing resistance against such measures, the variety of departments to be evaluated, the lack of competencies of students to be involved, and the amount of red tape it would generate as obstacles.

Yes, but there is also risk, a major risk involved. If evaluation is purely quantitative, first of all you may favor large universities and disadvantage smaller universities because obviously they don't have the same potential, and possibly we don't have the same quality to offer them. We may have had good quality if we confine ourselves to a number of specific subjects. So probably there is a need for specialization. There is also a risk, you know, whereby the situation that we see in Britain may develop, and this becomes something like a mad machine, and it could become purely a mathematical system. Because what matters is the number of publications, not the contents of publications. They meet requirements, and this does not mean that they are good lecturers and good researchers. So there is a risk, obviously. (Avignon, Senior, Male, Academic, Professional School)

Only 21 percent of the responses indicated that they were in favor of introducing more evaluation mechanisms to be able to reward merit and do something about the position of the "privileged caste." Some responses hinted at the shocks such measures would produce.

I think that they could have an extremely positive effect on the way things are done here and the way we work here. It could help create a little more open-mindedness, but I think that it also depends, to a large degree, on a change of the mentalities (we also need to change people's way of thinking). People need to be more adventurous, risk being a little more open-minded, instead of sticking rigidly to their particular specialty. They don't realize how intolerable and how pigheaded they can become. (Avignon, Senior, Male, Manager)

At the University of Twente, 45 percent of the responses revealed that there was about the right level of evaluation. Just over one quarter (27 percent) of the responses agreed largely with the present evaluation culture, but indicated that there should be a change in the kinds of evaluation and there should be more differentiation, for instance in terms of bonuses for departments or individuals. About one fifth (21 percent) of the responses mentioned that there should be less evaluation for reasons of efficiency, and calls for more qualitatively-oriented evaluations.

Yes, I think it's a bit overexaggerated at the moment, especially at the national level, not in our institution. We have a teaching and research assessment every five years, as separate exercises, so that's an average of two-and-a-half years for each cycle. That's quite a burden for a faculty or a research area. I would be in favor of having a combined teaching and research assessment once in every five years. (Twente, Senior, Male, Manager)

The feelings and views at Boston College are comparable to Twente in that 45 percent of the responses indicated that the current amount and type of evaluations was about right. Within this group of responses at Boston College, some remarks were made on the need to increase evaluation in the area of research. Also, 27 percent of the responses indicated that in principle they would endorse the current practice, but would recommend changes.

A more realistic form of evaluation is needed. The point is that there is no other activity that's more important than the evaluation of your employees. It gives them self-esteem; it gives them motivation. It is an opportunity to sit down face to face with them and discuss their career. But it never happens here. (Boston College, Senior, Male, Academic, Professional School)

Other suggested changes related to a more developmental approach, and more mentoring. Boston College differs from the Dutch university when it comes to the call for more or less evaluation. Only a very small minority at Twente pleaded for more evaluation and a critical discussion of research quality and productivity. In contrast, at Boston College 24 percent argued for more evaluation, particularly through serious collegial discussions on teaching, and only 9 percent pleaded for less evaluation.

At the University of Oslo a slightly different question was put forward. Here the respondents were asked if there was resistance to the accountability measures at the university. More than half (59 percent) confirmed the question.

Yes, absolutely. When this idea comes up, they say, "We don't like it. We don't like to have this control. We don't like to have these declarations. It is a lack of confidence in us, and it doesn't work. It is just a lot of paper." (Oslo, Senior, Male, Academic, Professional School)

Particularly at the University of Oslo there tended to be passive forms of resistance as expressed by resenting the measures rather than by active resistance. People questioned the value of assessment mechanisms and verbalized their disagreement with the process. They also expressed frustration and complained that there were too many forms to complete. Less than half (41 percent) did not resist the mechanisms in force, although some displayed a passive noncompliance by storing the evaluation results in drawers and not acting on them.

SUMMARY AND CONCLUSIONS

It is difficult to draw firm and direct conclusions given the large variety of national contexts in which accountability is introduced and/or changed, and the respondents' demographic variables, such as discipline, gender, age, and position. Nevertheless, when we look at the type of mechanisms in use, both at the organizational and the individual level, it is striking that most mechanisms would be categorized as soft measures (monitoring and explanation) and to a lesser extent as strong measures (justification). In terms of meeting accountability requirements, sticks and carrots are used, but in most cases it is just twigs and baby carrots.

Regarding the effects of accountability mechanisms, a large number of responses shows skepticism. There is some opposition to the bureaucratic procedures, the amount of work involved and the stress on quantifiable indicators. Many respondents doubt whether the procedures will indeed have the presumed impact. Across the countries, many respondents argue for less formal, more individualistic procedures, and plead for a culture in which informal procedures are accepted as part of the working environment. On the other hand, there are also arguments from a minority of respondents who want to introduce accountability mechanisms that reward good practices and punish low-quality performance.

With respect to the question of whether there should be more evaluation or not, more respondents indicate that it should be less rather than more. This is expressed by the aforementioned passive resistance at some universities, in particular the University of Oslo, and by condemnation of such interference by some at Avignon. A considerable number of respondents suggest changes in the existing practices that would, in their opinion, be more effective and/or efficient.

The responses clearly were influenced by the contexts in which the accountability debate took place and the experiences gained with accountability. The four universities apparently were in different stages of development. Boston College and the University of Twente seemed to be the two institutions in which accountability measures were institutionalized, although the Boston case showed much variety by department. Another difference was the fact that in the Dutch case, the university followed the national quality assurance requirements, whereas in the U.S. case, there was much more variety in mechanisms and procedures used by the departments. The University of Oslo seemed to be representative of universities in which accountability was to some extent implemented, but at the same time practices were mostly ceremonial. At the University of Avignon accountability was least visible; debates were taking place, but in practice not so many mechanisms were actually in place. In particular, the practices at the European institutions were reflections of developments at the national levels.

Connecting the findings at the case-study level to those at the national levels and the theoretical framework, there are some interesting findings. Romzek's (2000) remarks on the dynamics of accountability are definitely applicable in the context of our study. The case studies and the national-level descriptions of the developments regarding accountability clearly illustrate these dynamics. Some accountability measures have been dormant, but have been evoked in times of crises. The use of performance indicators by state-level authorities in the United States may illustrate this fact. Another type of dynamism is shown in most national cases that illustrate legitimate authorities' shift from invoking one type of accountability, proactive by legislative requirements, towards other output-oriented forms, such as accreditation, performance-based funding, and reporting performance indicators. A third type of dynamic, resulting in conflicting accountability expectations, did not come to the fore very often. These would have been particularly visible at the case study level. These conflicts did not occur because most accountability mechanisms belong to the category of "soft" mechanisms. They have not as yet harmed individuals or their activities.

We expected accountability to be a consequence of changing relationships between government and universities, the internationalization of higher education, efficiency and the movement towards value for money, and communication and information technology developments. However, the national and institutional case studies seem to indicate that the changing relationship between government and universities is the most important factor. The shift in types of steering relationships towards more institutional autonomy, and to some extent increasing market mechanisms, invoked new types of accountability mechanisms. Neither administrators nor academics wholeheartedly welcomed many of these. Nonetheless, there is possibly an indirect link between globalization and accountability, whereby globalization has affected government views regarding steering higher education. Thus, through this policy globalization has impacted on accountability. Yet the governmental policy papers have paid little attention to globalization as a motive for changing steering relationships. In practice, many of the governments have introduced accountability or quality assurance procedures.

NOTE

1. For further information consult their Web site: www.cne-evaluation.fr.

Chapter 6

Employment Flexibility

Privatization often leads to a reduction in funding for public sector agencies. One way that public sector employers deal with reduced funding is to change their employment practices, for instance increasing the number of part-timers, contracting out, and reducing the number of permanent workers. In sum, employers seek greater employment flexibility to deal with their fiscal situation. Senior university administrators require greater flexibility in their employment structures as the salary bill is usually the largest item in the budget. Some administrators pursue a reduction in full-time staff members by totally eliminating tenure or permanent employment, while most administrators simply require a reduction in the number of tenured academics to create a more flexible employment profile.

This chapter briefly discusses the link between globalization and worker flexibility before addressing permanent employment or tenure. The concept, origin, and changing nature of tenure is examined within the European and U.S. contexts. Although tenure is essentially a U.S. concept, variations of it are evident in a number of countries around the world. Tenure is slightly different from the concept of being a civil servant as is the case for academics in most European countries. Some writers argue that a civil servant has more permanency than a tenured person, while other writers argue just the opposite. This book treats the terms as interchangeable, contrasting them with hiring teachers or adjuncts on fixed-term contracts or hiring temporary workers for shorter time periods. Fixed contractual, temporary, and part-time employment schemes have generally increased in universities and society where public sector privatization has occurred.

THE LINK BETWEEN GLOBALIZATION
AND WORKER FLEXIBILITY

One aim of politicians and bureaucrats advocating globalization policies is to create a more flexible workforce (Sklair, 2001). This flexibility includes expecting workers to have various skills, demanding that workers occupy more diverse roles, reducing the number of permanent workers who are eligible for benefits and replacing them with contract workers who are less expensive to maintain. The shift to greater flexibility of academics is occurring in many Anglo-American countries as permanent employment becomes more difficult to obtain and fewer tenure-track positions are advertised. The notion of a secure job for life is fast disappearing in countries such as the United States, Canada, Britain, and Australia, with more academics working on short-term contracts between two and five years. In European universities there has been some reluctance to abolish the notion of academics as public servants even though some university rectors require greater worker flexibility.

Jane Buck (2001), President of the American Association of University Professors (AAUP), identifies the mid-1970s as the period when job security was no longer seen as a necessary right of workers in the United States. She notes that corporations began to more aggressively seek greater profits, eliminate workers, and restructure the workforce. In addition, the corporation leaders managed to attain positions on university governing boards and began demanding a review and even abolition of tenure. The AAUP notes that attacks on tenure increased during the 1980s and have not disappeared even though the AAUP has won some of the worst battles.

Most academics in France, Norway, and the Netherlands are in permanent employment.[1] Those who are not civil servants are mostly on research contracts or short-term teaching contracts. In these three countries there is a high degree of permanency in most jobs in the public and private sectors. Interestingly, many interviewees compared academics with the general population of workers and mentioned that since most of their fellow workers had permanent jobs it would seem odd if academics did not hold permanent positions. Analogously, within the United States and Australia the current economic and cultural climate is to deregulate, create greater flexibility, and not grant permanency, which results in many workers not having permanent jobs, including teachers and other senior public servants. In the U.S. and Australian universities some academics interviewed suggested that professors should be treated the same as other workers and wondered why academics are still granted permanency.

In the Netherlands the security of employment is changing to resemble that in the United States. The Netherlands appears to be pursuing global practices to a greater extent than the other two European countries. Two respondents express this.

It's rapidly changing in the Netherlands now. Our status as workers in this university will be more like in companies. There are quite a few restrictions on being fired. Even in the private sector it is not too easy to get rid of personnel, but they can. The differences between public and private sector employees are diminishing. So the civil servant rules are systematically changing in the direction of private companies, and that's a national policy. And the system of companies is to have some sort of open-ended contract where you can be fired if there are financial problems or the factory is closing down. There is a series of steps to be taken, but once these are guaranteed then that should serve for all employees, whether private or public. (Twente, Senior, Male, Manager)

There is a general tendency in the Netherlands that positions are less permanent and that people are more eager to change positions much more. It's changing in the general society, and I think it is also changing in the public service. (Twente, Junior, Male, Academic, Social Sciences)

Concurrently it appears that the Dutch model of employment is still quite different from the United States'. Peter Brain (2001) compares the two and notes that the annual hours demanded by employment with moderate to high incomes exceeds 2,300 hours in the United States'. Yet in the Netherlands, where productivity is equal to the United States, workers engage in employment an average of 1,350 hours annually. Brain praises the Dutch labor model that enables people to have only a slightly lower per capita living standard without the social destructiveness associated with the U.S. labor market model.

Professors in the United States' are aware of the destructive characteristics associated with the U.S. labor market that demands greater worker flexibility. Several AAUP presidents have expressed concerns regarding the economic changes affecting universities, and are cognizant that the worst excesses of the labor market are still to come (Perley, 1997; Buck, 2001). Although tenure is being attacked and greater flexibility in employment is being promoted within the United States, two thirds of all full-time faculty at U.S. colleges and universities remain tenured. In 1993, an AAUP survey discovered that 89 percent of full-time faculty were either tenured or on the tenure track (Yarmolinsky, 1996). Nonetheless, when digesting these figures it is important to understand that fewer faculty members are full time and the number of part-time faculty is rising at an alarming rate. Buck (2001) reports that in 1970 part-time faculty comprised only 22 percent of the professoriate or one in five faculty. Yet in 1995 the figure had risen to 41 percent, and in 2001 it was 46 percent. Shapiro (2000) notes, "of the 35,000 who entered the profession from 1995 to 1997, more than two-thirds were part-timers" (p. 15). Within Australia the shift from a full-time to a temporary, part-time academic workforce is gaining momentum, although it is not as dire as the situation in the United States. According to the Department of Education, Training and Youth Affairs (2000) the number of part-time employees in the Australian university sector rose by 18.2 percent between 1998 and 2000, with part-time staff now comprising 15 percent of the university workforce. More significantly, 78 percent of employment growth over the past 12 months has been in the area of temporary or part-time employment.

HISTORY AND CONCEPT
OF PERMANENT EMPLOYMENT

Civil Service Status in European Universities

Security of employment is enjoyed as a legal right by most European academics. Under French law, university professors may not be deprived of their chair unless their peers pronounce a judgment. A similar principle is evident within most western European countries (Morrow, 1968). However, according to Altbach and Lewis (1996) the notion of permanent employment is changing within many European countries, for instance nonpermanent appointments are becoming common in Germany and are increasing in Sweden and the Netherlands. Nevertheless, they found that job security in these countries is still significantly stronger than in the United States. In addition, they describe one of the most drastic changes as the abolition of the tenure system within the United Kingdom by the Education Reform Act in 1988 that allowed dismissal due to redundancy and replaced tenure with renewable contracts.

In most European countries such as France, Norway, and the Netherlands, academic staff are public officials and have the legal status of civil servants. De Weert and van Vucht Tijssen (1999) describe this as a "service" relationship, rather than contractual, which is regulated by public law. They contrast this with the situation in Anglo-Saxon countries where higher education institutions are not formally part of the state and have an autonomous status. Thus academic staff members have private contracts of employment under private law. This has implications for the way employment is negotiated.

The two types of employment relations differ in the way terms and conditions of service are determined. In the public type these are settled unilaterally, and academic staff are supposed to be loyal to the state in return for job security, usually on a lifetime basis. In the contractual type, the substance of the obligations of staff is settled bilaterally between employers and employees, either on an individual basis or, as if often the case, through collective bargaining between the representative bodies (De Weert & van Vucht Tijssen, 1999, p. 47).

The French and Norwegian systems have maintained this public relationship. However, De Weert and van Vucht Tijssen (1999) assert that the Dutch system is in transition from a public to a contractual relationship. The minister of education has not wanted to abolish the public character of higher education and transform universities into private enterprises. Nevertheless, the minister's decision to devolve responsibilities for salary negotiations to institutions is a step towards a more contractual relationship between universities and their employees.

In the Netherlands there is a desire to "modernize" the employment relationship. De Weert and van Vucht Tijssen (1999) define modernization as the introduction of "market-like agreements that enable employers to manage their institutions as flexible corporations" (p. 50). This flexibility is a crucial factor in the bargaining process and can extend to the use of more contract employment and may eventually mean the abolition of the civil service status for academic staff. The universities have acted as a block of employers in opposition to the trade unions representing staff and have pushed for greater flexibility. The trade unions have opposed the abolition of civil servant status and other flexibility measures. The resulting agreement has been a compromise of these different stands.

In sum, it is evident that the Dutch system is becoming more similar to the U.S. system where there is greater differentiation among academic staff and more flexibility for the employers. Both systems have implications for academic freedom, which will be discussed in Chapter 8. In regard to the Dutch universities, De Weert and van Vucht Tijssen (1999) indicate that a culture of academic freedom is being replaced by a culture where staff members are accountable for their contributions to the quality and output of teaching and research. In addition, the culture of professional trust, integrity, and a system where universities were to serve the "public good" is being replaced by a culture of marketplace "performativity."

Tenure in U.S. Universities

The notion of tenure was uniquely created in the United States and began with the 1915 Statement of the AAUP that called for permanent tenure after 10 years of service for all positions above the grade of instructor. In the 1940 Statement the AAUP proposed that tenure be installed as the cornerstone of academic freedom, and it called upon institutions to grant permanent tenure to all academics after a probationary period usually not exceeding seven years. Termination was permitted only at retirement, upon demonstration of adequate cause, or due to extraordinary financial exigencies. During that time half of all colleges and universities were hiring faculty on an annual basis. The AAUP Statement was just that: a statement of principle that did not have the force of law. In the 1940 Statement the AAUP clearly links tenure and academic freedom: "Tenure is a means to certain ends, specifically: (1) freedom of teaching and research and of extramural activities, and (2) a sufficient degree of economic security to make the profession attractive to men and women of ability. Freedom and economic security, hence, tenure, are indispensable to the success of an institution in fulfilling its obligations to its students and to society" (AAUP Web site).

The concept of tenure, although originating in the United States, has since been transplanted into various national systems and has become linked with academic freedom. One main linkage enables faculty job security, which allows faculty the freedom to speak explicitly and criticize social or internal university issues without fear of being fired. Leslie (1998) specifies that although tenure is nominally a universal norm among institutions in the United States, it has different meanings at each institution. He reiterates the Keast Commission's (1973) findings that there is no such thing as a "tenure system" within U.S. higher education, as tenure is applied inconsistently. In addition, Leslie asserts that the nexus between employment security and intellectual freedom is no longer as close as once thought. He indicates that collective bargaining is one way employment security has been negotiated. Furthermore, individual rights and liberties have been expanded through legal cases, which he perceives as more powerful tools than tenure to safeguard academic freedom. During the 1990s in Australia, the notion of tenure was replaced through enterprise bargaining with the concept of continuing employment. The union movement is relatively strong and is the main organization protecting employment security and academic freedom. However, the union was not able to stop the pressure by the government to move toward greater employment flexibility.

In contrast to Leslie's (1998) position that tenure can be protected through the judicial system of legal precedents and collective bargaining, Chemerinsky (1998) argues that the tenure system is a greater protection for academics than either the First Amendment or the protection that is accorded government employees. A major difference is that under the tenure system, "the university has the burden of starting the proceedings to terminate a tenured faculty member. At the very least, the need to bring formal proceedings is a disincentive for the university to act" (Chemerinsky, 1998, p. 645). He argues that any alternative to tenure is likely to lead to a decrease in the protection of faculty members and consequently of academic freedom. Perley (1997) is also concerned about relying on the protection of the First Amendment, noting that it forbids the government to infringe upon free-speech rights, and therefore protects academics in state colleges and universities but not in private institutions.

Yarmolinsky (1996) suggests that academic tenure is at the "far end of the spectrum in degree of permanence—not quite so close to permanent as civil service tenure" (p. 16). He remarks that tenure is intended to protect the nonconformist, and argues that tenure should also protect those who challenge it, as he did in the article. In addition, while attempting to alter the tenure system at the University of Minnesota, a regent used this notion of protecting freedom to criticize tenure, opposing the faculty attempting to defend tenure and ignoring the arguments of the regents. Greenwood (1998), one of those faculty members defending tenure, discusses the provision of job security as necessary to avoid the constant monitoring of employees and to gain greater commitment from scholars to the university.

A popular myth holds that tenure is an archaic ritual out of touch with our modern economy. In fact, it is a rational policy for attracting scholars who will have commitment to an institution and take time to nurture their students. Faculty without tenure must be individualistic in their approach to success, maximizing their publications and grant opportunities. It is only after tenure is granted that loyalty to an institution is possible and that one's own future becomes tied to that of the institution. (Greenwood, 1998, p. 24)

A further reason that tenure is under attack in several countries is due to rulings against mandatory retirement. In the 1990s in the United States, the elimination of mandatory retirement began to affect universities. Commenting on the University of Chicago, Provost Geoffrey Stone (2000) notes that due to the change in federal policy, there were probably some 30 fewer assistant professors than there would have been had mandatory retirement not been eliminated. He notes that there is an important distinction between tenure as a means to preserve academic freedom and tenure as a means to prolong a career. Universities have had to develop retirement packages that give faculty incentives to take early retirement or just retire at 65 or 70. Nevertheless, a number of faculty have remained, jeopardizing the hiring of younger faculty and intergenerational vitality essential to university health.

VALUE OF TENURE/PERMANENCY
IN EUROPEAN AND AMERICAN UNIVERSITIES

The particular question asked regarding tenure depended upon the country context. At Avignon and Oslo we asked: Would you like to keep the idea of university professors being public servants and having their positions permanent? If yes, why is that a value you would like to keep? At Twente we asked: Do you think it is an important principle to maintain professors as civil servants or in permanent employment in Dutch universities? At Boston College we asked: Do you think tenure for academics is an important principle to maintain in American colleges and universities?

Table 6.1 indicates that the majority of responses from all four universities are in favor of the principle of tenure or permanency, especially evident when the "Yes" and "Yes, But" categories are summed. Twente (32 percent) has the highest percentage of responses against permanency, while Oslo (0 percent) has no one who spoke against the principle. In addition, Oslo (23 percent) has the highest percentage of respondents uncertain about tenure, perceiving it as a dilemma, whereas Avignon (63 percent) and Oslo (53 percent) have the highest percentages in favor of the principle. When summing the "Yes" and "Yes, But" categories, the percentage of responses from Avignon (89 percent), Oslo (76 percent),

Table 6.1
Importance of Tenure/Permanency (percentages and numbers)

Universities	Yes	Yes, But	Dilemma	No	Total Responses
Avignon	63	26	7	5	101 (43)
Boston	44	30	14	11	99 (36)
Oslo	53	23	23	0	99 (30)
Twente	29	25	13	32	99 (31)

and Boston College (74 percent) show no substantial differences, with over three quarters in each favoring tenure. Twente (29 percent) has the lowest percentage in favor of tenure, and summing the "Yes" and "Yes, But" categories shows that overall only just over half (54 percent) are in favor.

Chemerinsky (1998) analyzed a survey by the Higher Education Research Institute at the University of California at Los Angeles (UCLA), which found that 43 percent of all faculty younger than 45 believed that tenure was an outmoded concept, compared with approximately 30 percent of all faculty older than 55. There were no significant age differences among Avignon and Boston College respondents. However, at Oslo and Twente there were similar findings to those at UCLA indicating that older faculty favor tenure more than younger faculty. At Oslo over twice as many older faculty 55 years or older (62 percent) were in favor of tenure compared with younger faculty, 30 to 44 years (28 percent). At Twente older faculty (55 years or older) were more likely to favor a preservation of permanency (50 percent) than younger faculty (45 years or younger, 9 percent; and 45 to 54 years, 36 percent). Younger faculty (45 years or younger and 45 to 54 years) were more likely to respond "No, permanency should be abolished" (21 percent) than older faculty (55 years or older, 17 percent). It appeared that the older, more administratively experienced respondents were likely to be more conservative, more compassionate, and to recognize that they had personally benefited from tenure. They may have witnessed and experienced the vicissitudes of careers and life cycles that make people vulnerable, and may also have been more aware of the competitive nature of recruiting highly qualified academics and the need to offer incentives like permanency to attract researchers to the university.

Positive "Yes" Responses

The most frequently mentioned reason behind positive responses in favor of tenure/permanency was academic freedom, which was mentioned most frequently at Boston College but also at Avignon and Oslo. The following quotes exemplify such comments.

Freedom to Critique Society

It is the issue of whether or not people have the license to engage in social critique. Tenure serves that purpose. (Boston College, Senior, Female, Manager)

Yes, because this is a way of protecting the financial and political freedom of the academics. (Avignon, Senior, Male, Academic, Social Sciences)

Academic freedom is something that is being actively discussed in the States, but not in Norway. I think there are situations where society really needs people who speak their mind. (Oslo, Senior, Male, Academic, Sciences)

Another often mentioned reason for maintaining tenure was related to academic freedom, but directed particularly at conducting controversial research or teaching ideas that may not be so popular.

Freedom to Research and Teach What You Want

There is also the pleasure for the students of coming to the university to listen to somebody who is passionate about his research and defends his ideas and opinions. And this is something that I feel is characteristic of the French universities. (Avignon, Junior, Male, Academic, Professional School)

You wouldn't speak out if your job were on the line. I mean I'd be very nervous about making big waves if I thought that I would lose my job. I need to feed my family. If you feel secure, then you don't mind pointing out where there are problems. I think most faculty use their academic freedom locally rather than globally. They use it more in what they do as a scientist or how they teach or what they suggest for students to research. (Boston College, Senior, Female, Academic, Sciences)

Yes, because this allows academics to retain their liberty to work as they please, which is very positive for the academic research side of things. (Avignon, Senior, Male, Academic, Social Sciences)

I know it's controversial, but freedom to do research that is unpopular, as long as it is not malevolent to the public, ought to be allowed. (Boston College, Senior, Male, Academic, Sciences)

Another mentioned reason referred to the ability to conduct a longer research program and allow the research cycle to naturally resolve so that pressure to publish would not dominate the need to investigate the "truth" or be creative in one's research.

Concern about Life Cycle of Research and Creativity

Yes, I do, for purposes of academic freedom but also for the purposes of creativity of the life cycle. There are times that I wrote like crazy, because I was finishing up a longitudinal study, and now I am at a point where I am designing a new study and raising funds. So not as much is coming out. And that's normal. And there should be times in your career when you read like crazy and then there are times when you spend your intellectual capital. And I think that is as it should be. (Boston College, Junior, Female, Academic, Professional School)

Interestingly, the above categories contained no responses from Twente. Compared to the responses from academics in the other three universities, no one from Twente mentioned the need to preserve permanency in order to guarantee academic freedom. This may have been because academic freedom was less threatened due to traditional Dutch tolerance of diversity and freedom of speech. However, a more important omission was the need to avoid the "publish or perish" syndrome and spend more time with students. Only a few mentioned the need to maintain a sense of community and commitment to the institution over time. One mentioned the ebbs and flows of conducting research and writing, and that short evaluation periods could be detrimental to long-term research careers. Generally the responses were more pragmatic. For instance, the need for job security was mentioned by quite a few respondents in all four universities and was often accompanied by a mention of the low pay academics received in most countries. In addition, issues concerning less stress and strain and the ability to do the job without fear of being sacked were mentioned.

Job Security in Exchange for Low Pay

Yes, this is a very French notion. It gives us a job security that is not the case for the whole country. So this is the benefit of being a public servant, although we could say that the disadvantage lies in the fact that higher education in the public sector is not very well paid. (Avignon, Senior, Female, Academic, Sciences)

I think in some respects you might look upon tenure as a quid pro quo for the fact that professors don't make as much money as they should and so at least you give the poor guys some security. They don't have to lie awake at night worrying if their jobs are going to be cut. (Boston College, Junior, Male, Academic, Sciences)

If you want a system that is less tenure based, then you need to increase the salaries, because the salaries are too low. It is hard to get the best people into science in Norway these days. And if they are now, in addition to having low salaries, facing lower job security, then I think universities are going to have a problem. (Oslo, Junior, Male, Academic, Sciences)

In all four universities the notion of lower salaries in exchange for security was mentioned by many academics. However, only the academics in Twente mentioned that job security was part of the culture of society. In France and Norway most people had job security and perhaps take it for granted, whereas among Dutch respondents there was a more conservative notion that recognized the importance of job security. The following quotes indicate the cultural context of job security in the Netherlands.

I think in the Netherlands there are a lot of people who find security important in their lives. And that has to be taken seriously by the university because it will find itself more and more in competition with other sectors of society to attract qualified personnel. I don't think permanency should be abolished even if it has brought an enormous lot of inflexibility into the system. There are people whom you really want to try to keep as long as possible, and they're very important people in the organization. Permanency is not as binding as it used to be. I think they can fire people with permanency more easily than they used to. (Twente, Junior, Female, Academic, Social Sciences)

We have in the Netherlands a policy of people who are employed for a longer period in industry and in the government. Therefore, we have to go parallel in our policies with industry. You can only get people here because they like research, and they want some certainty in their employment. The wages here are lower than in industry. If you didn't get the security, I'm sure that everyone will go to industry, and we have to be competitive. (Twente, Senior, Male, Academic, Sciences)

A further reason for maintaining tenure referred to the ability to form a community of scholars and work collaboratively.

Community of Scholars

This is one of the last places in America that people are in their jobs for a long time. And the creation of a community within a higher education institution requires, I think, longevity and job security. One of the ways of undermining tenure is not by abolishing it outright, but by hiring all these part-timers and non-tenure-track people, I think that is eroding community. (Boston College, Junior, Female, Academic, Professional School)

Yes, I would rather like the university to keep the idea of posts for life. Although I am aware of the risks involved with that, you get some people who don't produce very much any longer. I think I would rather try to find the means of involving them more if possible. I think it is also one of my favorite ideas as a way to make the university a little bit less individualistic than it is. (Oslo, Senior, Male, Academic, Professional School)

The argument is very simple. The state system has many functions, but the state is also a moral community or socially responsible for the basic values in society. For the university to take care of its basic responsibilities, people should be very, very, secure in their positions. It should not be possible for economic interests to threaten them or take resources away. And it should not be possible for any other parts of the state apparatus to intervene and hierarchically govern what goes on in universities. So universities should be extremely independent, and academics should have tenure. (Oslo, Senior, Male, Academic, Social Sciences)

Once again these responses came more from Boston College, Avignon, and Oslo, but not from Twente. Nonetheless, a response that appeared to be more common among the French academics referred to the notion of serving the public and the students in a continuing form.

Serving the Public

Yes, because as public servants, our role is precisely one of serving the public, and the university being a public service assures us continuity, even in difficult times. We will always exist, even when financial times are hard. (Avignon, Senior, Male, Academic, Professional School)

It is part of our whole mentality. In France, we are supportive of that view. In the educational field we have a role to play. We have the state and the citizens and the students, and we should serve the students for life. It is in keeping with our notion of state education. Education should be free and compulsory, so therefore the state has to provide the teachers for life and not have them as temporary workers. It can be seen as very narrow-minded, but it is something that we are extremely attached to, and it is part of the French psyche. As teachers, we know that we are very smug and secure, but we also feel that we deserve that security—it is part of our heritage of French republicanism and all that. (Avignon, Senior, Female, Academic, Social Sciences)

A further response that more French academics mentioned was the notion of time for reflection, which may not endure in a competitive, "publish or perish" environment.

Freedom to Reflect

Yes, I think the university should have that sense of freedom, freedom to learn; what we call the art of wasting your time, of reading, thinking, daydreaming—having the time for reflection. (Avignon, Senior, Male, Academic, Social Sciences)

These days younger academics, particularly in Boston College and Twente, are more likely to assert that universities cannot continue a leisurely notion of freedom incorporating daydreaming and reflection, as time is a commodity and too precious to be frittered away. This suggests that academics should not be given the time to think or reflect and that the only things that matter are concrete and tangible.

The "Yes, But" Responses

Academics against this notion of freedom were more likely to be against tenure or would at least want some modifications of the present system. Approximately one quarter of all respondents wanted some changes and felt that greater flexibility was needed in the system.

Sanctions and Flexibility

I think that there are certain points we need to reexamine, for example, there should be possibilities of sanctioning or excluding academics who make serious errors. But we would have to be very prudent with sanction procedures. (Avignon, Senior, Male, Academic, Sciences)

Yes, but at the same time I think we should have more positions that are contracted. It would mean more flexibility. Now we have so much money tied up in the salaries of the tenured professors that there is very little flexibility. (Oslo, Junior, Female, Academic, Sciences)

The "Dilemma" Responses

This is a similar category to the one above that called for modifications. In this category respondents perceived the question as a dilemma and could not give a clear yes or no answer. However, overall less than 20 percent responded in an ambivalent way and fell into this category.

Security Is Good but Leads to Lack of Competitiveness

In today's world where economic instability is a big problem, the guarantee that we will not end up unemployed can be very reassuring for some. But this also brings up the problem of recruiting our members of staff, because knowing that they run little risk of being fired, we need to make a very careful selection before employing them. But this is also a very "comfortable" position, and sometimes we end up falling asleep! So we could say that it gives us, as public servants, the privilege of working in a calm and stable job environment, but at the same time this environment lacks the competitiveness which often leads to improvement and a higher quality of work. (Avignon, Senior, Female, Academic, Professional School)

I think there are both pluses and minuses to tenure. I mean I have got it myself, so I am glad I have it. There are people who relax after they get tenure. You know, there has to be some kind of post-tenure review. I am committed. I am going to do a good job. The same job after I get tenure as I did before tenure, because that's just me, and it is the kind of standards I set for myself. But you look around and you see people with tenure who are relaxed a bit. I do see a tendency for universities to become much more businesslike these days, and so there probably needs to be tenure protection. (Boston College, Senior, Female, Academic, Sciences)

That is a difficult question. We need more postdocs, more flexibility. But at the same time, we live in Norway, and almost everyone has a permanent position. It is hard to say that academics should have a different type of contract. Even in the private sector, workers are permanent. Even the CEOs are often permanent. They can be fired from the board and get some redundancy package, and so they are taken care of. (Oslo, Senior, Female, Manager)

There are two sides of it, I think. Some permanency is not too bad. Sometimes you also think it's not so bad if there's some change. For those who have permanency it gives them the freedom to do the research of their choice, even if the university or their colleagues do not like the research. And from that sometimes you get very original and new ideas. In that respect I think it's a good idea. But sometimes there are people who don't function, and you must have the possibility to get rid of them. And yet the difference between these two types of people is also sometimes very subtle. (Twente, Senior, Male, Academic, Sciences)

Need to Change the Tenure or Permanency System

Some of the academics at Boston College who defended tenure due to its importance for academic freedom also emphasized the need for some system modification, although these respondents differed from those who expressed ambivalence towards tenure and were more certain that the system needed to change. The Boston College and Twente academics expressed the need to change tenure and increase academic productivity. These academics comprised the "Yes, But" category, yet did not contribute explicit examples of how to change the system.

We Need Remedies for the Deadwood

The downside is that once you are tenured you stop doing things. I think there are remedies to weed those folks out. If you do proper evaluations along the way, at promotion time and between promotion times, then you could just say, "Look you are not performing. You seem to have other activities. You better start doing something differently or your increment is going to go down or you'll lose your office." You know, you just have to have these sanctions. If it is fairly done and faculty members are involved in the decision, then it would be appropriate to have a kind of promotion committee or at least some other faculty to evaluate folks along with the chair. (Boston College, Senior, Male, Academic, Sciences)

You may offer permanency to your top professors and top academics, but it should be your own institutional choice to do so. In the current civil service system, you have a national rule about after working two years in a place, and then you automatically have the right to permanency. That's bad. I recognize the need of the university to have some sort of mix of short contracts, longer contracts, and when you want to keep your quality academics, you have to offer open-ended contracts and say, "Well, you can stay here." If not and they are good enough, then you feel the national and international competition, "Okay, byebye, I have a better offer in Hamburg." (Twente, Senior, Male, Academic, Sciences)

Need for a Different Type of Tenure

Academics at Boston stressed the need for a different type of tenure, drawing upon similar discussions in the news media. In the popular press and scholarly journals there were calls for sliding tenure and post-tenure reviews. At Twente there was some discussion concerning alternatives to being a public servant. Once again these comprised the "Yes, But" category as they accepted tenure but wanted a different type of system.

Sliding Tenure

I think sliding tenure is preferable. In other words there would be no such thing as permanent tenure, but you may get it in groups of three to five years. So it is not permanent, but it is semipermanent. It would maintain the vigor of both junior and senior faculty. I don't see academic freedom as a major issue these days. You know, I see it as sometimes a shield that is hidden behind and hides incompetence. (Boston College, Senior, Male, Academic, Professional School)

Reverse Tenure

Now, the best thing I ever heard about tenure, I think, was by George Will, and he said you should have reverse tenure. That is, tenure should be granted to assistant professors in the first 12 years to protect them as they are and to guarantee them that period of time to get their career going, their writing going when they are the most vulnerable, and then you start taking it away because you want to keep only the people that are really performing. (Boston College, Senior, Male, Academic, Social Sciences)

Rolling Five Tenure

There are a few universities that do it differently. Johns Hopkins Medical School has something called the Rolling Five, where individuals are appointed for five years and then the clock starts down. At the end of the five years if they are judged not to be productive by whatever criterion, then the clock will start down. They will get appointed for four years, then three, etc. Essentially they have a five-year notice and within five years they have to leave, but every year they are reevaluated, and the clock can be reset again during the five-year countdown. (Boston College, Senior, Male, Manager)

Mobile Tenure

You could say that the university could have permanent jobs, but not permanently in a particular department. I think we should be more mobile. So you are now five years in that group and you've done teaching and research in a particular field, now it is time to change and be in another department for five years. I see the problem that people are getting stuck in one place and it is difficult to get away and refresh yourself. I think we need more flexibility and a more dynamic situation. I think in the Netherlands we are used to having too much security. (Twente, Junior, Female, Academic, Social Sciences)

Negative View of Tenure/Permanency

The respondents that were opposed to tenure or permanency came mainly from Boston College and Twente, whereas there were none from Oslo and only a few from Avignon. Thus the following comments are predominantly from Boston College and Twente.

Need for Contracts

Not necessarily, no. The idea of renewable contracts is not such a bad idea. Professors could be reengaged provided all went well, every six years for example. The working contracts would have a length of between 6 and 10 years. (Avignon, Senior, Female, Academic, Social Sciences)

Need to Fire Incompetents

No, I've seen it abused way too much. You could have strong laws to protect academic freedom separate from tenure. Make sure there are sanctions applied to any university for violating academic freedom. What we don't need is for people to be using resources and getting high salaries while they are teaching courses that are 20 years out of date, where they don't contribute to scholarship or don't do community service. If my kids are going to a public university, I don't want to pay for people who are not going to give them a quality education, who don't keep their office hours. They don't give students good advice, they give them lousy teaching, and are so divorced from their field because they haven't done anything actively that the information they are presenting in class is not only poorly presented but out of date. (Boston College, Senior, Male, Academic, Professional School)

No, I don't think you should keep permanency. There are people who get older and slow down. I think you should be able as a university to say, "Okay, you did a great job, but now it's over." (Twente, Junior, Female, Academic, Sciences)

The overall sentiment of those opposed to tenure concerned the need for greater flexibility and the elimination of academics perceived as unproductive. There appeared to be few valid ways to evaluate and terminate academics not performing to a set standard. This was a problem that at least one third of academics from Twente, a smaller percentage from Avignon (5 percent), and Boston College (11 percent) wanted remedied. At Oslo academics were more protective of their colleagues. Perhaps the egalitarian ethos within the wider society caused academics to opt for a sense of community over the individualistic ethos that often arises with a focus on productivity and performance evaluation.

THREATS TO TENURE

Boston College: A Special Case

When respondents at Boston College were asked about tenure some referred to the threat of the *Ex Corde Ecclesia* ("from the heart of the church") and its possible impact upon academic freedom.[2] During the time of these interviews the Catholic bishops voted on this landmark document. *Ex Corde Ecclesia* was originally issued by the Vatican in 1990. Conferences involving bishops around the world were asked to adapt it to the tradition of higher education in their regions. In 1996 the United States conference approved its first document by a vote of 226 to 4; however the Vatican sent it back and asked for stricter language safeguarding Catholic identity and outlining the bishops' role in school supervision. Following the latest vote (233 to 31) the document was tightened by the bishops to gain greater authority over the 236 Catholic colleges in the United States. Kate Zernike (1999) reported that, "The bishops had revised the document several times up until minutes before the final vote as they tried to respond to an outcry from college presidents and colleagues who said the provisions are so stringent that schools might abandon their Catholic identity. The document's most hotly debated ordinance gives the bishops the power to decide who is fit to teach Catholic theology" (p. 1).

In addition, Marc Daniel (1999) reported that the Boston College president, the Reverend William P. Leahy, S.J., said, "There are troubling elements in the draft text, such as the mandate concerning Catholic theologians, the oath of fidelity to the church required for new college presidents, and the implications for trustees and faculty who are of other faiths" (p. A35).

It appears that certain American colleges comprised a more precarious position than others. According to Zernike (1999), "The document came primarily out of concern about more well known Catholic schools that have grown into more national universities, such as Georgetown, Boston College, and Notre Dame. As they have done so, they have raised more money and attracted a far more diverse faculty and student body. The Vatican and many bishops feared the diversity diluted their Catholic identity" (p. A35).

In their interviews some managers were asked an additional question that related directly to the *Ex Corde:* What impact do you think the *Ex Corde Ecclesia* will have on Boston College? Generally, the reaction of administrators indicated that it would have little or minimal impact due to a number of factors. There was a sentiment that the voices of Jesuit and Catholic colleges around the country were unified and that most colleges were run by a lay board of trustees, which was the case for Boston College. The board of trustees at Boston College consists of lay people and members of the Jesuit order—approximately eight Jesuits out of 39 on the board with a mixture of Catholics and non-Catholics. The President clearly indicated that the college would be run by the board of trustees and not by an outside authority. Nevertheless, one manager felt that it could still be an issue, and highlighted two concerns. First, a board consisting of mainly religious Jesuits could be created above the existing board of trustees. Second, that the new board would set the direction of the college, own the land, and approve all the financial decisions.

If you ever do that, you would never have the quality of people on the board that we currently have. They are helpful, skilled, experienced, loyal, and thoughtful people. If the current board were seen as a second tier board, you would never be able to get the presidents of major corporations to sit on it. At least this Catholic university just doesn't want to give up that kind of control to the religious, because they would get their orders from Rome. And the other troublesome thing, I think, to a lot of people is the requirement, in faculty appointments where the faculty member is to teach Catholic theology, that the appointment be approved by the local bishop. And that really strikes at academic freedom. (Boston College, Senior, Male, Manager)

A number of academics, without being prompted, mentioned the *Ex Corde* as an issue that may threaten academic freedom. Following are a few quotes from faculty concerning the *Ex Corde*.

This *Ex Corde* thing might set us back a decade. Because who wants to come to a college where the Bishop's going to overlook your syllabus? (Boston College, Senior, Male, Academic, Professional School)

The notions of freedom to investigate anything that you want to and be supported by your academic peers and freedom from political pressure to conform to various decisions are important. But I really feel that job security has to be maintained to protect us from creed and conformity and political ideology, in order for a sociologist, for example, to be able to investigate contraception and sexual "deviance" and things of that sort. (Boston College, Senior, Male, Academic, Social Sciences)

I think, frankly, that academic freedom is still an issue in a Catholic institution nowadays, when we have the Vatican hovering around, trying to interfere. We have the Vatican, and public universities have the legislature. They always want to interfere. The Vatican wants people to take an oath, but I don't think it's going to happen. I just don't think the college president would let it happen. And I think most of the American bishops know the university system well enough to know this wouldn't work. So I think what's going on is a lot of stalling. So eventually they'll sort of wear the Vatican down, and they'll turn to something else. (Boston College, Senior, Male, Academic, Social Sciences)

Clearly these quotes emphasize the importance of academic freedom, individual freedom, and not being committed to a particular ideology for the Boston College faculty who perceive the *Ex Corde* as a threat. However, in reality the only academics that are under threat from the *Ex Corde* are the theologians. It appears that there is not much concern among them because the bishops are not exerting their rights to intrude into the autonomy of Catholic universities. Nevertheless, the last quote points to the different types of threats to institutions that have occurred over time in the United States. The legislature often threatens public institutions, and the Vatican can threaten the freedom of private Catholic institutions.

Threats from Boards and Legislatures

A further major threat to universities comes from the board of regents or the trustees. This has gained prominence in the last couple of decades in the United Sates when conservative governors appointed board members whose views posed a threat to more liberal-minded faculty. The same divide is evident when conservative legislatures dictate policies on what should be taught in universities. It is often a conservative government that restricts the teaching of gay or lesbian studies, or topics on sexuality, or the introduction of black or women's studies, or discussion of evolution in biology. The interference into what should be taught or researched and who should be allowed to teach is a direct attack on the integrity of the academic community and its professionalism. It does not matter whether that interference is from the left or right of the political spectrum. The important point is *where* curricular decisions should take place and *who* has the expertise to make those decisions. There is a need to balance the interests of various groups in making curricular decisions. However, the mandating of curricular decisions by politicians and trustees can limit the debate on these issues, which should take place within the university. It also directly questions the importance of debate within the university, which is so essential for democracy within universities as well as for maintaining democracy within the larger society.

The intrusion of trustees or regents into the running of universities is noticeable at a number of U.S. universities. Arenson (2000) chronicled the battle between trustees and faculty at the State University of New York (SUNY). The battle over requiring a core curriculum was between conservative trustees appointed by a conservative governor pitted against a more liberal-leaning faculty. At the heart of the battle was the belief that decisions about what to teach were the preserve of the faculty, and they were losing control over those decisions. Arenson noted that Arthur Levine, president of Columbia Teachers College, perceived this intrusion by a lay board without curriculum expertise as a violation of academic freedom. She also reported that this was not the only university system that was seeing trustees encroaching on their turf. She identified other public universities where this was happening, for instance the George Mason University in Virginia and the City University of New York.

It is noteworthy that since the September 11, 2001, attacks on the World Trade Center and the Pentagon, there have been threats of dismissal and disciplinary action taken against faculty members who have criticized U.S. foreign policy at teach-ins. The American Council of Trustees and Alumni released a report on November 11, 2001, listing 117 examples of individual statements made on U.S. campuses, labeling them a "blame America first" response. The report, *Defending Civilization: How Our Universities Are Failing America, and What Can Be Done About It*, urges alumni, trustees, and donors to protest these actions, and extols the need for U.S. colleges to require the teaching of U.S. history and Western civilization (Blumenstyk, 2001). This is a further example of how groups outside the university can intrude on academic professionalism and attempt to deny faculty the freedom to critique U.S. foreign policy. This particular group, American Council of Trustees and Alumni, is a conservative, nonprofit organization, and it is not a professional association representing university trustees.

State legislators are also beginning to question the purpose and effectiveness of existing tenure systems. Post-tenure review is now a common part of tenure policies in the United States (Leslie, 1998). An example is the state of Virginia, where all institutions have to perform regular, rigorous, pre- and post-tenure performance reviews. In the 1990s these moves became more common as U.S. institutions were faced with substantial declines in state funding. According to Leslie, it was during this period that tenured faculty members were viewed as a financial liability. He noted that in 1998 more than half of all faculty held positions out of the tenure stream. Some policy makers have taken the bold step of totally eliminating tenure. This was the case at Florida Gulf Coast University, a new public university in the Florida system that began without tenure in August, 1997. This also occurred in older colleges, for instance Bennington College, that abolished tenure, and in approximately 20 percent of all independent four-year colleges in the United States that ceased to offer their faculty tenure (Chemerinsky, 1998).

Engstrand (1998) argued that one of the fiercest battles over tenure in U.S. higher education occurred at the University of Minnesota from late 1995 to June,

1997. The attack on tenure began when several regents requested a review of tenure. Engstrand pointed out that tenure is explosive as "it engages the issue of academic freedom, which scholars regard as the bedrock of their teaching and research" (p. 622). He noted that virtually every faculty discussion at Minnesota included fears for the future of academic freedom. The approach by the regents to review tenure and subsequent events galvanized the faculty to consider join-ing the union. The vote on the union was 666 in favor, 692 opposed, and 237 faculty did not vote. Engstrand wrote that the regents and the administration recognized that the close vote sent a clear message. In the end, "the Minnesota faculty adopted a post-tenure review system that included the possibility of up to a 25 percent salary reduction. They also streamlined the procedures for dis-cipline and separated base pay and performance pay" (Engstrand, 1998, p. 623).

Kingman Brewster (1972), former President of Yale University, defended tenure and was against any system of periodic review that could lead to dis-missal. He observed: "The more subtle condition of academic freedom is that faculty members ... should not feel beholden to *anyone*, especially department chairmen, deans, provosts, or presidents, for favor, let alone for survival" (p. 381). Today trustees and legislatures could be added to this list.

Some European universities may be constrained by the policies of their na-tional governments that may interfere with curricula decisions at the institu-tional level. In addition, policies that shift accountability from a professional system of peer expertise to a more managerial type of accountability may be an-other threat to academic freedom and security of employment. However, the ability of academics to voice their dissent and not be dismissed seems to be very much alive on the Continent. A French academic remarked that frequently pro-fessors still write letters to the editor in leading papers giving their opinions on educational policies or other political issues and sign their letters as Professor of __ at University of __, even explicitly criticizing the Ministry of Education (Lacotte, 2001).

CONCLUSION

The desire for greater employment flexibility is apparent in many countries; however, the movement against tenure is more prevalent in Anglo-American countries. An interesting strategy used by U.S. administrators is to ask faculty members to accept renewable term appointments and forgo tenure in return for a higher salary. Proponents of these agreements suggest that if faculty accept these arrangements they will be demonstrating that in a free market, faculty will forgo tenure. The AAUP (2000) is worried about these transgressions of tenure for a number of reasons; for instance, a fundamental concern is that this constructs tenure as a private exchange. The AAUP asserts that renunciation of tenure has much larger institutional and social consequences and that tenure was established for the common good of the academy and society. They reiterated the 1940 statement that "institutions of higher education are conducted for the common good and not to further the interest of either the individual teacher or the institution as a whole"(AAUP Web site).

One of the main purposes of tenure is to allow faculty to participate fully in civic and institutional life. The AAUP (1966) extends the obligations of academics to promoting "conditions of free inquiry and to further public understanding of academic freedom" (AAUP Web site). These are important obligations because the community puts a lot of trust in the professional integrity of professors, and in turn professors need to be free to speak their minds in order to protect the interests of the community. These are the tenets of a democratic society. The statement also noted that professors are "citizens engaged in a profession that depends upon freedom for its health and integrity" (AAUP Web site).

Tenure is not under as much threat in most U.S. universities as it may have been a decade ago. Nevertheless, the desire for more control over academics has emerged in the need for post-tenure review. Post-tenure reviews have raised another concern, according to the AAUP (1999). Post-tenure reviews substitute "managerial accountability for professional responsibility [and thereby altering] academic practices in ways that inherently diminish academic freedom" (p. 2). It is important for faculty, not business-trained managers, to review performance, which should be aimed at faculty development and only in rare cases at dismissal. The shift that is occurring puts the burden of proof on the faculty member to justify why they should retain tenure. There is also a shift towards managing faculty performance rather than professional independence (Benjamin, 1997). This leads to a diminution of professional integrity.

In the European context, only the Dutch system has moved toward greater flexibility. The Dutch interviewees seem to be approaching this transition from a civil service status to a private contractual status with considerable pragmatism. The shift in the Dutch system has not gone as far as in the U.K. system, which totally abolished tenure, or as in the United States, where many universities have introduced post-tenure reviews and the diminution of new tenure-track positions. Nevertheless, the Dutch have introduced more institutional autonomy for personnel recruitment policies and employment agreements, and the continuing debate in the Dutch parliament about further deregulation of employment matters for universities points to the question of how far their employment practices will go towards a contractual relationship.

Societies need professors who can approach their work with intellectual honesty and be committed to the work of the university. Concurrently, they should expect professors to be loyal critics of their university and be the conscience of the nation. The strength of a nation is in the healthy debate that it allows within institutions and in society in general. Academics are one of the few groups within society that have a special obligation to speak out and express their opinions. If they do not have tenure that gives them the freedom to speak without fear or favor, which group in society will have that special obligation?

NOTES

1. During the past decade, a significant shift has occurred in Norway and the Netherlands from a system where professors are appointed for life by the king or queen to a system where academics are appointed by the minister of education in Norway and by the university in the Netherlands.

2. An article by Paulson (2000), updating the impact of the *Ex Corde,* noted that the bishops do not want to exert control over Catholic colleges. This declaration by a top official of the National Conference of Catholic Bishops "essentially removes the teeth from a controversial measure approved by the bishops last year under pressure from the Vatican" (Paulson, 2000, p. A1). Paulson reported that some theologians at Boston College stipulated they would refuse to apply for permission to teach from Cardinal Bernard Law: "The combination of the lack of punishment for failure to seek permission and Law's assertion of his own open-mindedness seem to go a long way to answering the concerns raised by faculty members at Boston College and other Catholic universities. They had feared their academic freedom was threatened by the suggestion that professors seek license from a church to teach" (p. A1). However the implementation phase has brought new fears. McBrien (2001) described the quandary that individual academics face when deciding whether to apply to their bishop for the mandate to teach theology in their institutions or to defy this demand and face loss of employment or some other sanction by the Catholic Church.

Chapter 7

New Technologies

The prevailing discourse in support of new technologies in education, particularly regarding the Internet, asserts that they enable: 1) individualized learning; 2) learner autonomy in seeking and investigating sources of information; and 3) individual learners, peers, and learning facilitators to assume an active part in building knowledge through interactive networking. If the prevailing discourse is believed, then the mere performance of this technical innovation should be enough to alter the cultural teaching or learning model and lead to the emancipation of the individual. In this instance, the nature of instructional technologies would be the exact opposite of that espoused by mass media where learning is supposedly based on passive adherence to a standardized model.

The supporters of e-learning, virtual campuses, e-universities, and other forms of technoeducation or technopedagogy (as critiqued by Newson, 1996) repeatedly indicate that instructional technology enables students to learn with more flexibility, at their own pace, and at their own time. This has been abundantly documented by many studies. For instance, Collis (1999) distinguishes flexibility in location, program, types of interactions, forms of communication, and study material. Other research based on European universities identifies 20 dimensions of flexibility (Collis, Vingerhoets, & Moonen cited in Collis, 1999).

This undisputed potential of instructional technology, best embodied in the paradigm of the hypertext, facilitates learner-centered education. In other words, the application of information and communication technology in education may enable new individualized learning options in a constructivist perspective, that is: "Constructivism is concerned with the process of how we construct knowledge. How we construct knowledge depends upon what learners already know, which depends on the kinds of experiences they have had, how the learners have organized those experiences into knowledge structures and the learners' beliefs that are invoked when interpreting the events in the world" (Jonassen, 1995, p. 42).

According to this definition, the traditional classroom model incorporating instructor-learner interaction through lectures appears to be an inadequate educational model in terms of flexibility and individualization. This is compounded when we consider that education systems in all Western countries must now provide services for mature or disadvantaged students who may not be culturally or intellectually prepared for the traditional academic learning process.

Therefore, if the new technologies allow learners superior control over subject matter and promote intellectual autonomy through direct access to freely available sources of information without any recourse to an intermediary, then their development must be inevitably seen as a liberating force. Conversely, those who curb the use of new technologies and express certain reservations about their efficiency are merely pronouncing an attachment to a reprehensible pedagogic past and a refusal to see the benefits of modernity.

Obviously the reality here is infinitely more complex. First, it is important to acknowledge that no technology in itself is a vehicle of a cultural, social, or pedagogic project (Wolton, 2000). The technology may even serve as an alibi for reproducing the most conservative didactic models. Ehrmann (1999) is justified in warning us against technological fetishism: "Technologies such as computers (or pencils) don't have pre-determined influence; it's their *uses* that influence outcomes. This statement seems obvious, but many institutions act as though the mere presence of technology will improve learning. They use computers to teach the same things in the same ways as before, yet they expect learning outcomes to be better" (p. 26).

We should be wary about confusing pedagogic mediation and the production of technological media. In addition, we should be wary of placing the individual in the pedestal position of an autonomous learner. This may result in a major benefit to society and an antidote to the strategies of globalization, but there is much that still needs to be discovered about online pedagogy.

Second, the less idyllic aspects of digital networked communication should not be ignored. The technical norms governing digital communication are the same throughout the world, and the tools producing and delivering the information that circulates on the network have worldwide standards, which are precisely the means generating its penetration power. At no point does it consider the cultural particularities specific to the country accessing or using the information, resulting in the development of a normalizing effect, a model that clearly encourages globalization. Whether appreciated or not, standardizing the tools and networks used in education implies a form of technical piloting and inevitably leads to the formatting of thought itself. For example, the resources offered by Clipart or PowerPoint© give rise to certain aesthetic or functional stereotypes (Darras, Harvey, Lemmel, & Peraya, 2000) that are potentially harmful in an educational context. Ready-made productions are only one step away from ready-made thinking.

A large number of multimedia products created for and used in education require a substantial initial level of financial investment that is only feasible in a market extending beyond the national level, possibly involving the whole continent or even the whole planet. However, due to the low manufacturing and delivery costs of these products, and even the trend towards zero cost,[1] institutions are being increasingly pressured to create a world market for educational multimedia products,[2] even though at the moment practically everyone is losing money on this e-learning world market. Foster (2001) quotes researchers at InterEd who predicted that by the end of 2000, "75 percent of all U.S. universities will offer online coursework, and 5.8 million students will have logged on" (p. 122). Foster also refers to a recent survey commissioned by the National Education Association (NEA) in 2000 that states, "Currently, one in 10 higher education NEA members teaches a distance learning course [and that] 90 percent of NEA members who teach traditional courses tell us that distance learning courses are offered or being considered at their institution" (p. 122). In addition, Medina (2001) states that "The online education market is expected to balloon to more than $7 billion in the next two years" (p. B9). Hoping to reap some of this profit California, Chicago, Columbia, Cornell, Maryland, New York, and Wisconsin universities have created for-profit companies selling distance-education courses.

This global dimension is already an undisputed fact. A handful of multinational organizations are competing to dominate the online education market by forming strategic alliances that are similar to those witnessed in the e-business field. Noble (2000) notes that the University of Wisconsin has a partnership with Lotus/IBM, the University of California with America Online, and Columbia and Chicago with UNEXT.com. Columbia also established a for-profit online company called Morningside Ventures. Globally, ministers of education and individual universities are making strategic decisions in the development of online and distance education. Several aspects are noteworthy:

the establishment of nationwide poles of excellence in France around a few prestigious universities in specific sectors, for instance management, business studies, or IT, so as to create a national monopoly of distance learning in these specialties;

the creation of international conglomerates, such as Universitas 21, where prominent universities are partners in association with major corporations, which take charge of the infrastructure and electronic delivery of course materials because they have the facilities and the expertise;

the creation of "portals" integrating, though not necessarily producing, course materials that play the part of brokers for academic institutions interested in joining the scheme, the initiative for such portals being either governmental, as in the e-university in Britain, or corporate, as in many projects in the United States;

the negotiation of international agreements to export existing models (the Open University in Britain is a case in point) to overseas countries with the cooperation of local universities, as accomplished in Australia;

the creation of world-based databases for schoolbooks by major multimedia publishing groups, an initiative recently publicized in France by Universal Publishing.

These developments, whatever form they take, clearly signify that small players are already out of this global e-learning market, and that faculty may lose one of their most important prerogatives through the processes of globalization and economies of scale. As Maloney (1999) shrewdly notes: "One of the most serious concerns among professors regarding online education is loss of control over the curriculum, a main area of faculty responsibility and a hot issue in debates over the faculty's role in governing colleges and universities" (p. 21).

In this context of global competition, the threat is a domination of major academic institutions, and we agree with Bates that, "Even more of a threat is likely to come from multinational corporations in the area of telecommunications, entertainment and information technology, such as Microsoft, IBM's Global Networks and the Disney Corporation who are all targeting education as a natural growth area for value added services and products" (cited in Van der Wende & Beerkens, 1997, p. 14).

Undoubtedly the new technologies also encourage the design of relatively cheap, more rudimentary products, of certain originality in pedagogic terms and suitable for a limited market. The developers of these products heed the cultural specificity of the targeted public and are sometimes financed indirectly by public research funding or the salary of academics. Yet, these products are often in competition with products from the commercial sector. This type of competition is clearly unfair as multinational corporations have substantial budgets at their disposal and can therefore put forward visually seductive products that can easily tantalize an audience of learners brought up on video games. On a wider scale, this development is part of a strategy aimed at marketing cultural goods (Rifkin, 2000), which is perhaps the ultimate form of capitalism.

Finally, because the new educational technologies eliminate the cost of transmitting or carrying information, they enable the diffusion of the most advanced knowledge to be organized on a global scale. This technical opportunity can be perceived from opposite standpoints. If we remember that an increasing number of academics publish parts of their research online, this means that an increasing amount of material is now available to universities in developing countries that could never afford this through traditional publishing channels. Thanks to the Internet, they can access an immense online library, entirely free of charge as digital files pay no transport fees, duties, or taxes. Even the fiercest opponent of globalization will admit that there are benefits to be reaped in this context.

Institutions and firms also take a more commercial view of these potentialities. Students at various locations around the world can access the same seminar by a world expert on a particular subject. Certain technical facilities, for instance two-way video conferencing using broadband networks, allow students to see, hear, and have a discussion with these academics in real or deferred time. From the point of view of an information economist, an analysis of this electronic teaching model presents certain advantages, to which those who take a managerial approach to higher education cannot remain indifferent. This point is made very clearly by a recent online, multiple-choice survey concerning e-learning (Quadratin Multimedia, 2001). Following is the list of possible answers to the question: Your University/Institution/Program of Studies has embarked on/will be embarking on e-learning in order to:

limit the production costs of teaching.

offer a competitive deal in continuing education.

attract a greater number of students.

diversify the range of educational products on offer.

gain competitive advantages.

set and standardize the content of teaching.

attract an international audience.

None of the ingredients of a standard marketing strategy is missing: reduce production costs, standardize products, be more competitive, increase market share. Clearly, managers are looking forward to e-teaching; however, some academics are conscious of the potential danger for smaller universities if this strategy is applied. The following quote from a Boston College lecturer forcefully makes the point.

If people can get the same education in Sri Lanka as they can get in Boston, why pay to come to Boston. So I expect there will be tremendous turmoil with a lot of job loss. Those universities that are already on to it will take large chunks of market share and traditional stick-in-the-mud universities will lose market share. (Boston College, Senior, Male, Academic, Professional School)

Many studies suggest that administrators are tempted to promote computer-mediated teaching in the hope that it will offer better value for money in a labor-intensive field, although this claim remains unsubstantiated by academic research. To the question, "Will the infusion of technology make institutions more productive?" Van Dusen (1999) answers prudently and with commendable common sense: "The answer will lie in how these technologies are applied. If they are purchased as bolts-on to existing processes, improvement in the ratio of output to investment is unlikely. If, however, they are part of a strategic plan to restructure the institution, improvement in the ratio is possible" (p. 7).

Are such strategic plans to restructure institutions likely? Certainly this will not happen until an agreement is reached about the qualitative aspects of output. We are not discussing the effectiveness of instructional technology, but simply pointing out that investment and policy decisions in this domain are made by institutions in the name of budget-based rationalization (Newson, 1996) combined with a belief that this technology embodies the paradigm of modernity.

Whether approved of or not, the various pedagogic models fostered by instructional technology, as evident here, have the potential to reduce all sources of knowledge to a certain uniformity and hence risk creating minicenters of scholarly expertise through the idea of centers of excellence. As the majority of centers for producing knowledge are in the United States, this example clearly illustrates Al Gore's ideas on information superhighways as vectors of U.S. hegemony. This could justifiably lead to fear concerning the development of "an *actual* technological imperialism, with the risk of cultural imperialism too, if only one part of the world produces content for the other part to consume" (Oillo & Barraqué 2000, p. 33). As Nora and Minc (1978) commented more than 25 years ago: "Telematics, as opposed to electricity, will not carry inert electric current but information, and that means power" (p. 11).

If there is any hope it lies in the naiveté of this approach. The strategists who want to produce new technologies and borderless education, the Trojan horse of globalization, are forgetting one essential fact, as pointed out by Wolton (2000): "The most important thing is the way in which each culture personalizes a technological advance according to its own specific social, mental and cultural universe; anthropologists have been demonstrating this for a long time now" (p. 128). After all it is important to remember that the telephone was invented as a means of broadcasting operas and that a respectable Catholic provincial paper in France, *Les Dernières Nouvelles d'Alsace*, inadvertently initiated the development of sex forums on the Minitel network. Each culture can divert and subvert any technological device to respond to its own deeper needs.

Thus it is legitimate to explore the way this appropriation of technology, deliberately represented in the media and politics as a challenge to academic institutions, is negotiated by administrators and faculty within universities. What common features and what idiosyncrasies emerge among academics in the four countries in this study? All are subject to various pressures of differing intensity, for instance incitements from their institutions sometimes guided by a cost-effectiveness logic; pressure from political authorities always obsessed by the idea of lagging behind in a technological revolution; and pressure from students ready to submit to the heady promises of global modernism and who confuse the accumulation of information with the acquisition of knowledge.

In this chapter we attempt to identify how academics, faced with new technologies and these multiple pressures, are beginning to integrate them into their work. We attempt to understand the impact of new technologies upon the schemata of their profession. We want to ascertain whether staff are making any distinction between the fields of teaching and research in their attitudes towards instructional technology, and what are their criteria for adopting or rejecting computer-mediated teaching in lectures or seminars. Do they consider these technologies as mere "additives," for instance comprising the same category as videotapes, or as a potential threat to their status as the holders and mediators of knowledge? Do they ask themselves the basic question: Is there a change of paradigm in the nature of learning and teaching when one enlists the help of the new technologies?

We limited the field of observation to the university, its policies, and sometimes the relevant ministry or other governing body in the case of public institutions. In this study the academics may be restricted at various levels by the directives issued by their institutions, the national educational policy, and the expectations of their society, regarding students' use of the Internet culture and their computer literacy. These restrictions may be experienced differently according to the person's status, employment contract, degree of responsibility, and dependence on or independence from the institution's hierarchy. French civil servants with permanent higher education employment would consider any move urging them to change their teaching methods and include new technologies as an intolerable interference. A U.S. academic from a private university with performance linked to results would be expected to have a different attitude.

Finally, we indicate an important limit to any conclusions we may draw from this study. While certain answers provide us with plenty of reported information about the happenings in practice, what actually happens cannot be easily measured. Most answers represent perceptions, and it would be dangerous to confuse these with objective reality.

ANALYSIS OF CASE STUDIES

Encouragement by University to Develop Online Education

The first question raises doubts about university policies and practices regarding online education because academics did not always know the explicit policies of their university regarding information and computer technology (ICT). We asked: Has your university encouraged you to develop new programs or teaching units that utilize the Internet, e-mail, satellite television, or other forms of "new" technologies? In this instance we are not evaluating the institutional policy but the way it is perceived. Therefore it is necessary to provide some information regarding the different contexts where this question was asked in order to shed proper light on the replies.

Avignon

At Avignon the infrastructure exists, for instance all the buildings are wired, every academic's office has potential Internet access, and the lecture halls are properly equipped. On the policy-making level, the president, a computer scientist, has integrated the new technologies to a high level where administrative practices are concerned—this specific domain is under his authority—but he has never outlined any policy regarding the pedagogic use of ICT. He has given staff members specific responsibility for the new technologies; however, there is no evidence of their influence and they have had no palpable effect.[3] All of this should be borne in mind when we analyze the responses. The first observation, when determining whether respondents identify a corporate policy of encouragement to use new technologies, is that a significant proportion of responses is positive. This is rather surprising as no such encouragement actually exists insofar as teaching is concerned. Moreover, this supposed encouragement is rarely perceived as a form of trespassing. The legendary attachment of French academics to the notion of total liberty in teaching methods led us to expect the opposite. The following response is illustrative of those who insist that the choice of usage is left solely to the initiative of the teacher and not the institution; however, this group very much comprises the minority.

It is the formulation of the question that is poor, because in fact it isn't them, not the university, that encourages. For example, in geography we are teaching satellite image analysis. It is something we have done for a long time. (Avignon, Junior, Male, Academic, Social Sciences)

In other words, it is not a deliberate university policy that decides the usage of educational technology by academics. A finer analysis of the responses shows that there is a consensus concerning the idea of a desirable availability of teaching tools and technical equipment. Thus the possibility of having personal access to the Internet and e-mail is clearly appreciated, but it is perceived as a sign of improved facilities and working conditions that are not linked to their responses regarding significant changes to teaching practices.

There is an implicit encouragement. Here, since we are in the new buildings, we are all connected to the Internet, to electronic mail, to e-mail. Therefore, there is a certain kind of inducement in that way. So far, in my teaching I have not received any particular encouragement. (Avignon, Junior, Male, Academic, Professional School)

Not surprisingly, a few respondents regret that the university is not doing enough in terms of providing technological equipment.

To begin with, there are not enough classrooms or even offices equipped with Internet access, even though we moved into new buildings. (Avignon, Senior, Female, Academic, Social Sciences)

There is a feeling that the discourse about the lack of funding for equipment is a way of avoiding the real issue, that is, the change in teaching methods that new technologies would entail. Very few pose the problem in didactic terms. Overall there is a noticeable gap between a largely favorable discourse towards the new equipment, that is, the seduction of the Internet and the utility of e-mail in the professional sphere, and a silence or reticence concerning the pedagogical implications the new technologies may engender. Respondents accept the idea that the institution has the right and duty to create the material conditions of pedagogical renewal based on new technologies, yet the majority does not acknowledge the institution's right to accomplish this directly. Any such right is further weakened by the academics involved who do not appear to have a clear idea of what form any such renewal would take.

Oslo

Oslo falls midway between Avignon, on one end, and Boston College and Twente, on the other end. The majority of respondents at Oslo feel that there is encouragement or at least the infrastructure available to use the new technologies (22 out of 32 responses); however, there does not appear to be much use of the technology in teaching.

Yes, I think the university wants it and we have to use our competence in teaching, especially in distance teaching and further education. Although we have the infrastructure, still a lot of our teaching is very traditional lecturing. (Oslo, Senior Male, Academic, Professional School)

Nevertheless, there are some academics who are already using the new technologies:

Some work is going on the Internet and we have a contract with the ministry to use the Internet with science teachers. We are also using the television and two-way communication. We are going to test it out this year. (Oslo, Senior, Male, Academic, Professional School)

In contrast, about one third feel that the university does not encourage them and that if there are any developments in that direction, it has to be on their own time.

No, the university does not encourage us. It has to be my own curiosity, I think. But it takes time to develop the skills. (Oslo, Senior, Female, Academic, Sciences)

The responses to the next question on whether there are negative or positive consequences to using the new technologies in teaching suggest that there will be considerable resistance to actually taking the time to learn to use the new technologies because the vast majority identified negative consequences in using the Internet for teaching. Unless there is increased pressure to learn or encouragement through reduced teaching loads or other incentives, it is not likely that academics at Oslo will be developing much teaching online.

Boston College

The case in Boston College is noticeably different, and it illustrates the technological gap between French and U.S. universities. The network infrastructure within the university currently provides a high-speed connection to all classrooms, offices, and rooms in halls of residence, and offers access to campus network resources for off-campus users. However, this is only one aspect of Boston College's determined commitment to technology. In addition, the university hired a new vice president for technology who envisages a wireless campus, a policy currently being implemented. She envisages students sitting in the quadrangle with their laptops, reading their e-mails, conversing with each other, and being productive in and out of the classroom. She believes the Internet is a wonderful teaching tool and would like faculty to engage in a form of teaching that differs from traditional methods and incorporates the various technological resources offered.

The university is implementing *Desktop 2000*, a comprehensive strategy for maintaining the distributed computing resources of Boston College. The scope of the project and its long-term dimensions are obvious signs of a deliberate policy from the establishment targeting information resources. Information Technology, which manages Boston College's computing, communications, and electronic information resources, defines its objectives as providing "leadership in shaping technology plans and strategies to support the mission and goals of the university" (Desktop 2000 Web site). Additional facilities are offered to students in the Student Learning and Support Center, for instance access to a variety of software applications and assistance in solving hardware and software problems.

When asked if the institution was encouraging the new technologies, respondents from Boston College almost unanimously identified this comprehensive strategy. The overwhelming response was that there was encouragement (33 responses) and this was demonstrated by the existing infrastructure, the technical assistance, and the equipment available to faculty and students (31 responses). There were no negative comments or dissenting voices.

We've had a lot of emphasis on technology for at least the last six years. We have had lots of workshops and our building was the first "smart" building. It is only now that there is talk in the technology plan of evaluating us on our use of technology. The resources have been available but most of us have used them primarily in our research and not in our teaching. (Boston College, Junior, Female, Academic, Professional School)

I think there is a lot of encouragement for the use of technology. We have a couple of people who are very interested in that. They have some grants. They have done a lot with faculty development work. They have done a lot to get faculty on board with trying to use more technology. So I think it's a goal and I think there's been support for trying to do that. (Boston College, Senior, Male, Academic, Professional School)

Most respondents are conscious of strong incentives on the part of the institution and approve them. In contrast to French academics, they did not question the institution's role in this respect, nor did they feel anyone was trespassing on their prerogatives.

However, one incidental point deserves particular comment. Though the question only mentioned the role of the university, some respondents noted three roles rather than two, that is, the institution, teachers, and students. However, they did not agree on the position of the third role, the students.

I think our students are pushing more than the faculty, although the university has made a big commitment to technology. (Boston College, Senior Female, Academic, Social Sciences)

I have interactive learning through the Internet now. I have a discussion group with both my classes that I use, but you know, my students are very reluctant to use it unless they are absolutely required to do it. They don't like doing that. They are conscious of how they write and what they say. (Boston College, Senior Female, Academic, Social Sciences)

This aspect is certainly beyond the scope of this study; nonetheless, two questions must be posed: "How significant is the role of students, supported by their institution, in this increased pressure to use educational technologies? To what extent do they see themselves as customers of educational services, and as such how far do they feel entitled to demand standards of efficiency and modernity of which ICT is a part?" Even in the U.S. context a response may not be as unanimous as it appears at first glance, but the image of this pressure is apparently present in the minds of some academics.

My daughter and her cohorts in high school have been on the Web for years. When she does research she's used to going on the Web, she e-mails her friends all over the country, and my point is that when she gets to college, she's going to have an expectation of students and faculty. So we have a competitive necessity there to be responsive to the emerging technologies and appropriate applications of those technologies. The challenge for us is how do we maintain our dedication to a personal learning community and use the emerging technologies to enhance that aspect of Boston? (Boston College, Senior, Male, Manager)

The notion that universities have "a competitive necessity to be responsive to new technologies" is not shared by all respondents but is illustrative of a trend in thought at Boston College. A further point raised by this quote concerns the assumption that it is not easy to reconcile this drive towards technopedagogy and the dedication to a personal learning community, as if the two commitments were mutually exclusive.

Twente

The University of Twente, which describes itself as "the entrepreneurial university," is similar to Boston College in terms of the stance and reaction of respondents, though they are perhaps less emphatic in Twente. The infrastructure exists and is considered to be a right, all students have access to the Internet. In addition, there is a Center for Telematics and Information Technology that has the status of a research center and a department of educational science under the title of Educational Science and Technology. A team of researchers formed the Dutch contingent for an international survey on computer use in education. One respondent mentioned a university committee whose stated aim is the development of educational technology.

I'm the head of the committee that tries to further the use of the Internet and computer-assisted instruction. I think now we are trying to put the entire curriculum in terms of the electronic learning environment. We also have part-time courses for people using these ideas for vocational training skills. We also have courses in public administration, sociology, and public economics. We will offer them through the Internet and we hope to start that in September of next year. (Twente, Senior, Male, Academic, Social Sciences)

These convergent elements show the explicit, unambiguous policy within Twente, for instance the assimilation of new technologies into the student curriculum. In the previous quotation, the expression "electronic learning environment" is significant as it illustrates a revealing change of position: the learner is now at the center. Twente does not cease with the construction of technical infrastructure, but also encourages the development of innovative pedagogic projects based on the new technologies.

Yes, we have a system here called Teletop or a telelearning project and now it's for first- and second-year students. They are given their education through the Internet or through this Teletop system. And in the next year that will expand to the whole curriculum so that each teacher here has to work with ICT or the Internet to do their teaching. (Twente, Junior, Male Academic, Professional School)

The majority of respondents (27 out of 31) are aware of this situation, but as is often the case, the most interesting point emerges indirectly from the findings. Those who express a certain skepticism regarding university policy are not conservative or indifferent, but are academics who clearly state they do not need encouragement from the institution to develop technological projects.

I don't think the university is encouraging it. We are encouraging ourselves. We are, for example, also a center for Holland on the international study of computer use in education. And for that study we have built a Web site. Then it becomes very easy to exchange data files, reports, chapters, and things like that. (Twente, Junior, Male Academic, Professional School)

I don't know if the university has pushed us, but we're very active in that domain. It's because of our own interests. In about 80 to 90 percent of our research projects, information communication technology plays a prominent role. All the time we're trying to explore what the potential of information communication technology is for making curriculum changes, and what are the implications for the curriculum and teacher development approaches and things like that. (Twente, Senior, Male Academic, Professional School)

Even though this is not the position of the majority it does indicate a certain activism in the technological domain. This is not nearly as clear in the other universities, although replies to the following question may lead to a qualification of this statement.

Consequences of Using the Internet for Teaching

We asked: What do you see as the positive and negative consequences of teaching students who do not come to the university, using the Internet for the entire course? This question is radical as it specifically focuses on teaching students exclusively through the intermediary of the Internet, excluding personal contact with a teacher. In essence, respondents were asked to state their views on the virtual classroom, bearing in mind the traditional model. The question refers to students but does not specify the type of students. The arguments that respondents used to qualify their replies[4] were interesting, considering the three main criteria: What type of teaching, for instance lectures, seminars, or tutorials, can or cannot be transferred onto the Internet? What type of subject, for instance technological subjects, humanities, or so on, is best taught on the Internet? What type of students, first year, advanced, or mature, may be capable of learning via the Internet?

Before embarking on a detailed analysis of these replies, a preliminary observation should be mentioned. In Twente there is committed activism towards educational technology, although almost none of the respondents had experienced teaching a course exclusively through the Internet. If e-teaching can be perceived as a cardinal virtue, it is only in the sense that it is more talked about than practiced.

From this perspective the situation in all four universities is virtually identical, which means that the responses obtained are largely speculative. Therefore we comment upon representations of potential teaching practices, and analysis of the responses is delicate. The answers of one respondent suggest an opposition on principle but also state the advantages of the new methods. In addition, it is hazardous to interpret silences. For instance, very few respondents mention the idea that developing computer literacy among students is a civic duty for modern universities. The following quote is an unexpected exception.

To educate students without learning how to use a computer, even for normal administrative and educational work, would be a bad education. To go into working life today, they need these skills. (Oslo, Senior, Female, Manager)

Should the conclusion be that the cohort of university students takes for granted computer literacy, or that the academics are not preoccupied by the necessary skills for working life? What can be asserted is that the global balance between opposition or reticence and the perception of advantages varies significantly between situations. Dutch and U.S. academics are less reluctant than French and Oslo academics. At Boston College the answers are almost evenly balanced between those that mention the benefits of teaching through the Internet and those that question its efficiency. In Twente skepticism is marginally stronger, whereas in Avignon and Oslo the majority of respondents see disadvantages or restrict acceptability to very specific conditions.

As expected, the pros and cons were similar in all four universities: the proportions vary but the ingredients are the same. First, there is a staunch belief that face-to-face interaction is a prerequisite in teaching.

I think that one must live with one's time, but on the other hand, I am convinced that nothing will replace the relationship between student and teacher. (Avignon, Senior, Male, Academic, Professional School)

I never would teach totally by the Internet. Somehow the basis of teaching is still interaction between people. And I don't want a virtual classroom. No, I think in terms of teaching that some human contact is definitely in order. Students want instantaneous information and that I see as a problem. This expectation that you can somehow push a button and information will become instantaneously available to you is problematic. So much scholarship involves digging and discovery, and not everything is on the Internet. (Boston College, Junior, Female, Academic, Social Sciences)

There is at least something a little bit sociable about coming to class. I mean the chatter we have before the lecture starts and even in the large lecture, there is some give and take with the students. So I worry that students might be spending too much time just at their machines. (Boston College, Senior, Female, Academic, Social Sciences)

If a program is totally on the Internet, then I think that there would certainly be negative aspects to it. I feel it's very important that in the course there is also the face of a human person. A good teacher can enthuse you about the subject. That is my own experience. (Twente, Senior, Male, Administrator, Social Sciences)

I don't think it can substitute for a living conversation. (Oslo, Senior, Female, Academic, Social Sciences)

The five preceding quotations are variations of the same familiar theme: that humanity is the essence of teaching. These are summarized in a vibrant, highly emotional article recently published by a U.S. academic in the Australian press: "No computer on the face of this earth can replace the affirmation that your child receives—no computer can generate the sparkle in your child's eyes—when I affirm the intellectual power of their remarks. Although it is perhaps true that human beings can learn under any condition, the fact remains that learning at its very best is quintessentially an interpersonal experience" (Thomas, 2001, p. 4).

In addition, what most academics explain at length is succinctly summed up by two French researchers: "Human intervention is a necessary aid to an individual's construction of knowledge" (Mounyol & Milon, 2000, p. 189). However, if responses of this type are analyzed further, a less controversial element is found and merits attention. This concerns the notion that the construction of knowledge has a social dimension that operates not only through dialogue with the teacher but also through exchanges with other learners arising during class sessions.

Teaching or learning is a social process. It is not only an individual process. And it is most important for the teacher to be there, actually there, at critical moments. (Oslo, Senior, Male, Academic, Social Sciences)

E-teaching is reproached as it fails to recognize the social and collective dimension of learning and leaves the learners on their own in front of an interface.

I think it is very important for students to have social contact and this will never be possible by using the Internet. (Twente, Junior, Female, Academic, Social Sciences)

It may be claimed that educational technologies offer the means to re-intro-
duce this collective dimension into the learning process through forums or collective projects. Nevertheless, the fear expressed by these academics is legitimate
since it indicates the limit of the technophiles' obsessive preoccupation with individualized learning.

Personally I'm very positive about the effects of the use of ICT on learning as a whole
and the effectiveness of learning. It's important that students get more opportunities to
have their individual learning plans so that they can learn at their own time, at their own
pace, and at their own speed. And I think ICT can contribute to that kind of arrangement
of the learning process. (Twente, Junior, Academic, Professional School)

In the replies of these academics are the beginnings of a possible paradox or
insoluble equation. Clearly there are advantages of using education technologies for handling large numbers of students arriving at the university.

It is useful for students since it increases the possibility for a larger number of students
to get a university education. (Oslo, Senior, Male, Academic, Professional School)

In other words, the possible pedagogic benefits to be drawn from the use of
ICT could be linked to scale. This is a familiar argument illustrated contrariwise
by an academic from Boston College who demonstrates a certain cynicism regarding economic realities.

The jury is still out about whether the use of technology in teaching will greatly enhance
the effectiveness of student learning, particularly in the kinds of classes that we offer,
which are typically not very large classes. Boston prides itself on not having huge, mas-
sive undergraduate classes like other big state universities in the U.S. (Boston College,
Senior, Male, Academic, Professional School)

Clearly the message is that mass teaching may have recourse to technology,
but elite teaching can afford the luxury of human mediation. On the one hand,
there is ready-to-wear teaching, and on the other, there is haute couture.

Very few respondents perceive the problem in terms of real situations and
tend to observe the use of digital technology from an ideal point of view. An exception is the clearsightedness of this young colleague from Twente.

I mean, first of all we tend to compare distance education with the best of face-to-face education, which we hardly ever offer. The best we have is probably a small-scale tutorial
with a feminist professor and how many students have had that? But if you compare the
average distance education with what our students have on average—that is to say, a big
lecturing class with little or no personal attention, face-to-face but no interaction between
students, although they're sitting next to one another—that would be a more fair comparison and a good sort of debate. (Twente, Junior, Female, Academic, Social Sciences)

This point is indeed central, though frequently ignored, that the human interaction engendered by face-to-face teaching is largely absent from the first
years of studies in the U.S. and European state universities. This is the very heart

of the paradox, clearly illustrated by the situation in French universities. Iron-ically, it is the model of the big lecture, excluding virtually all verbal interaction, that dominates French university teaching, and it is precisely in the first years that respondents clearly express a refusal to teach using the Internet because it excludes verbal interaction!

Should the conclusion be that undergraduates have enough intellectual au-tonomy and self-reliance to learn through a lecture but not through an inter-active program on the Internet? Or that the spoken word has a seminal value that the screen apparently lacks? Or is the note-taking of a student in a big lec-ture hall more active than the same student interacting with a learning program through an interface?

If the problem is addressed from a graduate and postgraduate perspective, the same paradox appears with the terms reversed. For instance, a large proportion of respondents agree that advanced students, sometimes physically a long way from the university, have the necessary intellectual independence to benefit from a teaching system that uses educational technologies. They have enough criti-cal judgment to evaluate the sources of information and do not require any per-manent methodological assistance.

I think there is a difference between educating undergraduate students or older learners. For older learners, this is perfect. They know what they want to learn. They can study and read on their own. They put forward their own questions and discussion by e-mail with their fellow students and with the tutors. But for first and second year students, it's different. It's better for them to have interaction, real contact between the teacher and the student. (Twente, Junior, Male, Academic, Social Sciences)

These are precisely the students who benefit from tutorials and stimulating intellectual exchanges with experts in the context of conventional teaching sit-uations.

Thus the basic point revealed by this study is that most academics have a cu-rious, self-deceiving attitude. They pretend not to see that the model to which they are legitimately attached is a mere caricature of itself for quite a few un-dergraduates in state universities. These same academics largely refuse to envisage interactivity as an alternative, albeit an imperfect one, to the human interaction that is so often a mere parody of real exchange.

There may be a simple explanation for this strange, deliberate behavior by academics. They find it difficult to accept "the epistemological and cognitive con-sequences of a new system of memory" (Jeanneret, 2000, p. 24). If they sanc-tioned these new ways of fixing and diffusing the knowledge they produce, this would question the status of the academic's word. The breakthrough of a new form of registering thought is bound to have some inevitable institutional im-plications for a profession whose power and recognition have always been based on the spoken word; however, it is too early to measure them. Among the more open-minded academics, this decidedly vast question provoked further comment on the cost effectiveness and flexibility of these technologies.

It takes so much time for me to put everything onto the Internet and I don't think it would be worth it. (Oslo, Junior, Female, Academic, Social Sciences)

I've put so much time into preparing materials but they are still not as good as the real teacher. I think there's a place for maybe 5 to 10 percent of a program using the Internet, but there it stops. (Twente, Senior, Female, Academic, Social Sciences)

Well, one big disadvantage is that an electronic teaching environment is so expensive to create, and in your design you may have a major flaw and it's very hard to be flexible; you are stuck with it. When you have a teaching team, the investment costs are low and the flexibility is much higher. The other part is that we do not really know how the learning process is going on. (Twente, Senior, Male, Manager)

Presumably these academics have personal experiences and have made an effort to conceive the demands of the interactive teaching program. Their analysis of the situation does not extend to its underlying economic conclusion, although the use of the term "investment" in their responses is revealing. Thus the conclusion, which has already been evoked and is familiar to all in the e-learning business, is that investments are only profitable when they are made on a large scale. Once again there is a confrontation with the problem of globalization and the concentration of knowledge sources. The respondents rarely contributed these types of analyses and more frequently contributed the standard reactions of rejection or support. This is because few academics actually measured the implications of this situation. The following quotes were found after much sifting.

The new technology has its own type of logic and you have to be familiar with it in order to utilize it effectively. I think some people use old-fashioned types of teaching with the new technology and it doesn't really work. (Oslo, Senior, Male, Academic, Professional School)

The text of my course on new technologies takes up one or two disks. I could put it on an Internet site if I wanted to, but that is no solution. We need a new pedagogical approach. So far, I haven't yet found the didactic strategy that fits the new technology. (Avignon, Senior, Male, Academic, Professional School)

This is the real root of the problem and is often hard to get near. A wider consensus of opinion accepts the use of the Internet as a complementary information source that comes after the information supplied by academics or books.

It gives you access to a lot of resources that you otherwise wouldn't have access to. There are databases where they could easily click into and get out important literature. (Oslo, Senior, Male, Academic, Social Sciences)

Not surprisingly there are many reservations expressed in the face of this nonvalidated information.

On the Web you can find lots of good stuff, but there is also a lot of garbage out there. When I set a text, I know the edition and I know what it is and that it has a good introduction, and the stuff on the Web is of mixed quality. (Boston College, Junior, Female, Academic, Social Sciences)

This invites two remarks: 1) the university as an institution has not totally abandoned its suspicious attitude towards sources of knowledge emanating from anywhere other than itself; and 2) the university as an educational body has not fully grasped the extent of its new mission, which is to make students more critical and autonomous where these new sources are concerned. This is where the most fundamental change wrought by the ICT resides. In a world where information was scarce the university as an institution had hardly any competitors. As the Boston College colleague remarks, "When I set a text, I know the edition," but when information abounds, coming from countless and unverifiable sources, it is no use blaming the media. On the contrary, a new stance must be adopted. Students must be taught to master the tools allowing access to information through search engines and information retrieval syntax, and must adopt a critical approach regarding these sources. In addition, the university must realize that teaching students to ask the right questions is more important than helping them know the right answers. On this particular point, our colleagues are silent.

Impact of ICT on Workloads

The next question resides on less controversial ground. The goal is to understand to what extent academics use Internet and e-mail for teaching purposes and whether it has increased their workload. Initially, if a rough qualitative indicator is relied upon, for instance the 50 percent increase in the number of e-mails exchanged in the Avignon server[5] between September 1999 and September 2000, then the replies to the question must be treated with particular caution. In this domain practices evolve so quickly that any conclusions drawn from this survey are no doubt obsolete already. Hence certain global trends will be highlighted. At Boston College and Twente the use of e-mail for teaching purposes is taken for granted and is current practice. In Oslo certain reservations were expressed, particularly for the undergraduate population, whereas in Avignon, barely one third of the academics questioned included this as an avowed practice in their teaching.

Rather than insisting on quantitative, relatively unimportant details, it is important to attempt to pinpoint the impact this practice has on those who have adopted it. Once again, dealing with large numbers appears to be the dividing line, and the argument put forward is now frequent and familiar. That is, the e-mail is an interpersonal means of communication, founded on the one-to-one model, which immediately puts it out of bounds for a large number of students. The flip side of this is that a relatively small number of academics use e-mail as a tool for the diffusion of information, and they do so on the basis of a one-to-many model. This completely reverses the previous argument by asserting that the more students there are, the more effective the medium appears.

With a click I can e-mail a class of 293 students. That's quite effective. (Boston College, Senior, Male, Academic, Social Sciences)

I can communicate a message to my class very quickly. I can, for example, put my notes up on the Web so that they can download my outline and my graphics for class. (Boston College, Senior, Male, Administrator, Social Sciences)

An example of the phenomenon using new technologies for purposes other than those for which they were originally designed is evident here. A further question asked is whether or not the advantages of e-mail encourage students to ask many trivial, time-consuming questions. Some respondents think this is the case.

Yes, I think it has increased the workload because now we get questions we wouldn't have gotten in the past. So there's more communication. Of course, in the past there was more direct communication but I think more communication has produced extra questions and extra work. (Twente, Junior, Male, Academic, Social Sciences)

Respondents also commented on the substitution effect.

I now live on e-mail and get them endlessly. I'm not sure it has increased my workload. I could easily spend two hours a day on e-mail but I don't. I used to come in and it was not unusual for me to have 25 phone messages. I barely would have five now. It is all on e-mail. I think my workload has just shifted around. (Boston College, Junior, Female, Academic, Professional School)

No, it doesn't increase or decrease. It's part of your working hours. It improves efficiency of communication. It's sometimes a burden. Sometimes you get a lot of e-mails and other times you may have gotten a lot of visitors or a lot of phone calls. Certainly for me, it's more substitution than increasing my workload. (Twente, Senior, Male, Administrator)

A surfacing argument is that every time a new media appears there is comment that it will replace the old one. In reality the new media creates new communication practices that do not replace the old ones. However, this case study does not enable any clear-cut conclusions, because the appropriation of e-mail by academics and students alike cannot be analyzed independently of the way they generally communicate. The models of teacher and student relationships are specific to each national culture, each establishment, or each department. Information technology undergraduates in a U.S. university do not have the same type of relationship with their teachers as classics students in a French university. The use of e-mail simply reflects preexisting patterns, practices, and expectations, no doubt putting a certain emphasis on them because they make the teacher more accessible.

However, there is one new aspect in this mode of communication, linked to temporality and the rhythm of exchanges. Whether liked or not, academics cannot pretend to ignore that students expect greater reactivity from them.

One of my graduate students gave me a two-page memo of his model and I had read it over the weekend, so I said, "Fine, let's meet on Tuesday." And what I did is I e-mailed him the seven questions I had. I said, "Come prepared to answer these questions." Now if I hadn't done that, what could it mean? He'd come in and I'd have to verbalize and he'd have to think about it and we'd take two hours, whereas this way it took me ten minutes to send an e-mail and he would come in here and we'll do it in half an hour. (Boston College, Senior, Male, Academic, Social Sciences)

It means, incidentally, that I must check my electronic box even in August [vacation time]. And that has changed my work conditions considerably. Before, we thought that from mid-July, we were on vacation (what you did with your vacation, beach or research, was your own affair). You had no one demanding to know what you were doing. You were free. That is no longer the case, because you have theses to direct and your electronic box is full even until the end of August. (Avignon, Senior, Male, Academic, Professional School)

This final reaction is directly in line with the general analysis from sociologists concerning these new media. Real time is a modern form of technological slavery, as portable phones, e-mail, and laptop computers with modems make you available everywhere, and at every moment, and provoke constraints and obligations, instead of the publicized freedom they are supposed to generate.

Any University Policy about ICT and Teaching Workloads?

One further point needed to be investigated. We asked: How far have the universities taken into account the new technological dimensions of the teaching profession, and is there a workload policy concerning the use of ICT for teaching purposes?

Underneath the innocent technical surface, this question is asking for the definition of the workload for an academic. Should this be measured exclusively in terms of teaching hours, as in the French case, or are there other criteria to be considered? It has been shown that the investment from a human level into the preparation of multimedia interactive teaching material has two specific characteristics:

It requires an enormous amount of time, out of proportion to a normal teaching load. Brabazon (2001) writes from her experience: "*Somebody* needs to design the content and layout. *Somebody* needs to write the Web pages. *Somebody* needs to ensure that hypertext links are up-to-date. *Somebody* needs to create evaluative criteria. *Somebody* needs to administer the students' results" (p. 3).

It cannot be conceived as the work of one individual as it requires a range of different skills from the members of a working team, for instance an ergonomist, a pedagogy specialist, a developer, a graphics designer, and a specialist in the particular discipline involved.

With this in mind, what type of contract or agreement, either formal or informal, can the academic make with the institution and what is the policy of the institution?

This question was not perceived as relevant. This was clearly the case in Avignon where the majority responded with a simple "no," or considered the question vaguely incongruous, doubting that such a policy could even exist. This was a predictable attitude as it is hard to imagine how the university could have a policy that took seriously a practice that is still extremely marginal. The institutionalization of the new technologies and their inclusion in any professional duties of academics is far off in all four universities. It is not surprising that at Twente and Boston College the approach is different, proven by the relatively high proportion of academics (45 percent and 35 percent respectively) that recognize their institution is taking an interest in the question. Yet neither of these universities appears to have an overall policy regarding the definition of an academic's workload. The department concerned is responsible for this, and thus the decisions appear to lack transparency and sometimes coherency.

I don't think the university recognizes what our workloads are even *without* technology. So I really don't think they are going to notice *with* technology. To my knowledge they haven't discussed a policy concerning workloads. (Boston College, Junior, Female, Academic, Professional School)

The university gives a lot of autonomy to departments about workloads. They don't even have a standard course load. I mean they are willing to accept that this person will be doing three courses a year and this other person will be doing five courses a year. The person the department thinks is heavily involved in research will probably teach less. It's pretty much left up to the department. (Boston College, Senior, Male, Academic, Social Sciences)

A reduction in the workload of academics is the most frequent form of compensation granted to those who decide to embark upon innovative projects involving educational technology. This is not a rule but is negotiated within the department.

I submitted a proposal and was awarded a grant for three years to introduce certain technology into the classroom. I was given a one-course reduction in each of the three years, not each semester but one for each of the three years of the grant. So that was a recognition that I was able to get. The dean gave this, not my department chair. (Boston College, Senior, Female, Academic, Social Sciences)

Such reductions in workload are minimal and quite out of proportion with the real workload demanded by the creation of interactive multimedia teaching modules. Hence there is a discrepancy between the institution's declared policy encouraging academics to explore the potentialities of educational technologies and an almost total absence of any application of this policy in real terms. There is a simple explanation for this. Departmental autonomy means the universities are largely deprived of any real power to direct and, above all, implement pedagogical reform.

I don't think there is real recognition in the sense that it would imply that you would have a decreased workload somewhere else and this is certainly not happening. So in a formal way there would be some kind of recognition, but in fact there's no real recognition. (Twente, Junior, Male, Academic, Social Sciences)

However, a single exception concerns financial incentives, in the form of stipends or grants, rather similar to the financing of research projects. These remain the prerogative of the university or the ministry.

There are incentives in the sense of summer teaching grants. I think people who had proposed to do something with technology would be viewed favorably for these kinds of incentives. They've just announced some $15,000 teaching grants for the summer. (Boston College, Senior, Male, Academic, Social Sciences)

For example, Avignon is now signing an important research contract concerning a virtual campus in the field of culture. It involves heavy funding, but the academics producing the course material will only receive a minor reduction in their workloads. It is obvious that this policy of financial incentives may not be adequate, since it may be people or more time that are needed.

Yes, sure, sure. We have a policy document on telematics in education. And we recognize that it will be a major investment in hours of teaching staff. Investment is usually counted in guilders, but it's not guilders that you need all the time; it is people on the job. You have to give them some room to train themselves to gain new knowledge. And so you need more people in between to help them with their daily workload. (Twente, Senior, Male, Administrator)

Apparently the awareness of the institution has not reached this stage. The reason for this may be that in most universities only two criteria are used to determine an academic's workload, that is, the number of hours spent in front of the students and the number of articles or books published. However, the personal investment involved in the creation of interactive e-teaching modules does not follow this logic.

If this reality is not rapidly taken into account by the universities, they could find themselves in an uncomfortable situation. The business sector will hire academics and invest the skills and materials necessary for the implementation of such projects, provided they are economically feasible. This will lead to the development of widespread globalization strategies and the creation of an e-knowledge market. Ironically, this could happen through the unwitting collaboration of universities, as they participate in joint ventures where these types of policies will be outside their control.

CONCLUSION

This last remark enables a recentering on the major theme within this book and a reformulation of conclusions concerning educational technologies in the perspective of globalization. Does this notion really exist in institutional strategy and academic thinking? Is it viewed as a challenge or a threat? Twente and

Boston College have apparently assimilated the phenomenon of educational technologies more extensively, though not necessarily more deeply, than Oslo and particularly Avignon. However, two constant factors can be observed.

On the one hand, institutions are in advance, technologically, of the people who work there. All universities have a policy regarding equipment and infrastructure that enables staff to access worldwide electronic information sources and communicate easily internally and externally. This is one of the avowed aims of all universities. In other words, they provide the tools, encourage their use, and sometimes reward the pioneers who use them, yet this never appears to influence the conventional definitions of the academic workload. Regarding pedagogy, the position of the different universities is more cautious. There are statements of principle, general policy documents, the creation of small experimental units, but no interference. The directive attitude of the institution stops at the entrance to the department, or at any rate to the lecture hall. It may be argued that the universities are becoming aware of the risk associated with adopting such an unambitious approach. "If people can get the same education in Sri Lanka as they can get in Boston, why pay to come to Boston?" This somewhat provocative question would certainly be formulated differently by a European academic, but it clearly shows that a global market for university education does exist and that ideas of national "catchment areas" or captive markets make no sense in the age of networks. On the other hand, this awareness faces a certain degree of human resistance, largely based on an image of the teaching profession that is difficult to reconcile with the use of educational technologies. There is something paradoxical about this resistance of academics, insofar as it is based on their attachment to a model of the teacher-student relationship that has largely ceased to exist, at least for undergraduates.

However, there are signs of less conservative attitudes. Whenever the use of educational technologies is prompted by sheer pragmatism or even common sense, they are used due to their efficiency, user-friendliness, and power of accessibility. This is true, for instance, of the pedagogical use of mailing lists with attachments. Academics also explore the Web, albeit tentatively and cautiously, not to say diffidently, as a worldwide multimedia digital library. Finally, some pioneers attempt to integrate self-made interactive materials in their teaching strategies, often with a trial and error approach. They are not representative of their institutions and are likely in the near future to compete with sophisticated ready-made products requiring heavy investments and only profitable for electronic publishers on a global market. Clearly the contenders do not play in the same league. Indeed, most academics are not even aware that there is a contest. They still view universities as enjoying some extraterritorial privilege, which is a dangerous form of delusion. If academics are attached to a certain set of values, they will not preserve them by rejecting educational technologies, but by enlisting them on their side. AOL, Microsoft or Vivendi Universal are not barbarians. They have no intention of destroying universities; but simply with the unwitting compliance of academics, they will bypass them.

NOTES

1. The increasing practice of downloading large files through broadband networks will reinforce this phenomenon and will reduce production and delivery costs for the use of network resources, where costs are steadily decreasing.

2. In the most favorable cases, a minimum effort is being made towards "localization" or tailoring products for a particular culture.

3. Two successive academics were in charge of ICT, which was largely nominal, and they developed no specific projects except for representing the university in regional or national committees or seminars.

4. The advantages, disadvantages, or reasons for use quoted by respondents may be compared to the list suggested in an online survey on e-learning; see http://www. quadratin.fr/noirsurblanc/.

5. See http://www.crir.univ-avignon.fr/melstats.html.

Chapter 8

Conclusion: What Is the Future for Universities on the Global Stage?

We conclude this book by reflecting on our findings and on the main question we investigated: To what extent have globalizing practices penetrated the four case study universities? We also present the views of our respondents on the future of their universities. Finally, we contemplate the possible consequences of globalization for universities in general.

This book began with the premise that globalization has an impact on higher education. We noted that globalization has different meanings for different people and hence should be handled cautiously. To some, globalization is equated with neoliberal competition and managerialism. Elements of this image are high private investments for those attending universities, businesslike approaches to the management of higher education institutions stressing effectiveness and efficiency, and a focus on profitable research activities rather than conducting research for the advancement of knowledge. This type of globalization is often critiqued by academics who fear the demise of traditional academic values that stress the collegial model of cooperation instead of competition and a search for knowledge for its own sake. However, other academics argue that competition is necessary to attain quality in research and education, another highly appreciated academic value. Other types of globalization appear less harmful at first sight. For instance, easier and faster communication around the world can be interpreted as an advantage. Yet the disadvantages of information technology should not be neglected. The tremendous growth of information and communication casts some doubts, for instance, on the reliability of the information.

These preliminary explorations revealed that closer investigation was needed to fairly assess globalization, given the variety of interpretations, presumed benefits, and drawbacks associated with this phenomenon. We chose to move beyond the theoretical debates concerning globalization and instead explore the actual occurrences of globalizing practices in different contexts. Implicit in our expectations was that varying interpretations affect the behavior and views of those involved, and also that the particular context, including university, department, and position, was of importance. The central question in this book concerned the responses of academics and administrators to globalizing practices in different contexts. How do they act and what are their views on globalizing practices?

In answering this question four case studies were conducted, in which we interviewed 131 staff members at universities in France (University of Avignon), the Netherlands (University of Twente), Norway (University of Oslo), and the United States (Boston College). These countries and universities differ considerably in a number of respects. Generally, the countries differ in their social and economic policies. Specifically, the higher education systems differ in their academic traditions, participation rates, governance, and other aspects of their structures. The universities differ in their age, location, and size. Consequently, we gained much insight into the globalizing practices in respective university departments through the views of diverse staff members. There is a broad pallet of issues related to globalization. We decided to explore five: privatization and entrepreneurialism, governance, tenure, accountability, and information and communication technologies. The higher education literature shows that these issues are closely connected to the phenomenon of globalization. Furthermore, these elements were on the political agenda of the countries and institutions we visited.

MAIN FINDINGS

Privatization, Competition, and Entrepreneurialism

While all samples reported increased internal and external pressures to be more entrepreneurial, performance oriented, and accountable, fully developed competitive pressures are few and often resisted. In addition, fully competitive markets are still rare and collaborative efforts are still in their infancy, although consortia and other types of cooperation emerged over a decade ago.

In the three public universities, there was relatively less government funding, yet they still predominantly rely upon public funding, with modest increases in user pays, marginal private delivery and outsourcing to private firms, immature formal accountability mechanisms and undeveloped "consumer beware" attitudes, with little if any true deregulation. Most movement toward greater private competition has been pragmatic, rarely strategic. Many reform policies imitate others or follow leadership opinion makers, such as the OECD. However, when there is strong economic or political resistance or strong organizations, for example where unions are strong or the political culture supports public sector efforts, privatization is fragile, cyclical, and weak. The fragile character of privatization recently became evident after the events of September 11,

2001, arousing a debate regarding the disadvantages of privatization and the need for a renaissance of public control and regulation.

Governance

The higher education literature suggests that managerial ideologies are a globalizing practice and have aided the establishment of institutional regimes, for instance strengthened executive leadership. However, the analysis in Chapter 4 indicates at least two qualifications. First, there are significant differences between universities throughout the world, as evident in the universities in this study. Governance structures appear to be path dependent. Why should these varying institutions automatically mold their internal structures in the same direction when they are exposed to managerialism? Second, there are differences between, on the one hand, formal change and accompanying rhetoric and, on the other, everyday practice. Managerialism may be a talking point within many countries and universities, but has it actually affected daily policy making and management?

The case studies of the four universities clearly show a difference between formal rules and daily practices, and between imposed changes and everyday business. There is a tendency to strengthen executive leadership or to centralize certain aspects of decision making, but this has not automatically changed the role of academics in decision making. The depth that these changes have penetrated the universities is variable. In most, at the "shop floor" level moderate changes, if any, were perceived. However, Boston College, since the early 1970s, has become a very managed university with little faculty input into decision making beyond the departmental level.

A related conclusion drawn from the country reports and the four case studies concerned the importance of traditions within universities. Managerialism appears to have entered the universities to some extent; yet in the practice of selecting rulers the majority of respondents from all four universities indicate an inclination to maintain previously established procedures. At Boston College and Twente, tradition balances consultation with appointment to gain greater central effectiveness, while at Avignon and Oslo, tradition means that elections are sacrosanct and academics prefer to be involved in decision making. Managerialism as a broad ideology has not yet had a major impact on the European universities, perhaps due to new concepts being implemented by people that are used to the old rules and customs.

Accountability

Undoubtedly, the countries under study show elements of increasing accountability. However, this statement requires two qualifications. First, there is a wide variety of accountability practices in the countries and institutions. In some higher education systems performance indicators, either at the national, state, institutional, or program level, have been introduced. In other systems quality assurance mechanisms have been accepted, ranging from nationwide assurance policies for teaching and research to experimental and voluntary auditing at the institutional level. Due to the Bologna Declaration, accreditation mechanisms will eventually be implemented in the European institutions, either adding to or replacing the existing quality assurance procedures. In addition, internal quality assurance and enhancement procedures differ considerably between systems, with some showing clear signs of businesslike accounting practices in the form of justification of the spending of resources, while others show soft accounting practices in the form of reporting.

Second, although accountability is more visible, the actual practices show mostly soft forms of accountability. Using the distinction of Leithwood, Edge, and Jantzi (1999) between descriptive, explanatory, and justifiable accountability, we conclude that overall, descriptive accountability dominates and justifiable accountability is hardly implemented. It remains to be seen whether the policy rhetoric of increasing accountability has not been translated into actual policies or whether academics and/or administrators have been able to strip accountability policies of their thorns. There are some signs in these institutions that the actual policies were indeed less threatening from a normative perspective, or less impressive from a neutral position, than the intentions showed. Concurrently, academics and administrators exhibit some skepticism regarding certain forms of accountability, which hints at implicit or explicit resistance to these practices. Only at Boston College do the accountability mechanisms include any sanctions. These are in the form of small salary increments to those who perform at a higher standard than the norm. These were not seen as particularly effective in changing behavior because they were considered to be negligible and distributed to almost all faculty members.

Employment Flexibility

Chapter 6 on employment flexibility began by asking the question: To what extent have European universities moved towards the American model, that is a corporate style of university? We are aware that not all U.S. universities have a businesslike manner, but in general they are seen as the front-runners in this respect. One trend in the area of employment flexibility concerns the elimination of tenure. For example, in the early 1990s British universities eliminated tenure for all academic staff and began hiring on continuing contracts. Academics with these contracts are close to having a permanent job, but the contracts give employers greater opportunities to terminate someone who is not performing at a satisfactory level. Universities in Anglo-American countries are relying increasingly on adjunct or part-time professors and introducing post-tenure reviews to increase faculty productivity.

At Avignon and Oslo academics are almost unanimously in support of keeping academics as public servants. This tradition is deeply ingrained in the psyche of France and Norway where almost all workers have permanency. Surprisingly, approximately three quarters of the Boston College academics are also in favor of tenure. Yet the academics in Twente are less in favor of permanency, with slightly over half of the responses indicating a desire to maintain public service status. There was also more discussion at Boston College and Twente about modifying the employment system. The main reason for wanting a more rigorous system was to improve productivity. At Boston College more alternatives were given, probably due to the popular press giving the issue more attention. Academics mentioned sliding tenure, post-tenure reviews, and reverse tenure. The latter is an interesting concept as it grants people tenure when they start out as academics, then removes it after a period of 12 years, and thereafter assesses performance annually to determine if they should keep their job.

An analysis of the practices within universities shows that employment flexibility has changed somewhat; however, evidence of fully applying businesslike models of employment is not yet visible. There are incremental changes, varying widely between the systems and institutions, that show an inclination towards emphasizing performance in the judgment of academics for tenure and post-tenure review.

Information and Communication Technologies

Technology and education have always been improbable bedfellows. Their love-hate relationship has been largely based on a mixture of fascination, suspicion, and misunderstanding. The arrival of digital technology characterized by global, all-inclusive dimensions, offers the possibility to create a virtual e-learning environment. Currently academics are confronted with an unprecedented challenge and increasing pressures from their institutions and society at large.

The complexity of this challenge, seen in the perspective of our study, lies firstly in the ambivalent aspect of these instructional technologies. For instance, on the one hand, they allow individuals to navigate through this material at their own pace. On the other hand, world-based operators control these technologies, imposing global standards and global strategies. This expected ambivalence is reflected in our findings, but it is important to differentiate between the various levels and aspects. At the institutional level, a distinction should be made between concerns about a technological infrastructure and the implementation of a consistent policy in the field of technopedagogy. The infrastructure is unanimously taken for granted by academics. The noticeable differences among the universities in the degree of technological sophistication simply reflect differences in the way these technologies have penetrated each country. However, the implementation is more difficult to evaluate.

Except for Avignon, policy statements and guidelines exist, but it appears that the central decision makers must be reluctant to impose these plans. Some troublesome aspects concern tensions between the financial incentives used by institutions to encourage academics to create e-courses and e-learning and the increased workload initiated by such pedagogical work. Moreover, universities do not appear to have fully measured the significant impact that e-teaching may have on the academic's workload. These differences, tensions, and uncertainties may explain why academics in general are more cautious and hesitant than national policy makers; although academics perceive benefits as well, for instance e-mail is extensively used and appreciated by academics.

Introducing the computer as a third person in the teacher-student relationship is a different matter. Virtual campuses may run the risk of delusion. Only a few academics are actually engaged in such projects. Most respondents in our study consider interactivity an inadequate substitute and a poor complement to teacher-student interaction. However, it is striking that e-learning is viewed by corporations such as Microsoft or AOL as a future money-making sector. To put it bluntly, they think it works. Therefore, either their analysts or our academics have missed an important issue.

MAIN UNIVERSITY TRENDS

University of Avignon

Avignon academics appear mildly content and their working conditions appear to be improving in recent years. There are a number of impending challenges, including greater financial rigor, curricula changes, management professionalism, and increasing accountability. Despite these changes, Avignon remains a public, state, tenured system that protects the university and its academics from the full rigors of neoliberal globalization. Avignon academics appreciate the present state of the university as it provides a stable and predictable environment, a sense of participation, and some degree of collegiality. However, most interviewees appear to be aware of the dangers in the current system, for instance complacency or too rigid a system of job protection for optimal academic creativity and efficiency. Yet they are not opposed to reforms that leave key principles intact.

Remarkably, many academics invoke the French Revolution and the traditions of democracy and long-standing expectations of being a civil servant to justify their views. The French public service model, involving the election of presidents and deans, appears to have a long life ahead of it. There seems to be no desire to move towards the Anglo-American, pragmatic perspective where most senior management are appointed and from outside the university.

University of Twente

Twente is a pragmatic university. It was established in a region that was economically depressed and for survival the university needed to develop a synergy with this region to rejuvenate its economy. The university has done well and has gained the title of "the entrepreneurial university." The university morale is positive because it has been highly successful in generating income and maintaining a high reputation in teaching and research. The university perceives itself as connected to the industries in the surrounding region.

Despite this apparent security, Twente like most other universities is facing challenges ushered in by this global era. The impact of global trends can be clearly seen in this university case study. In every area investigated there are signs that Twente is moving closer to the kind of "best practices" that are touted in the United States and the United Kingdom. Even government agencies in the Netherlands are developing "best practice" in the area of quality and accountability mechanisms that others may like to emulate. The Netherlands appears to be moving away from some Continental practices and closer to Anglo-American practices. This is seen especially in the changes to its governance structures. Nevertheless, due to the Dutch cultural style of honoring consensus and shying away from authoritarian tendencies, their decision-making structures are not as close to the extreme model of managerialism exhibited by Boston College in its governance practices.

University of Oslo

The University of Oslo appears to be maintaining many of its traditional values while in the midst of some major changes. It is modernizing its finance system, professionalizing its administration, and reorganizing the structure of the university to become more efficient. These changes have reduced the amount of time academics spend in meetings and to a certain extent on administrative tasks, and have given more power to the heads of departments, the deans, and smaller boards that now include greater external representation. To a certain extent this has diminished the democratic impulse; however, democracy remains in the election of academics into administrative positions and in the election of members of the various boards. Democracy has become more representative, rather than participatory in the town meeting sense.

Many of the changes that have been introduced in the University of Oslo are subtle. There is a feeling that managerialism is penetrating the university and that it is mixed with bureaucracy and collegiality. There is a fear that appears to be underlying some of the comments: As individuals start using the vocabulary of managerialism and begin seeing the goals of the university through economic lenses, this way of thinking will seep into the way academics and administrators begin to view the university and its goals. This economic way of thinking can have negative consequences for the role many academics envisage for the university.

Paradoxically, with this emphasis on economics and efficiency, there has been an increase in administrative staff and accountability procedures. Consequently, academics appear to be spending more time completing forms. However, sanctions or incentives have not yet accompanied the accountability measures that have been introduced into the university. This means that academics have not had nearly the amount of pressure to produce or even account for their time as their colleagues in Anglo-American countries. Discipline reviews and teaching evaluations have not been administered in a punitive fashion and have not been systematically introduced to determine rankings or in an attempt to eliminate bad teachers. The desire expressed by most academics was that any measures to evaluate individuals, departments, or universities should be done in a supportive way to improve quality rather than to punish anyone. There was a general disdain for the British or U.S. style of accountability measures that appear to lead to an emphasis on *countability,* as one academic put it, rather than on the quality of what one publishes. The "publish or perish" syndrome is a trend that many Norwegian academics would like to avoid.

Boston College

Boston College could be seen as balancing the impact of globalization trends. Among the four universities studied, Boston College exhibits more global trends, is the most wired campus, and is beginning to use more technology as part of its instructional repertoire. This university has adopted many of the corporate practices of management and accountability. However, Boston College is not an extreme example of a "globalized university," which may be exhibited by other U.S., some British, and Australian universities.

Boston College does not see the necessity to move towards greater flexibility in employment, regarding tenure and academic freedom as important. It wants to increase the number of tenured faculty and not move towards the use of more adjuncts, even though that would be more economical. Concurrently, it values many traditional academic principles, and due to its Jesuit origins is proud of its liberal arts and humanistic education. Its mission is to reach out to the community, to involve its students in voluntary service, and to pursue social justice programs. There are some countervailing forces that make it difficult for Boston College academics to create a scholarly community the way they may like. The major pressure on them is to publish and obtain research grants, which leads to a more competitive rather than a cooperative environment. The quest for Boston College to move up the league tables and compete with the top research universities in the United States is one that leads to a more individualistic culture, rewarding the high flyers, not the campus citizens, or those who reach out into the surrounding communities. Also, its near bankruptcy in the early 1970s led it down a path of central control of the finances and a much more managerial decision-making structure than most other U.S. universities have adopted. In the area of governance, it shows how the globalizing practice of managerialism can eliminate the voice of the faculty, with no faculty senate to debate academic policies and little dialogue between the senior managers and the faculty about the running of the university.

THE IMPACT OF GLOBALIZING PRACTICES

The first chapter in this book began with the comment that globalization has different meanings for different people and that there are strong supporters and strong opponents. Our findings have not changed this comment. On the contrary, the case studies provide a variety of views where advocates and opponents report on the benefits, costs, and objections to globalizing practices. Surprisingly, however, there are few systematic variations among academics despite their differences in sex, age, and disciplines. In other words, we found considerable consensus of views within each university, whether professors or junior academics, or whether male or female. Acknowledging the considerable variety of practices within the institutions in this study, at the level of the average academic staff and managers, the recent changes due to government reform efforts, responding to pressures of globalization, have not yet impacted fully on the Continent, and may never do so. Globalizing practices can be useful and provide opportunities to improve basic practices of universities, but they can also threaten key university values that have brought prosperity to universities and society.

There are some impacts of globalizing practices, yet they appear not to be solely the consequence of neoliberal tendencies inextricably connected to economic globalization. According to our findings, the impact of globalizing practices cannot be uncoupled from other important developments in higher education and society in general. We must take into account the changing role of governments, the technological developments, internationalization as such, or Europeanization that have taken place simultaneously with globalizing practices.

Eventually, it depends upon how one perceives these kinds of phenomena, their effects, and their mutual relations. We proposed the following metaphor to illustrate this. Suppose we imagine the universities as dollops of color on a palette using red, yellow, green, and blue dollops, and a dollop of black representing globalization. Then we mix an equal amount of black in with those four colors. Two conclusions can be drawn regarding the action of black on the four colors. First, the black will change the hues of the original colors to the same degree, concluding that the universities have undergone similar change due to globalizing practices. However, second, the mixture results in different colors. For instance, a mixture of red and black does not yield the same color as yellow and black. Of course, the ultimate color depends upon the precise composition of the mixture of colors. The effect of globalization on universities has not been as good or as bad as may have been expected, and the globalizing factors have not been applied to the same degree in all systems or institutions. The findings of the case studies demonstrate clearly that changes at the shop floor level have normally been less penetrating than at other levels. When combining the rich data of the case studies, it can be concluded that higher education, including its diverse institutions, has changed due to globalizing practices. The result is not a kind of fatalistic tendency that turns the world of higher education into a gray mass of homogeneity. The dynamics of higher education show still a huge variety in patterns and cultures.

THE WAY AHEAD: RESPONDENTS' EXPECTATIONS ABOUT THE FUTURE

We asked: What would you like to see as the role of universities/colleges in society in the future? The respondents contributed a variety of perspectives concerning the future of the university. We divided these into three categories. The first category of answers clearly shows a wish to return to or preserve the traditional image of the university. Keywords in these responses from Avignon, Boston College, and Oslo University were: academic freedom, intellectual curiosity, generation of ideas, elitism, critical thinking, and civil society.

Academic Freedom

I think that more than anything else it has to be the bastion for academic freedom. It has to be a place where we can all pursue research wherever it takes us and we can speak our minds within the boundaries of civility. It should be the place in which we push research to the frontiers. (Boston College, Senior, Male, Academic, Social Sciences)

I see the university first of all as a place of higher learning, where free thinking and philosophical reflection take place. In other words, it's a place where thoughts should have a possibility to develop and mature and where criticism should flourish. It should be the conscience of the nation. (Oslo, Senior, Male, Academic, Sciences)

Generation of Ideas

Universities are places where ideas are generated. They are places of scholarly pursuit. It's a mistake to equate them to businesses. It's a mistake to overmanage them. They should be kept free to pursue ideas. (Boston College, Senior, Female, Academic, Sciences)

Elitist Institution

I am not really elitist, but one problem now is that there are too many students who are here that shouldn't be here. First of all, they are not interested, and I think that universities should be places for those who want to spend enough time to understand what is going on. (Oslo, Senior, Female, Academic, Sciences)

I'm not sure. I think to start with, I'd like to see changes not only in the future, but starting right now. I would like the role of the university to be a prestigious one, obviously. I would like to see the university go back to its intellectual and academic roots, and to keep a certain autonomy, and even a superior status in society. The university needs to set an example. (Avignon, Junior, Male, Academic, Professional School)

Creation of Civil Society

There has been a lot of talk, perhaps exaggerated, but I think there is a grain of truth in the idea that there has been a decline of public life, civic life, and there is a need to replenish that and rebuild that. I think there's a major role for the universities in that, in encouraging collective participation in public life. (Boston College, Senior, Male, Academic, Social Sciences)

I wish every young person in the world could have a liberal arts education, save the trade stuff for later. I think it's so important because I think the university should be there to produce not just a set of smart people who can solve problems, but to me the big thing is tolerance. So to me the role of a university is really to make people at least intellectually tolerant. (Boston College, Senior, Male, Academic, Social Sciences)

Numerous respondents show ambiguity regarding the future of the university. Their answers can be interpreted as an indication that they would prefer the preservation of traditional values and functions of the universities; however, it appears that they want to give a modern twist to the traditional function. In other words, they predict a future for the university where the traditional functions gradually transform into modern versions. Some respondents seem to indicate that the newer functions are not at odds with the more traditional functions. Serving society can be achieved by educating the civil society and conducting contract research activities for society. Some answers indicate that these respondents want the university to change and become clearly different from what the university used to be. Keywords in such views are: greater international involvement, more training for the global workforce, becoming entrepreneurial, linking with industry, and more vocationalism.

Global Workforce

We train the elite of the nation but now they have to be trained for the global workforce as decision makers. But we are going to be increasingly in competition with other universities in the world. Students will be able to choose to go to the next city or another country in Europe or the United States. So we will face a new challenge. We get requests to cooperate with universities in different parts of the world, but we have to find a quality university as a partner. You can then offer a first degree here coupled with a Master's degree in France or the United States. But there has to be a balance between the partners and that is difficult. (Twente, Senior, Male, Manager)

Contributions to Industry, the Region, and the Society in General

I would like to see universities and colleges to collaborate more with industry in the advancement of education and knowledge. (Boston College, Senior, Female, Manager)

I would like to see the university contribute to making our society a more open-minded one, and one that opens up more to the rest of the world. French universities are still very conservative in their international involvement. For example, we don't speak enough foreign languages at the university, and I would like to see history classes take place in English or Italian for example, and I think that this is a very important part of integrating ourselves into the European community. (Avignon, Senior, Male, Academic, Social Sciences)

We should find a way of implementing our knowledge and technology transfer towards the regions around us. We can do that by stimulating the entrepreneurship of our students and even of our staff. In that sense we will have a large number of spin-off companies from this university towards the region. (Twente, Senior, Male, Manager)

FUTURE SCENARIOS

Despite the existence of various forms of pressure on universities to adopt globalizing practices, one of the most significant findings of the study is that many academics are either not affected by these trends or are unaware of the impact these pressures are having on their institutions. An explanation for this could be, firstly, that those involved are strongly resisting the globalizing practices. Secondly, that these globalizing forces are strong, but that academics and administrators are able to bend these forces so that they are not fully exposed to the effects.[1] Thirdly, that there is no empirical connection between globalizing practices and higher education practices. The remainder of this chapter follows two lines of reasoning. First, universities have to adapt to these external forces, whether that adaptation is in the form of acquiescence or manipulation in order to survive (see Oliver, 1991, for a typology of strategic responses). If universities do not follow this strategy, they will become marginal. Second, most elements of globalizing practices are harmful to the essence of universities. These forces should be resisted in order to preserve the characteristics of academe.

Scenario 1: Adjust or Disappear

This scenario is based on the idea that it is time for universities to adjust gradually to the changing expectations of society. If universities do not take up this challenge, they will end up as marginal institutions in society; or even worse from the perspective of those whose hearts lie with these institutions, they will not survive at all. Adjusting to globalizing practices does not mean the university has to sell its soul to the devil of globalization. Many of the traditional values of academe can be preserved and concurrently necessary adaptations can be realized. Clark's (1998) picture of the entrepreneurial university may serve to illustrate this view. Whereas the entrepreneurial universities he depicts clearly internalize elements of globalizing practices, they remain compatible with a stimulated academic heartland. Clark concludes that departments should be given leeway to "fuse their new administrative capability and outreach mentality with traditional outlooks in their fields" (p. 142). He also advises that academic norms operate close to the surface: they define whether "changes are 'up-market' or 'down-market'" (p. 142). In a similar vein, Sporn (1999) shows that the universities she studied in the United States and in Europe were able to adapt to rapidly changing environments. Each university has done this in a mix of entrepreneurial characteristics, for instance professionalized university management and clear mission statements, and traditional characteristics, for instance shared governance, committed leadership, and a differentiated structure. The examples imply that there is not one path to success. A sound mix of traditional and modern characteristics will allow the university to survive and thrive in the future.

Scenario 2: Resist and Survive

Globalization forces will not disappear. Universities will continue to be challenged by a changing world that will become more integrated with each new technological advance in communications technology. The borderless world is a reality in many aspects of our lives and will become more so in the future. How will universities survive in this borderless world?

What are the values that we want universities in the future to maintain? Writers agonize over the loss of the humanistic dimension and the need to strengthen the "soul" or essence of the university (Hickling-Hudson, 2000; Kelly, 2000; Gidley, 2000). Williamson and Coffield (1997) want institutions of higher education to nurture personal integrity, honesty, and democratic ways of working. "It is still dissent that is pivotal if the university is about creating an alternative future" (Inayatullah, 2000, p. 227).

How can these values survive in the face of managerialism and the more competitive, commercial environment? Rooney and Hearn (2000) warn us about commodifying knowledge, maintaining openness and collaboration in the search for new knowledge, and maintaining trust in learning relationships. Hickling-Hudson (2000) wants universities to cooperate with communities and to honor the scholar-activist who engages with society in the quest for solutions to community problems.

Universities have already adapted and become more involved with communities. For the most part, they are no longer perceived as ivory towers where scholars can sit in isolation and espouse solutions for the world's problems or ignore the outside world altogether. The engaged activist-scholar is one we would want to preserve and to flourish in the future. However, we would want the activist-scholar to be more attached to creating a just society, rather than one that panders to business and the desire for a more consumer-oriented society. There are many dangers universities must avoid lest they follow the path of consumerism. One of these is the secrecy that develops in corporatized universities and the commodification that comes with commercialized universities. That is a dangerous path. Can academics resist this direction?

The main buffer against the student as consumer and knowledge as a commodity is an adequate amount of public funding of universities or funding from private sources that is unattached, allowing academics to maintain the disinterested nature of their scholarship and teaching. It is vitally important for university academics to pursue knowledge for knowledge's sake, to be driven by a research agenda that is of one's choosing and out of one's curiosity rather than to be paid to engage in research by a company, a government, or an individual. The pressures to deliver predetermined results can be paramount when there is direct payment for the research. At the same time, there can be other types of research that involve the community in setting the agenda. It can be more applied research, which tries to solve practical problems. However, this type of research should not dominate the university.

So university academics have to be of this world and detached from it. They have to critique society as well as generate new ideas for it. It is important for them to enter into trusting relationships with students and collaborate with the community to form a learning society. They have to be open and transparent in their internal relations and with the community at large. They cannot be secretive and driven only by market forces if professors are to maintain their soul, their passion, and their integrity.

We believe that there is an enduring need to assert the role of universities in developing active and critical thinking citizens. Smith and Webster (1997) argue that university education is about creating thoughtful citizens. They say that universities must be concerned with "the conduct of critical enquiry and rational debate, nurturing abilities such as a capacity to distinguish opinion from evidence and to evaluate an argument dispassionately, to learn independently and in groups, to develop abilities to present coherent arguments, to improve the sophistication of one's thinking, to open one's imagination and reflexive capabilities, to improve analytical capacities and to think conceptually" p. 108). The future will reveal whether these crucial values persist in universities as they increasingly become globalized institutions.

NOTE

1. The distinction between resisting and adapting to external challenges has much in common with the explanation for the long life of universities as institutions. Is it because universities have resisted change for so long or is it because universities have adapted to external conditions (see Kerr, 1982, and van Vught, 1989)?

Appendix I: Description of Sample

BOSTON COLLEGE

The respondents interviewed (a total of 37) consisted of 11 faculty from a professional school, 10 from the sciences (biology, chemistry, geology and mathematics), 13 from the social sciences/arts (economics, English, history, political science, sociology and theology), and 3 senior administrators. Some faculty were in the positions of dean and department head. The senior administrators were in the positions of vice president or associate vice president. The 34 faculty interviewed ranged in rank from professor (20), to associate professor (9), and assistant professor (4). There was a mixture of men and women (21 males and 16 females). All faculty had either a Ph.D. or Ed.D. Thirteen faculty were over the age of 55, 14 were between the ages of 45 and 54, and 7 were younger than 45 years of age. Two of the senior administrators were over the age of 55 and the other one was younger than 45 years of age. The tables below show that males and females were fairly equally distributed across the disciplines and ranks, although more professors were

Qualifications and Discipline Location at Boston College (numbers)

Qualifications	Professional School	Social Sciences	Sciences	Administration	Total
PhDs	11	13	10	2	36
Masters	0	0	0	1	1
Total	11	13	10	3	37

Gender and Rank/Position at Boston College (numbers)

Gender	Full Professor	Associate Professor	Assistant Professor	Senior Administrator	Total
Male	14	4	1	2	21
Female	6	6	3	1	16
Total	20	10	4	3	37

males, more associate and assistant professors were females, and more senior administrators were males (as is the case in reality at Boston College).

UNIVERSITY OF AVIGNON

Those interviewed (a total of 32) consisted of 10 from the social sciences (comparative and English literature, economics, geography, history and international relations), 9 from the sciences (biology, chemistry, computer sciences, geology and physics) and 10 from the professional areas of communication studies, law, applied languages, and education. Three senior administrators were interviewed: the president, the current most senior administrator (secrétaire-général), and the previous secrétaire-général. In French universities, females are underrepresented in the university generally and particularly among professors, as this

Qualifications and Discipline Location at Avignon (numbers)

Qualifications	Social Sciences	Sciences	Professional	Administration	Total
PhD	9	9	6	1	25
Masters	1	0	4	2	7
Total	10	9	10	3	32

Gender and Rank/Position at Avignon (numbers)

Gender	Professor	Maitre	Assistant	Senior Administrator	Total
Male	12	7	2	2	23
Female	0	7	1	1	9
Total	12	14	3	3	32

sample indicates. All the 12 professors were males, females (7) and males (7) were evenly represented at the maitre de conférence level, and there were 3 assistant instructors (2 males and 1 female). The majority (15) were between the ages of 45 to 54, the next largest group (10) was over 55 years of age, and there were 7 younger than 45 years of age.

UNIVERSITY OF OSLO

The 31 interviewees consisted of 10 academics from the sciences (biology, botany, zoology, chemistry and physics), 9 academics from the social sciences (political science, anthropology, geography, philosophy, psychology, sociology, and women's studies) and 10 academics from education. Some of these academics were in elected positions as deans and heads of departments. In addition, a director and prorector were interviewed from the central administration. Those interviewed ranged from professors to assistant professors, and were a fairly even balance of 16 males and 15 females. Out of this group, three had Master's degrees and the rest had doctoral degrees. Fifteen participants were over the age of 55, 12 were between the ages of 45 and 54 and 4 were younger than 45 years of age.

Qualifications and Discipline Location at Oslo (numbers)

Qualifications	Social Sciences	Sciences	Education	Administration	Total
PhD	9	10	8	1	28
Masters	0	0	2	1	3
Total	9	10	10	2	31

Gender and Rank/Position at Oslo (numbers)

Gender	Full Professor	Associate Professor	Assistant Professor	Senior Administrator	Total
Male	12	3	0	1	16
Female	8	5	1	1	15
Total	20	8	1	2	31

UNIVERSITY OF TWENTE

A total of 31 individuals were interviewed, including 2 senior administrators. The group interviewed consisted of 11 academics from the social sciences (edu-

cational, public administration and public policy, philosophy of sciences, and sociology), 10 from the sciences (chemical engineering) and 8 from educational
sciences and technology. The two tables below show that almost all of the participants had Ph.Ds. Those with Master's were located in education and administration. Six respondents were over the age of 55, 14 were between the ages of
45 and 54, and 11 were younger than 45 years of age. Males and females were
unevenly distributed across the ranks with no females among the senior administrators or full professors. Females were in the categories of associate and
assistant professors. In 1999 females made up 29 percent of full-time staff within
the university. This figure includes academic, administrative, and technical staff.
In this sample, female academics were 21 percent of the academic staff, which
was only a slight overrepresentation of female academics at the University of
Twente, where the actual percentage was 19 percent in 1999. In the Netherlands
as a whole at the end of 1996, female academic staff made up 23 percent of the
total academic staff but were only 5 percent of professors and 7 percent of associate professors (Boezerooy, 1999).

Qualifications and Discipline Location at Twente

Qualifications	Social Sciences	Sciences	Education	Administration	Total
PhD	11	10	5	1	27
Masters	0	0	3	1	4
Total	11	10	8	2	31

Gender and Rank/Position at Twente (numbers)

Gender	Full Professor	Associate Professor	Assistant Professor	Senior Administrator	Total
Male	11	8	4	2	25
Female	0	2	4	0	6
Total	11	10	8	2	31

Appendix II: Interview Protocol

These questions refer to any changes that you may have observed over the last five years in your institution.

GOVERNANCE

1) How would you describe the way your institution is governed (centrally managed, collegial or democratic, or something else)? Have there been any changes to this basic model in the last five years or since you have been employed here?
2) If there have been changes, what impact have these changes had on the role of academics in decision making?
3a) Would you like the faculty to be more involved in the governance of your institution or in decision making?
3b) Would you like to have a faculty senate reinstated here?

ACCOUNTABILITY

4) What kinds of accountability measures (for example, research indices, quality reviews, teaching evaluations) are used by your board of trustees to monitor departments/sections of the institution?
5) What kinds of accountability measures (performance indicators, annual reviews, student course evaluations) exist within the college to monitor the teaching and research of individual academics?
6) In your opinion, how effective have these mechanisms (both institutional and individual) been in either monitoring quality or improving the quality of teaching and research within the institution?
7) Would you like to see more or less evaluation of academics within the institution?

COMPETITION AND GENERATING FUNDS

8) Has your institution asked you to gain funds from external sources?

9) Do you see academics in this college becoming more entrepreneurial, either individually or as departments, in gaining funds?

10) What are the advantages or disadvantages of academics becoming more entrepreneurial?

11) Has the college put pressure on academics to improve their research performance to make the institution more competitive with other colleges/universities?

"NEW" TECHNOLOGIES

12) Has your institution encouraged you to develop new programs or teaching units that utilize the Internet/e-mail, satellite television, or other forms of "new" technologies?

13) What do you see as the positive and negative consequences of the use of "new" technologies in teaching and research in your university?

14) Have you used e-mail to communicate with students, and has it increased or decreased your workload?

15) Is there any recognition by the university of the workload involved in the use of new technologies, and has the university discussed a policy concerning workloads of those using e-mail and the Internet for teaching purposes?

GENERAL QUESTIONS

16) What would you like to see as the role of universities/colleges in American society in the future?

17) Do you think it would be of value to democratically elect your department heads/deans or even the president of the university as is done in many European universities?

18) Do you think tenure for academics is an important principle to maintain in national colleges and universities?

Bibliography

Aamodt, P.O. (1990). A new deal for Norwegian higher education. *European Journal of Education* 25(2): 171–185.

Aamodt, P.O., Kyvik, S., & Skoie, H. (1991). Norway: Towards a more indirect model of governance? In G. Neave & F.A. van Vught (Eds.), *The Changing Relationship Between Government and Higher Education in Western Europe* (129–144). Oxford: Pergamon Press.

Abecassis, A. (1994). The policy of contracts between the state and the universities. A quiet revolution. In Organisation for Economic Cooperation and Development (OECD) (Ed.), *Evaluation and the Decision Making Process in Higher Education: French, German and Spanish Experiences* (13–18). Paris: OECD.

Aitkin, D. (2000, Sept. 6). A bedrock that's not set in stone. *The Australian:* 33.

Albrow, M. (1993). Globalization. In W. Outhwaite & T. Bottomore (Eds.), *Blackwell Dictionary of Twentieth Century Social Thoughts* (248–249). Oxford: Basil Blackwell.

Alexander, F.K. (2000). The changing face of accountability. Monitoring and assessing institutional performance in higher education. *Journal of Higher Education* 71(4): 411–431.

Altbach, P.G. (2001). Higher education and the WTO: Globalization run amok. *International Higher Education* 23: 2–4.

Altbach, P. & Lewis, L. (1996). The academic profession. In P.G. Altbach (Ed.), *The International Academic Profession* (3–48). Princeton, NJ: The Carnegie Foundation for the Advancement of Teaching.

American Association of University Professors. (AAUP). (1940). *Statement of Principles on Academic Freedom and Tenure.* Washington, DC: AAUP.

American Association of University Professors. (AAUP). (1966). *Statement on Professional Ethics.* Washington, DC: AAUP.

American Association of University Professors. (AAUP). (1999). *Post-Tenure Review: An AAUP Response.* Washington, DC: AAUP.

American Association of University Professors. (AAUP). (2000). *Incentives to Forgo Tenure. A Statement by Committee A.* Washington, DC: AAUP.

Anderson, D. & Johnson, R. (1998). *University Autonomy in Twenty Countries.* Canberra: DEETYA, Higher Education Division.

Anderson, H. (2001, Jan. 27–28). France finds more time for the good life. *The Weekend Australian:* 20.

Appadurai, A. (2000). Grassroots globalisation and the research imagination. *Globalisation, Special Edition of Public Culture* 12(1): 1–19.

Arenson, K. (2000, Jun. 6). SUNY fight over curriculum mirrors larger debate. *New York Times:* B1.

Bacharach, S.B., Bamberger, P., & Conley, S.C. (1991). Negotiating the 'see-saw' of managerial strategy. A resurrection of the study of professionals in organizational theory. *Research in the Sociology of Organizations* 8: 217–238.

Balligand, J.-P. (1998, Sept. 29). Le globalization l'état et le marché [Globalization, the state and the market]. *Le Monde:* 26.

Barry Jones, R.J. (1995). *Globalization and Interdependence in the International Political Economy.* London: Pinter.

Bauer, M., Askling, B., Marton, S.G., & Marton, F. (1999). *Transforming Universities: Changing Patterns of Governance, Structure and Learning in Swedish Higher Education.* London: Jessica Kingsley.

Becher, T. & Kogan, M. (1992). *Process and Structure in Higher Education.* London/New York: Routledge.

Benjamin, E. (1997). *Some Implications of Tenure for the Profession and Society.* Washington, DC: AAUP.

Bess, J.L. (1992). Collegiality: Toward a clarification of meaning and function. In J.C. Smart (Ed.), *Higher Education: Handbook of Theory and Research* VIII (1–36). Bronx, NY: Agathon Press.

Bleiklie, I. (1996). Reform and change in higher education system. Unpublished, University of Bergen.

Bleiklie, I., Hostaker, R., & Vabo, A. (2000). *Policy and Practice in Higher Education. Reforming Norwegian Universities.* London: Jessica Kingsley.

Blumenstyk, G. (2001, Nov. 30). Group denounces 'blame America first' response to September 11 attacks. *The Chronicle of Higher Education:* A12.

Boer, H. de (2002). On nails, coffins and councils. *European Journal of Education* 37(1): 7–20.

Boer, H. de & Denters, B. (1999). Analysis of institutions of university governance: A classification scheme applied to postwar changes in Dutch higher education. In B. Jongbloed, P. Maassen, & G. Neave (Eds.), *From the Eye of the Storm: Higher Education's Changing Institution* (211–233). Dordrecht: Kluwer Academic Publishers.

Boer, H. de, Denters, B., & Goedegebuure, L. (1998). On boards and councils: shaky balances considered. The governance of Dutch universities. *Higher Education Policy* 11(2/3): 153–164.

Boer, H. de, Denters, B., & Goedegebuure, L. (2000). Dutch disease of Dutch model: An evaluation of the pre-1998 system of democratic university government in the Netherlands. In R. Weissberg (Ed.), *Democracy and the Academy* (123–140). Huntington, NY: Nova Science Publishers.

Boer, H. de, Goedegebuure, L., & Meek, L. (1998). In the winter of discontent—business as usual. *Higher Education Policy* 11(2/3): 103–110.

Boer, H. de, & Huisman, J. (1999) The new public management in Dutch universities. In D. Braun & F.-X. Merrien (Eds.), *Towards a New Model of Governance for Universities? A Comparative View* (100–118). London: Jessica Kingsley.

Boezerooy, P. (1999). Higher education in the Netherlands: Country report. *CHEPS Higher Education Monitor* 310. Enschede: University of Twente Higher Education Policy Series.

Brabazon, T. (2001). Internet teaching and the administration of knowledge. *First Monday* 6: 1–10. Retrieved November 20, 2001, from www.firstmonday.org/issues/issue6_6/brabazon.

Brain, P. (2001, May 8). The opportunity cost of misplaced faith. *The Australian Financial Review:* 3.

Brewster, K. (1972). On tenure. *AAUP Bulletin* 58(4): 382–383.

Buck, J. (2001, Feb. 24). *Academic freedom for a free society.* Paper presented at the ASC/CBC Joint Leadership Conference. Kansas City, MO.

Burtchaell, J.T. (1998). *The Dying of the Light: The Disengagement of College and Universities from their Christian Churches.* Grand Rapids, MI: W.B. Eerdmans Publishing.

Callan, P.M., Doyle, W., & Finney, J.E. (2001, Mar.–Apr.). Evaluating state higher education performance. *Change:* 10–19.

Carlson, S. & Carnevale, D. (2001, Dec. 14). Debating the demise of NYUonline. *The Chronicle of Higher Education:* A31, A32.

Central Intelligence Agency. (CIA). (2001). *The World Factbook—United States, Australia, the Netherlands, Norway and France.* Retrieved September 29, 2001, from www.odci.gov/cia/publications/factbook/geaos/us/as/nl/no/fr.html.

CEPES. (1993). France. *Higher Education in Europe* 19(1).

Chapman, J.W. (Ed.). (1983). *The Western University on Trial.* Berkeley: University of California Press.

Charle, C. (1994). *La Republique des Universitaires: 1870–1940.* Paris: Seuil.

Chemerinsky, E. (1998). Is tenure necessary to protect academic freedom? *American Behavioral Scientist* 41(5): 607–626.

Chevaillier, T. (1998). Moving away from central planning: Using contracts to steer higher education in France. *European Journal of Education* 33(1): 65–76.

Chipman, L. (2000, Mar. 8–14). Academic freedom can prevail. *Campus Review:* 17.

The Chronicle of Higher Education. (1997). *The Chronicle of Higher Education Almanac 97–98.* Retrieved November 7, 2000, from www.chronicle.com/data/infobank.dir/almanac.dir/97alm.dir/97almain.htm.

Clark, B.R. (1983). *The Higher Education System: Academic Organization in Cross-National Perspective.* Berkeley: University of California Press.

Clark, B.R. (1998). *Creating Entrepreneurial Universities: Organizational Pathways of Transformation.* Oxford: IAU Press, Pergamon.

Coady, T. (1996). The very idea of a university. *Australian Quarterly* 68(4): 49–62.

Coaldrake, P. & Stedman, L. (1999). Academic work in the twenty-first century: changing roles and policies. Occasional Paper Series 99-H. Canberra, ACT: DETYA, Higher Education Division.

Cohen, M. (1999/2000). The general agreement on trade in services: Implications for public post-secondary education in Australia. *Australian Universities' Review* 42(2)/43(1): 9–15.

Collis, B. (1999). Pedagogical perspectives on ICT use in higher education. In B. Collins & M.C. Van Der Wende (Eds.), *The Use of Information and Communication Tech-*

nologies in Higher Education: An International Orientation on Trends and Issues (51–86). Enschede: University of Twente, Center for Higher Education Policy Studies.

Comité National d'Evaluation. (1991). *L'Université d'Avignon et des Pays du Vaucluse: Report d'Évaluation.* Paris: Comité National d'Évaluation.

Considine, M. (2001a). *Enterprising States: The Public Management of Welfare-to-Work.* Cambridge: Cambridge University Press.

Considine, M. (2001b). Commentary: APSA presidential address 2000: The tragedy of the common rooms? political science and the new university governance. *Australian Journal of Political Science* 36(1): 145–156.

Cunningham, S., Tapsall, S., Ryan, Y., Stedman, L., Bagdon, K., & Flew, T. (1998). *New Media and Borderless Education: A Review of the Convergence Between Global Media Networks and Higher Education.* Canberra: Australian Government Publishing Service.

Currie, J. (2001). *Privatization and academic freedom in Australian universities.* Paper presented at the Association for the Study of Higher Education (ASHE) 26th Annual Conference, Richmond, VA.

Currie, J. & Newson, J. (Eds.). (1998). *Universities and Globalization: Critical Perspectives.* London: Sage.

Daalder, H. (1982). The Netherlands: Universities between the 'new democracy' and the 'new management.' In H. Daalder & E. Shils (Eds.), *Universities, Politicians and Bureaucrats: Europe and the United States* (173–232). Cambridge: Cambridge University Press.

Daalder, H. & Shils, E. (Eds.). (1982). *Universities, Politicians and Bureaucrats: Europe and the United States.* Cambridge: Cambridge University Press.

Dahl, R.A. (1989). *Democracy and its Critics.* New Haven, CT: Yale University Press.

Daly, H. (1994). Farewell lecture to the World Bank. In J. Cavanagh, D. Wysham, & M. Arruda (Eds.), *Beyond Bretton Woods: Alternatives to the Global Economic Order* (109–117). Boulder, CO: Institute for Policy Studies and Transitional Institute.

Daniel, M. (1999, Nov. 18). Report. *The Boston Globe:* A35.

Darras, B., Harvey, D., Lemmel, C., & Peraya, D. (2000). Construction des savoirs et multimedias. In B. Darras (Ed.), *Multimedia et Savoir. MEI, Médiation et information* 11 (10–57). Paris: L'Harmattan.

DeAngelis, R. (1992). The Dawkins revolution. *Australian Universities' Review* 35(1): 37–42.

DeAngelis, R. (1993). Funding the Dawkins revolution in higher education: The first five years—policy, problems, prospects. *Flinders Studies in Policy and Administration* 9: 43.

DeAngelis, R. (1996). Universities. In A. Parkin (Ed.), *South Australia, Federalism and Public Policy* (217–230). Canberra: Federalism Research Centre, The Australian National University.

DeAngelis, R. (1998). The last decade of higher education reform in Australia and France: Different constraints, differing choices in higher education politics and policies. In J. Currie & J. Newson (Eds.), *Universities and Globalization: Critical Perspectives* (123–139). Thousand Oaks, CA/London: Sage.

DeBats, D. & Ward, A. (1999). *Degrees of Difference: Reshaping the University in Australia and the United States.* Sydney: Centre for American Studies, University of Sydney.

De Groof, J., Neave, G., & Svec, J. (1998). *Democracy and Governance in Higher Education*. The Hague: Kluwer Law International.

Department of Education, Training and Youth Affairs (DETYA) (2000). *Higher Education Selected Staff Statistics* (Tables 1, 4).

Desktop 2000. Enterprise Technology Resource Management Project. Retrieved May 28, 2001, from www.Boston.edu/Boston.org/tv/etrm.

Dill, D.D. (1997). Accreditation, assessment, anarchy? The evolution of academic quality assurance policies in the United States. In J. Brennan, P. De Vries, & R. Williams (Eds.), *Standards and Quality in Higher Education* (15–43). London: Jessica Kingsley.

Dill, D.D. (1998). Evaluating the 'evaluative state': Implications for research in higher education. *European Journal of Education* 33(3): 361–378.

Dill, D.D. (1999). Academic accountability and university adaption: The architecture of an academic learning organization. *Higher Education* 38(2): 127–154.

Dill, D.D. (2000). *The Nature of Academic Organisation*. Utrecht: Lemma Publishers.

Dill, D.D. & Peterson Helm, K. (1988). Faculty participation in strategic policy making. In J.C. Smart (Ed.), *Higher Education: Handbook of Theory and Research* IV (319–355). New York: Agathon Press.

Dimmen, A. & Kyvik, S. (1998). Recent changes in governance of higher education institutions in Norway. *Higher Education Policy* 11(2/3): 217–218.

Dionne, E.J.J. (1998, Aug. 11). A 'third way' is in vogue on both sides of the Atlantic. *Herald International Tribune*: 6.

The Economist. (2001a, Sept. 9). Globalisation and its critics: 1–30.

The Economist. (2001b, Nov. 10). Reading the tea leaves: 39.

The Economist. (2001c, Aug. 4). Putting the brakes on: Globalisation through French eyes: 42.

Ehrmann, S.C. (1999). Asking the hard questions about technology use and education. *Change* March/April: 25–29.

Elliot, L. (1998, Sept. 13). Capitalism on a fast road to ruin. *Guardian Weekly*: 19.

Engstrand, G. (1998). 'Tenure wars': The battles and the lessons. *American Behavioral Scientist* 41(5): 607–626.

Exworthy, M. & Halford, S. (Eds.). (1999). *Professionals and the New Managerialism in the Public Sector*. Buckingham: Open University Press.

Feigenbaum, H., Henig, J., & Hamnett, C. (1999). *Shrinking the State: The Political Underpinnings of Privatization*. Cambridge: Cambridge University Press.

Folger, J.K. (1977). Editor's note to 'Increasing the public accountability of higher education.' *New Directions for Institutional Research* 16: vii–xii.

Foster, L. (2001) Review essay: Technology: Transforming the landscape of higher education. *The Review of Higher Education* 25(1): 115–124.

Frederiks, M.M.H., Westerheijden, D.F., & Weusthof, P.J.M. (1994). Effects of quality assessment in Dutch higher education. *European Journal of Education* 29(2): 181–199.

Friedberg, E. & Musselin, C. (Eds.). (1992). *Le Gouvernement des Universités: Perspectives Comparatives*. Paris: L'Harmattan.

Friedman, T.L. (2000). *The Lexus and the Olive Tree*. New York: Random House.

Geurts, P.A., Maassen, P.A.M., & van Vught, F.A. (1996). The Dutch professoriate. In P.G. Altbach (Ed.), *The International Academic Profession* (493–528). Princeton, NJ: The Carnegie Foundation for the Advancement of Teaching.

Gidley, J. (2000). Unveiling the human face of university futures. In S. Inayatullah & J. Gidley (Eds.), *The University in Transformation: Global Perspectives on the Future of the University* (235–245). Westport, CT: Bergin & Garvey.

Glassick, C. (1997). *Scholarship for Higher Education*. Canberra: Higher Education Council.

Goedegebuure, L., Kaiser, F., Massen, P., Meek, L., Vught, F. van, & Weert, E. de (Eds.). (1994). *Higher Education Policy. An International Comparative Perspective*. Oxford: Pergamon Press.

Goedegebuure, L. & Vught, F. van (1994). Alternative models of government steering in higher education. In L. Goedegebuure & F. van Vught (Eds.), *Comparative Policy Studies in Higher Education* (1–34). Utrecht: Lemma.

Gorbachev, M. (2001, Jan. 6–7). Mikhail Gorbachev delivers the new president a reality check. *The Weekend Australian:* 17.

Gornitzka, A., Huisman, J., Massen, P., Van Heffen, O., Klemperer, A., Van De Maat, L., & Vossensteyn, H. (1999). *State Steering Models with Respect to Western European Higher Education*. Enschede: CHEPS.

Graham, W. (2000). Academic freedom or commercial license? In J.L. Turk (Ed.), *The Corporate Campus: Commercialization and the Dangers to Canada's Colleges and Universities* (23–30). Toronto: James Lormier and Company.

Gray, J. (1998, Sept. 13). Unfettered capital spells global doom. *Guardian Weekly:* 1,4.

Greenwood, D. (1998, Jan.–Feb.). Problems in the university? Tenure, they say. *Academe:* 23–24.

Guin, J. (1990). The reawakening of higher education in France. *European Journal of Education* 25(2): 123–145.

Halimi, S. (1998, Oct. 1). Le naufrage des dogmes liberaux [The shipwreck of liberal dogma]. *Le Monde Diplomatique:* 18,19.

Halsey, A.H. (1982). *Decline of Donnish Dominion: The British Academic Professions in the Twentieth Century*. Oxford: Clarendon Press.

Harley, D. (2001). Higher Education in the Digital Age: Planning for an Uncertain Future. *Syllabus* 15(2): 10–12.

Haug, G. (1999, Dec.). *Visions of a European future: Bologna and beyond*. Paper presented at the 11th EAIE Annual Conference. Maastricht.

Henkel, M. (2000). *Academic Identities and Policy Change in Higher Education*. London: Jessica Kingsley.

Henry, M., Lingard, R., Rizvi, F., & Taylor, S. (1997). Globalization, the state and education policy making. In S. Taylor (Ed.), *Educational Policy and the Politics of Change*. London: Routledge.

Hickling-Hudson, A. (2000) Scholar-activism for a new world: The future of the Caribbean university. In S. Inayatullah & J. Gidley (Eds.), *The University in Transformation: Global Perspectives on the Future of the University* (150–159). Westport, CT: Bergin & Garvey.

Hirschman, A.O. (1982). *Shifting Involvements: Private Interests and Public Action*. Oxford: Martin Robertson.

Honan, J.P. & Teferra, D. (2001). The U.S. academic profession: Key policy challenges. *Higher Education* 41(1/2): 183–203.

Hood, C. (1991). A public management for all seasons? *Public Administration* 69(Spring): 2–19.

Hood, C. (1995). Contemporary public management. *Public Policy and Administration* 10(2): 104–117.

Hoppe-Jeliazkova, M.I. & Westerheijden, D.F. (2000). *Het Zichtbare Eindresultaat*. Den Haag: Algemene Rekenkamer.

Hughes, O. (1994). *Public Management and Administration: An Introduction*. London: St. Martin's Press.

Huisman, J. & Jenniskens, I. (1994). The role of Dutch government in curriculum design and change. *European Journal of Education* 29(3): 269–279.

Huisman, J. & Theisens, H. (2001). Marktwerking in het hoger onderwijs. *B & M, tijdschrift voor beleid, politiek en maatschappij* 28(3): 165–176.

Huisman, J., Westerheijden, D., & Boer, H. de (2001). *De tuinen van het hoger onderwijs*. Enschede: Twente University Press.

Inayatullah, S. (2000). Corporate networks or bliss for all: The politics of the future of the university. In S. Inayatullah & J. Gidley (Eds.), *The University in Transformation: Global Perspectives on the Future of the University* (221–233). Westport, CT: Bergin & Garvey.

James, B. (1998, Sept. 25). The elusive 'third way': Europe's socialists rarely agree on definition. *Herald International Tribune:* 1,7.

Jeanneret, Y. (2000). *Ya-t-il (Vraiment) des Technologies de l'Information?* Paris: Presses Universitaires du Septentrion.

Jonassen, D.H. (1995). Computers as cognitive tools: learning with technology, not from technology. *Journal of Computing in Higher Education* 6(2): 40–73.

Jongbloed, B. & Vander Knoop, H. (1999). Budgeting at the institutional level: Responding to internal pressures and external opportunities. In B. Jongbloed, P. Maassen, & G. Neave (Eds.), *From the Eye of the Storm: Higher Education's Changing Institution* (141–164). Dordrecht: Kluwer Academic Publishers.

Kaiser, F. (2001). *France: Country Report*. Enschede: CHEPS Higher Education Monitor.

Kaiser, F. & Neave, G. (1994). Higher education policy in France. In L. Goedegebuure, et al. (Eds.), *Higher Education Policy: An International Comparative Perspective*. Oxford: Pergamon Press.

Kaiser, F., Van der Meer, P., Beverwijk, J., Klemperer, A., Steunenberg, B., & Van Wageningen, A. (1999). *Market type mechanisms in higher education: A comparative analysis of their occurrence and discussions on the issue in five higher education systems*. Enschede: CHEPS.

Karmel, P. (1992). The Australian university into the twenty-first century. *Australian Quarterly*, Autumn: 49–70.

Katzenstein, P.J. (1985). *Small States in World Markets: Industrial Policy in Europe*. Ithaca/New York/London: Cornell University Press.

Kelly, P. (2000). Internationalizing the curriculum: For profit of planet? In S. Inayatullah & J. Gidley (Eds.), *The University in Transformation: Global Perspectives on the Future of the University* (161–172). Westport, CT: Bergin & Garvey.

Kerr, C. (1982). *The Uses of the University* (3rd ed.). Cambridge: Harvard University.

Kim, H. & Fording, R.C. (1998). Voter ideology in western democracies, 1946–1989. *European Journal of Political Research* 33: 73–97.

Kogan, M. (1986). *Education Accountability. An Analytic Overview*. London: Hutchinson.

Kong, D. (2000, Sept. 3). College try: As tuition keeps soaring, families put their all into finding ways to foot the bill. *The Boston Globe:* F4.

Korean Ministry of Education. (2001). Review of National Policies on Education. *Follow-up to OECD Recommendations for Higher Education.* Seoul: Korean Ministry of Education.

Kyvik, S. (2000). Academic work in Norwegian higher education. In M. Tight (Ed.), *Academic Work and Life: What it is to be an Academic and How this is Changing* (33–72). Amsterdam: Elsevier Science.

Kyvik, S. & Odegard, E. (1990). *Universitetene i Norden foran 90-tallet. Endringer i Styring og Finansiering av Forskning [The Nordic Universities Towards the 90s. Changes in Governance and Research Funding].* Copenhagen: Nordisk Ministerrad.

Lacotte, C. (2001, Nov. 15, personal communication). Academic at the University of Avignon.

Langlois, G., Litoff, J., & Iiacqua, J. (2001). Reaching across boundaries: The Bryant College-Belarus Connection. *Syllabus* 15(3): 12–14.

Lanzara, G.F. (1998). Self-destructive processes in institution building and some modest countervailing mechanisms. *European Journal of Political Research* 33: 1–39.

Larsen, I.M. (2001, Oct.). *The role of the governing board in higher education institutions.* Paper presented at the Governance Structures in Higher Education Institutions seminar. Porto: CIPES/HEDDA.

Larsen, I.M. & Gornitzka, A. (1995). New management systems in Norwegian universities: The interface between reform and institutional understanding. *European Journal of Education* 30(3): 347–362.

Lawday, D. (2001, Aug. 11–12). New French resistance: France is standing firm against a global culture dominated by the United States. *Australian Financial Review:* 1,3.

Lawrence, S.V. (2001, Nov. 15). Going out of business. *Far Eastern Economic Review:* 38.

Leithwood, K., Edge, K., & Jantzi, D. (1999). *Educational Accountability: The State of the Art.* Gutersloh: Bertelsmann.

Leslie, D.W. (1998). Redefining tenure: Tradition versus the new political economy of higher education. *American Behavioral Scientist* 41(5): 652–679.

Lijphart, A. (1984). *Democracies: Patterns of Majoritarian and Consensus Government in Twenty-one Countries.* New Haven, CT: Yale University Press.

Lingard, R. & Rizvi, F. (1998). Globalization, the OECD, and Australian higher education. In J. Currie & J. Newson (Eds.), *Universities and Globalization: Critical Perspectives* (257–273). Thousand Oaks, CA: Sage.

Lowi, T. (2001). Our millennium: Political science confronts the global corporate economy. *International Political Science Review* 22(2): 131–150.

Maassen, P.A.M. & Vught, F.A. van (1988). An intriguing Janus-head: two faces of the new governmental strategy for higher education in The Netherlands. *European Journal of Education* 23(1/2): 65–76.

Maloney, W.A. (1999). Mortar campuses go online. *Academe* Sept/Oct: 19–24.

Marceau, J. (1993). *Steering from a Distance: International Trends in the Financing and Governance of Higher Education.* Canberra: Australian Government Publishing Service.

Marginson, S. (1997). *Educating Australia: Government, Economy and Citizen Since 1960.* Cambridge: Cambridge University Press.

Marginson, S. and Considine, M. (2000). *The Enterprise University: Power, Governance and Reinvention in Australia.* Cambridge: Cambridge University Press.

Marginson, S. & Mollis, M. (1999/2000). Comparing national education systems in the global era. *Australian Universities' Review* 42(2)/43(1): 53–63.

McBrien, R.P. (2001). Theologians at risk? Ex corde and catholic colleges. *Academe* Jan.–Feb.: 13–16.

McBurnie, G. (2001). Leveraging globalization as a policy paradigm for higher education. *Higher Education in Europe* 26(1): 11–26.

McDaniel, O.C. (1996). The paradigms of governance in higher education systems. *Higher Education Policy* 9(2): 137–158.

McInnis, C. (1996). Change and diversity in the work patterns of Australian academics. *Higher Education Management* 8(2): 105–117.

McInnis, C. (2000). Towards new balance or new divides? In M. Tight (Ed.), *The Changing Work Roles of Academics in Australia. Academic Work and Life: What It Is to Be an Academic, and How This Is Changing* (117–145). Amsterdam: Elsevier Science.

McKew, M. (2001, Jul. 17). Glyn Davis ... VC elect. *Bulletin:* 42–44.

McNicol, I.H. (2001, May 25). Universities are private already. *Letter to the Times:* 15.

Medina, J. (2001, Aug. 5). Despite school closing, online colleges beckon. *Boston Sunday Globe:* B9,B12.

Ménand, L. (2001, Oct. 18). College: The end of the golden age. *New York Review of Books:* 44–47.

Merrien, F.-X. & Musselin, C. (1999). Are French universities finally emerging? Path dependency phenomena and innovative reforms in France. In D. Braun & F.-X. Merrien (Eds.), *Towards a New Model of Governance for Universities? A Comparative View* (220–238). London: Jessica Kingsley.

Midgaard, K. (1982). Norway: The interplay of local and central decisions. In H. Daalder & E. Shils (Eds.), *Universities, Politicians and Bureaucrats: Europe and the United States* (275–328). Cambridge: Cambridge University Press.

Mignot Gerard, S. (2000, Sept. 9). *The paradoxical victory of representative leadership in universities: the French model.* Paper presented at the EAIR Forum. Berlin.

Miyoshi, M. (1998). Globalization, culture and the university. In F. Jameson & M. Miyoshi (Eds.), *The Cultures of Globalization* (247–270). London: Duke University Press.

Morrow, G.R. (1968). Academic freedom. In D.D. Dill (Ed.), *International Encyclopedia of Social Sciences* 1&2 (4–10). New York: The Macmillan Company/The Free Press.

Mounyol, T. & Milion, M. (2000). Flexibilité d'un support pédagogique multimedia. In H. Samier (Ed.), *Les Universités Virtuelles* (173–192). Paris: Hermes.

Musselin, C. (1997). State/university relations and how to change them: The case of France and Germany. *European Journal of Education* 32(2): 145–164.

Musselin, C. (2001). *La Longue Marche des Universités Françaises.* Paris: Presses Universitaires de France.

Myers, R.S., Frankel, M.C., Reed, K.M., & Waugaman P.G. (1998). *Accreditation and Accountability in American Higher Education.* Bonn: Federal Ministry of Education, Science, Research and Technology (BMBF).

National Centre for Post Secondary Involvement. (NCPI). (2000). Market-driven accountability in post-secondary education. *Change* May/June: 53–56.

National Office of Overseas Skill Recognition. (1992). *Country Education Profiles: France: A Comparative Study.* Canberra: Australian Government Publishing Services.

National Tertiary Education Union. (NTEU). (2000). *Unhealthy Places of Learning: Working in Australian Universities.* South Melbourne: The National Tertiary Education Union.

Neal, J.E. (1995). Overview of policy and practice: Differences and similarities in developing higher education accountability. *New Directions for Higher Education* 91: 5–10.

Neave, G. (1988a). On the cultivation of quality, efficiency and enterprise: An overview of recent trends in higher education in Western Europe, 1986–1988. *European Journal of Education* 23(1/2): 7–23.

Neave, G. (1988b). The making of the executive head: The process of defining institutional leaders in certain European countries. *International Journal of Institutional Management in Higher Education* 12(1): 104–114.

Neave, G. (1991). The reform of French higher education, or the ox and the toad: A fabulous tale. In G. Neave & F.A. van Vught (Eds.), *The Changing Relationship Between Government and Higher Education in Western Europe*. Oxford: Pergamon Press.

Neave, G. (1994). The evaluation of the higher education system in France. In R. Cowen (Ed.), *The Evaluation of Higher Education Systems* (66–81). London/Philadelphia: Kogan Page.

Neave, G. (1998). The evaluative state reconsidered. *European Journal of Education* 33(3): 265–284.

Neave, G. & Vught, F.A. van (1991). Conclusion. In G. Neave & F.A. van Vught (Eds.), *Prometheus Bound: The Changing Relationship Between Government and Higher Education in Western Europe* (239–255). Oxford: Pergamon Press.

Newson, J. (1992). The decline of faculty influence: Confronting the effects of the corporate agenda. In W. Carroll, L. Christiansen-Ruffman, R. Currie, & D. Harrison (Eds.), *Fragile Truths: 25 Years of Sociology and Anthropology in Canada* (227–246). Ottawa: Carlton University Press.

Newson, J. (1996). Technopedagogy: A critical sighting of the post-industrial university. In (Ed.), *Research Monograph Series in Higher Education: Vol. 3. The Canadian University in the Twenty-First Century* (45–66). University of Manitoba: Research Monograph Series in Higher Education.

Newson, J. (1998). Conclusion: Repositioning the local through alternative responses to globalization. In J. Currie & J. Newson (Eds.), *Universities and Globalization: Critical Perspectives* (295–313). Thousand Oaks, CA: Sage.

Noble, D. (2000). Digital diploma mills: Rehearsal for the revolution. In J.L. Turk (Ed.), *The Corporate Campus: Commercialization and the Dangers to Canada's Colleges and Universities* (101–121). Toronto: James Lormier and Co.

Nora, S. & Minc, A. (1978). *L'Informatisation de la societé: Rapport à M. le Président de la Republique.* Paris: La Documentation Française—Ed. du Seuil, coll. "Points."

NOU. (1988). *Med Viten og Vilj [Hernes Report].* Oslo: Kultur-og vitenskapsdepartementet.

Oillo, D. & P. Barraque (2000). Universités virtuelles, universités plurielles. In H. Samier (Ed.), *Les Universités Virtuelles* (17–36). Paris: Hermes.

Oliver, C. (1991). Strategic responses to institutional processes. *Academy of Management Review* 16(1): 145–179.

Oliveri, N. (2000). When money and truth colllide. In J.L. Turk (Ed.), *The Corporate Campus: Commercialization and the Dangers to Canada's Colleges and Universities* (53–62). Toronto: James Lormier and Company.

Organisation for Economic Cooperation and Development. (OECD). (1987). *Universities Under Scrutiny.* Paris: OECD.

Organisation for Economic Cooperation and Development. (OECD). (1988). *Reviews of National Policies for Education. Norway.* Paris: OECD.

Organisation for Economic Cooperation and Development. (OECD). (1994). *Evaluation and the Decision Making Process in Higher Education: French, German and Spanish Experiences.* Paris: OECD.

Organisation for Economic Cooperation and Development. (OECD). (1996). *Reviews of National Policies for Education. France.* Paris: OECD.

Organisation for Economic Cooperation and Development. (OECD). (1997). *Thematic Review of the First Years of Tertiary Education. Country Note: Norway.* Paris: OECD.

Organisation for Economic Cooperation and Development. (OECD). (1998a). *Open Markets Matter: The Benefits of Trade and Investment Liberalization.* Paris: OECD.

Organisation for Economic Cooperation and Development. (OECD). (1998b). *Redefining Tertiary Education [Redefinir l'Enseignement Tertiaire].* Paris: OECD.

Organisation for Economic Cooperation and Development. (OECD). (1998c). *National Accounts of OECD Countries: Main Aggregates 1989/2000.* Paris: OECD.

Organisation for Economic Cooperation and Development. (OECD). (1990). *Financing Higher Education: Current Patterns.* Paris: OECD.

Organisation for Economic Cooperation and Development. (OECD). (2000). *Education at a Glance: OECD Indicators.* Paris: OECD.

Paulson, M. (2000). Bishops say theologians may teach without OK. *The Boston Globe:* A01.

Perley, J.E. (1997). Tenure remains vital to academic freedom. *The Chronicle of Higher Education* 43(30): A48.

Perlez, J. (2000, Sept. 20). Suave rival has words for the U.S.: 'En garde.' *The New York Times International:* A9.

Pollitt, C. (1990). *Managerialism and the Public Services.* Oxford: Blackwell.

Pollitt, C. (1993). *Managerialism and the Public Services. The Anglo-American Experience.* Oxford: Blackwell.

Polster, C. (2000). The advantages and disadvantages of corporate/university links: What's wrong with this question? In D. Doherty-Delorme & E. Shaker (Eds.), *Missing Pieces II: An Alternative Guide to Canadian Post-Secondary Education* (180–185). Ottawa: Canadian Centre for Policy Alternatives.

Porter, P. & Vidovich, L. (2000). Globalization and Higher Education Policy. *Educational Theory* 50(4): 449–465.

Press, E. & Washburn, J. (2000). The kept university. *The Atlantic Monthly* 285(3): 39–54.

Quadratin Multimedia. (2001). *Enquête E-Learning Europe–Questionnaire.* Retrieved June 3, 2001, from www.quadratin.fr/noirsurblanc/.

Ragin, C.C. (1987). *The Comparative Method: Moving Beyond Qualitative and Quantitative Strategies.* Berkeley: University of California Press.

Rhoades, G. (1998). *Managerial Professionals: Unionized Faculty and Restructuring Academic Labor.* Albany: State University of New York Press.

Rhoades, G. & S. Slaughter. (1998). Academic capitalism, managed professionals, and supply-side higher education. In R. Martin (Ed.), *Chalk Lines: The Politics of Work in the Managed University* (33–68). Durham: Duke University Press.

Rifkin, J. (2000). *The Age of Access.* New York: J. Tarcher.

Rodrik, D. (1997). *Has Globalization Gone Too Far?* Washington, DC: Institute for International Economics.

Romzek, B.S. (2000). Dynamics of public sector accountability in an era of reform. *International Review of Administrative Sciences* 66(1): 21–44.

Rooney, D. & Hearn, G. (2000). Of minds, markets, and machines: How universities might transcend the ideology of commodification. In S. Inayatullah & J. Gidley (Eds.), *The University in Transformation: Global Perspectives on the Future of the University* (91–102). Westport, CT: Bergin & Garvey.

Sassen, S. (2000). Spatialities and temporalities of the global: Elements for a theorization. In A. Appadurai (Ed.), *Globalisation, Special Edition of Public Culture* 12: 215–232.

Scharpf, F. (1987). *Crisis and Choice in European Social Democracy.* Ithaca: Cornell University Press.

Scholte, J. (2000). *Globalization: A Critical Introduction.* London: Macmillan.

Schwartz, H. (1994). Small states in big trouble: State reorganization in Australia, Denmark, New Zealand, and Sweden in the 1980s. *World Politics* 46: 527–555.

Scott, P. (1998). *The Globalization of Higher Education.* Buckingham: SHRE/Open University Press.

Seddon, T. & Marginson, S. (2001). The crisis trifecta: Education. In C. Sheil (Ed.), *Globalization: Australian Impacts* (202–218). Sydney: UNSW Press.

Senate Standing Committee on Education (2001). *Universities in Crisis.* Canberra: Australian Government Printing Office.

Shapiro, J. (2000, Aug.). Death in a tenured position. *University of Chicago Magazine:* 15–18.

Singh, M. (2001, Mar. 27–29). *Re-inserting the 'public good' into higher education transformation.* Paper presented to the Globalisation and Higher Education: Views from the South Conference. Cape Town, South Africa.

Sklair, L. (2001). *The Transnational Capitalist Class.* Oxford: Blackwell.

Slaughter, S. (1993). Introduction to special issue on retrenchment. *The Journal of Higher Education* 64(3): 247–249.

Slaughter, S. (1998). National higher education policies in a global economy. In J. Currie & J. Newson (Eds.), *Universities and Globalization: Critical Perspectives* (45–70). Thousand Oaks, CA: Sage.

Slaughter, S. & Leslie, L.L. (1997). *Academic Capitalism: Politics, Policies and the Entrepreneurial University.* Baltimore: John Hopkins University Press.

Smeby, J.-C. & Stensaker, B. (1999). National quality assessment systems in the Nordic countries: Developing a balance between external and internal needs? *Higher Education Policy* 12(1): 3–14.

Smith, A. & Webster, F. (1997). Conclusion: An affirming flame. In A. Smith & F. Webster (Eds.), *The Postmodern University? Contested Visions of Higher Education in Society* (99–113). Buckingham: Society for Research into Higher Education/Open University Press.

Sporn, B. (1999). *Adaptive University Structures. An Analysis of Adaptation to Socioeconomic Environments of U.S. and European Universities.* London: Jessica Kingsley.

Staropoli, A. (1996). Evaluating a French university. *Evaluation and the Decision Making Process in Higher Education: French, German and Spanish Experiences* (55–59). Paris: OECD.

Stensaker, B. (1997). From accountability to opportunity: the role of quality assessments in Norway. *Quality in Higher Education* 3(3): 277–284.

Stone, G. (2000, Aug.). Tracking tenure at Chicago. *University of Chicago Magazine:* 17.

Thomas, L. (2001, Jan. 31). Humanity is the essence. *The Australian:* 4.

Tjeldvoll, A. (1992). Evaluation of higher education research in Norway. In V. Chinapah (Ed.), *Evaluation of Higher Education in a Changing Europe* (43–56). Stockholm: Stockholm University.

Tjeldvoll, A. (1998). The service university in service societies: The Norwegian experience. In J. Currie & J. Newson (Eds.), *Universities and Globalization: Critical Perspectives* (99–121). Thousand Oaks, CA: Sage.

Tjeldvoll, A. & Holtet, K. (1998). A service university in a service society: The Oslo case. *Higher Education* 35: 27–48.

Tonder, J.-K. & Aamodt, P.O. (1993). Between the market and the welfare state: How to adjust Norwegian higher education to new principles. In United Nations Educational, Scientific, and Cultural Organization (UNESCO) (Ed.), *European Centre for Higher Education Academic Freedom and University Autonomy*. Papers on Higher Education Series (248–257). Bucharest: CEPES/UNESCO.

Trow, M. (1994). Managerialism and the academic profession: The case of England. *Higher Education Policy* 7(2): 11–18.

Trow, M. (1996). Trust, markets and accountability in higher education: A comparative perspective. *Higher Education Policy* 9(4): 309–324.

Tudvier, N. (1999). *Universities for Sale: Resisting Corporate Control over Canadian Higher Education*. Toronto: The Canadian Association of University Teachers/James Lormier and Company.

Turnbull, S. (1999, Oct. 30–31). Weekly, France bucks the toiling trend. *The Weekend Australian*: 32.

Turner, D. (1996). Changing patterns of funding higher education in Europe. *Higher Education Management* 8(1): 101–111.

University of Oslo. (1995). *Strategisk Plan, 1995–99 [Strategic Plan 1995–99]*. Oslo: The University of Oslo.

University of Twente. (1998). *Annual Report*. Enschede: University of Twente.

U.S. News & World Report. (1999). *America's Best Colleges: Exclusive Rankings*. Retrieved September 2, 2000, from www.usnews.com/usnews/edu/college/rankings/rankindex.htm.

Van de Graaff, J. & Furth, D. (1978a). Introduction. In J. Van de Graaff, B.R. Clark, D. Furth, D. Goldschmidt, & D.F. Wheeler (Eds.), *Academic Power. Patterns of Authority in Seven National Systems of Higher Education* (1–12). New York: Praeger.

Van de Graaff, J. & Furth, D. (1978b). France. In J. Van de Graaff, B.R. Clark, D. Furth, D. Goldschmidt, & D.F. Wheeler (Eds.), *Academic Power. Patterns of Authority in Seven National Systems of Higher Education* (49–66). New York: Praeger.

Van Dusen, G.C. (1997). The virtual campus: Technology and reform in higher education. *ASHE-ERIC Higher Education Report* 25. Washington, DC: George Washington University.

Vangsnes, S. & Jordell, K. (1992). Norway. In B.R. Clark & G.R. Neave (Eds.), *The Encyclopedia of Higher Education* (524–533). Oxford: Pergamon Press. van Vught, F.A. (Ed.). (1989). *Government Strategies and Innovation in Higher Education*. London: Jessica Kingsley.

Vossensteyn, H.J.J. & Dobson, I.R. (1999). Hey, big spender! Institutional responsiveness to student demand. In B. Jongbloed, P. Maassen, & G. Neave (Eds.), *From the Eye of the Storm: Higher Education's Changing Institutions* (189–210). Dordrecht: Kluwer Academic Publishers.

Vught, F.A. van, (1997). Combining planning and the market: An analysis of the government strategy towards higher education in the Netherlands. *Higher Education Policy* 10(3/4): 211–224.

Wagner, A. (1996). Financing higher education: New approaches, new issues. *Higher Education Management* 8(1): 7–17.

Wagner, R.B. (1989). *Accountability in Education. A Philosophical Inquiry.* New York/London: Routledge.

Weert, E. de, & Tijssen, L. van vucht (1999). Academic staff between threat and opportunity: Changing employment and conditions of service. In B. Jongbloed, P. Maassen, & G. Neave (Eds.), *From the Eye of the Storm: Higher Education's Changing Institution* (39–63). Dordrecht: Kluwer Academic Publishers.

Wende, M.C. van der (2001). Internationalisation policies: about new trends and contrasting paradigms. *Higher Education Policy* 14(3): 249–259.

Wende, M.C. van der & Beerkens, H.J.J.G. (1999). Policy strategies on ICT in higher education. In B. Collins & M.C. Van der Wende (Eds.), *The Use of Information and Communication Technologies in Higher Education: An Internatinal Orientation on Trends and Issues* (21–50). Enschede: University of Twente, Center for Higher Education Policy Studies.

Westerheijden, D.F. (1997). A solid base for decisions. *Higher Education* 33(4): 397–413.

Williamson, B. & Coffield, F. (1997). Repositioning higher education. In F. Coffield & B. Williamson (Eds.), *Repositioning Higher Education* (116–132). Buckingham: Society for Research into Higher Education/Open University Press.

Wilson, N. (2001, Jan. 20–21). Selling off the farm. *The Weekend Australian:* 24.

Wolton, D. (2000). *Internet, et Après? Une Théorie Critique des Nouveaux Medias.* Paris: Flammarion, coll. 'Champs

Yang, R. & Vidovich, L. (2001, Aug. 20). *Globalisation, Higher Education and Murdoch's Context: A Briefing Paper for Senate.* Perth: Murdoch University.

Yarmolinsky, A. (1996). Tenure: Permanence and change. *Change* May/June: 16–20.

Yoneyazawa, A. & Yoshida, K. (2001). *Financial Structure of Higher Education in Japan.* Cheongu, Choonbuk, Korea: World Council of Comparative Education Societies.

Zernike, K. (1999, Nov. 18). Report. *The Boston Globe:* 1,A35.

Index

About the Authors

JAN CURRIE is Associate Professor, School of Education, Murdoch University, Australia.

RICHARD DEANGELIS is Senior Lecturer in Political Science at Flinders University, Australia.

HARRY DE BOER is Research Associate at the Center for Higher Education Policy Studies, University of Twente, the Netherlands.

JEROEN HUISMAN is Senior Lecturer at the Center for Higher Education Policy Studies, University of Twente, the Netherlands.

CLAUDE LACOTTE is Maitre de Conferences in the Faculty of Sciences and Applied Languages at the Université d'Avignon, France.